A FRAMEWORK FOR COGNITIVE SOCIOLINGUISTICS

A Framework for Cognitive Sociolinguistics attempts to lay out the epistemological system for a cognitive sociolinguistics—the first book to do so in the English language. The intention of this volume is not to provide a simple catalog of sociolinguistic principles or of theoretical postulates of a cognitive nature, but rather it aims to build a verifiable metatheoretical basis for cognitive sociolinguistics. This book is articulated through a series of propositions, accompanied by annotations and commentaries that develop, qualify and exemplify these propositions. As for the research questions that would be central to a cognitive sociolinguistic endeavor, the following incomplete catalog could be enumerated: What do speakers know about their language? What do they know about communicative interaction? What do speakers know about sociolinguistic variation? Where does that knowledge reside and how is it configured? How does social reality influence the origin and processing of language? How does language use affect the configuration, evolution and variation of language? What do speakers know about their socio-communicative context? How do speakers perceive sociolinguistic reality? What are speakers' attitudes and beliefs regarding linguistic variation? How does sociolinguistic perception influence speakers' communicative behavior at all levels? How does language contribute to the construction of identity?

Offering a fresh perspective on the frequently taught and studied topic of cognitive linguistics, *A Framework for Cognitive Sociolinguistics* can easily be incorporated into existing courses in the areas of both cognitive and sociocultural linguistics.

Francisco Moreno-Fernández is Professor of Hispanic Linguistics at the University of Alcalá (Spain) and Executive Director of the Instituto Cervantes at Harvard University. He is co-editor of *Spanish in Context*, founder of *Lengua y Migración/Language & Migration*, and a member of the editorial boards of many journals, including *Intenational Journal of the Sociology of Language*, *Journal of Linguistic Geography*, *Journal of World Languages*, *Revista Internacional de Lingüística Iberoamericana*, and *Lingüística Española Actual*.

A FRAMEWORK FOR COGNITIVE SOCIOLINGUISTICS

Francisco Moreno-Fernández

NEW YORK AND LONDON

First edition in English published 2017
by Routledge
711 Third Avenue, New York, NY 10017

and by Routledge
2 Park Square, Milton Park, Abingdon, Oxon, OX14 4RN

Routledge is an imprint of the Taylor & Francis Group, an informa business

© 2017 Taylor & Francis

The right of Francisco Moreno-Fernández to be identified as author of this work has been asserted by him in accordance with sections 77 and 78 of the Copyright, Designs and Patents Act 1988.

All rights reserved. No part of this book may be reprinted or reproduced or utilised in any form or by any electronic, mechanical, or other means, now known or hereafter invented, including photocopying and recording, or in any information storage or retrieval system, without permission in writing from the publishers.

Trademark notice: Product or corporate names may be trademarks or registered trademarks, and are used only for identification and explanation without intent to infringe.

First edition in Spanish published 2012 by Iberoamericana/Vervuert.
Sociolingüística cognitiva. Proposiciones, escolios y debates. Madrid/Frankfurt: Iberoamericana/Vervuert, 2012.

Translation from Spanish: Rafael Orozco and Rachel Varra.
Stylistic reviewer: Rachel Varra.
Revision, updating and adaptation: Francisco Moreno-Fernández.

Library of Congress Cataloging in Publication Data
Names: Moreno Fernandez, Francisco, author.
Title: A framework for cognitive sociolinguistics/Francisco Moreno-Fernandez.
Other titles: Sociolinguistica cognitiva. English
Description: First edition. | New York, NY: Routledge, [2016] |
Originally published in Spanish: Sociolinguistica cognitiva: Proposiciones, escolios y debates, 2012. | Includes index.
Identifiers: LCCN 2016008739| ISBN 9781138681972 (hardback: alk. paper) | ISBN 9781138681989 (pbk.: alk. paper) | ISBN 9781134815319 (epub) | ISBN 9781134815388 (mobipocket/kindle)
Subjects: LCSH: Sociolinguistics. | Cognitive grammar.
Classification: LCC P40 .M67413 2016 | DDC 306.44—dc23
LC record available at http://lccn.loc.gov/2016008739

ISBN: 978-1-138-68197-2 (hbk)
ISBN: 978-1-138-68198-9 (pbk)
ISBN: 978-1-315-54544-8 (ebk)

Typeset in Bembo and Stone Sans
by Florence Production Ltd, Stoodleigh, Devon, UK

Printed and bound in the United States of America by Publishers Graphics, LLC on sustainably sourced paper.

On the border,
you may look backward
and not remember.
> *Midlife's Haikus* (2011)

En la frontera,
puedes mirar atrás
y no acordarte.
> *Haikus de la media vida* (2011)

CONTENTS

List of Illustrations   *ix*
Preface   *xi*
Acknowledgments   *xiii*

    Introduction   1

1   The Dynamic and Complex Nature of Language   15

2   Social Reality and Perception   34

3   Worldview, Discourse and Society   59

4   Cognitive Foundations of Linguistic Variation   74

5   Sociosemantics and Cognition   89

6   Sociogrammar and Cognition   109

7   Sociophonology and Cognition   127

8   Methodology for a Cognitive Sociolinguistics   145

9   The Sociolinguistic Interview   159

10   The Perceptual Dynamics of the Sociolinguistic Interview   179

11 The Perception of Linguistic Variation 191

12 The Perception of Linguistic Contact 206

Epilogue *224*
Index *226*

ILLUSTRATIONS

Figures

2.1	Social Reality as Objective Environment and Perceived Environment	38
2.2	*Regulatory-Creating* Dynamics	39
2.3	Network Types: Centralized (A), Decentralized (B), Distributed (C)	48
2.4	Networks with Varying Degrees of Internal Cohesion	48
2.5	Social Networks of a Ghanaian Immigrant (Left) and a Young Catalan Lady (Right)	49
4.1	The Relationship Between Schema, Prototype and Linguistic Exemplar	81
5.1	Series of Cup-Like Objects	93
5.2	Lexico-Semantic Network of "Human Body," Obtained from 48 Chicago Spanish Speakers	97
7.1	Radial Arrangement of the Structure Corresponding to the English Phonemes /r/ and /l/	131
7.2	Schema of -s in Spanish in Communities of Conservative Implosive Consonantism	136
7.3	Schema of -s in Spanish, in Innovative Implosive Consonant Communities (I)	136
7.4	Schema of -s in Canary Islands Spanish	137
7.5	Schema of -s in Spanish, in Innovative Implosive Consonant Communities (II)	137
9.1	Network of Thematic Modules Configuration for Adolescents and Young Adults, Based on Labov (1981)	164
9.2	Subjective Perception of Colloquial Conversation Situation	170

9.3	Subjective Perception of the Sociolinguistic Interview from the Interviewer's Perspective	171
9.4	Subjective Perception of the Sociolinguistic Interview from the Interviewee's Perspective	172
9.5	Subjective Perception of an Interview with Multiple Observers from the Interviewee's Perspective	173
9.6	Subjective Perception of an Interview with Multiple Subjects from the Main Interviewee's Perspective	173
9.7	Objective Perception of a Speech Event from the Transcriber's Perspective	175
10.1	Representation of the Sociolinguistic Interview's Internal Dynamics Guided by Three Criteria: Performance, Positioning and Organization	187
11.1	Folk Linguistic Theory of Language, Based on Preston (2004)	196
11.2	Levels for a Typology of Speakers of an International Language. NSC: Native Skills Cluster; LSC: Limited Skills Cluster; FLLC: Foreign Language Learners Cluster	201
12.1	Intensity of Accommodation on Various Linguistic Levels, from Most (Center Circle) to Least (Outer Circles) in a Situation of Language Contact Resulting from Immigration	215

Tables

2.1	Characterization of Social Groups and Social Networks	44
3.1	Hierarchy of Modality	63
5.1	Basic Types of Sociosemantic Differences	102
9.1	Comparison Between Colloquial Conversation and Semiformal Interview According to Situational and Discursive Parameters	161
9.2	Conversational Interaction Typology According to Length and Spontaneity	176
12.1	Classification of Linguistic Varieties According to Stewart's (1962) Attributes	212
12.2	Scale Linguistic Complexity of the Host Community	217

PREFACE

Someone once asked me whether the main objective of my research was to understand language or to understand the human being. After a moment of reflection, I matter-of-factly said, "to understand the human being." And I must confess that I have returned to that question time and again throughout my academic career. It is not that I doubted my response: my interest as a scientist lies in coming to know reality as fully as possible. So, if language is a human attribute, I consider it an obligation to be interested in the human being as the framework of so unique an attribute; if things were any other way, whatever understanding we gained about linguistic reality would surely be only partial. My continued return to that question, I think, has had to do with having received an education in linguistics in which the "autonomy" of the discipline was held up as one of the greatest accomplishments of modern language study. After more than century of linguistic history, it seems that the "success" of autonomy and immanence did not merit so prolonged a celebration, among other reasons, because linguistics can only be explanatory if it enters into dialogue with other disciplines.

These pages have been written with the conviction that the study of language has to be approached from a multidimensional and integrative perspective. Having such an approach does not mean that we do not have a preferential center of interest, which in this case would be language as it relates to its social and cultural environment. It could be said that, as we focus on the social aspect, however, we are disregarding from the start our commitment to integration and multidimensionality. Yet, if it is accepted that the linguistic is necessarily social—that is, that language, its composition, processes and functions can only be language because of its social and cultural dimensions and that linguistics, as a way of understanding language, cannot be anything but "socio-linguistic"—we are still able to advocate for a multidimensional conception. And since the social component of language is not incompatible with the linguistic, properly speaking, neither of course would the neurolinguistic, the psychological or the historical be incompatible with it. Thus, the analysis we aspire to achieve is not formalistic or functionalist, but relational, beginning with the moment that language, each of its components and its dynamics, are explained with respect to its natural, cultural, social and situational environment.

ACKNOWLEDGMENTS

I would like to thank several people and organizations for permission to reproduce copyright material. First of all, a heartfelt thank you to Klaus Vervuert, general editor and owner of Iberoamericana/Vervuert publishing company. Not only has he generously given permission to reproduce those figures that I had designed for the Spanish version *Sociolingüística cognitiva. Proposiciones, escolios y debates* (2012. © Iberoamericana. © Vervuert), but he was also the first person to believe in this book when it existed as but a Spanish-language tome and has continued to provide support throughout its preparation for an English-speaking audience.

Thank you to Pompeu Casanovas, director of the Comares series "La Razón Áurea," as well as to José Luis Molina, Chris McCarty, Claudia Aguilar and Laura Rota, authors of "La estructura social de la memoria" (In: *Interacción, redes sociales y ciencias cognitivas*, edited by Carlos Lozares), who gave permission to reproduce Figure 2.5: "Social networks of a Ghanaian immigrant and a Catalan young lady."

Thanks also go to Wiley for permission to reproduce Figures 9.1 and 11.1. The former figure, "Network of thematic modules configuration for adolescents and young adults" based on William Labov's proposals, was included in *Sociolinguistics. Method and Interpretation* (Oxford: Blackwell. © 2003 by Lesley Milroy and Matthew Gordon). The latter figure, "Folk Linguistic Theory of Language," belongs to the chapter by Dennis Preston "Language with an Attitude" (in *The Handbook of Language Variation and Change*, pp. 40–66, edited by Jack Chambers, Peter Trudgill and Natalie Schilling-Estes (Oxford: Blackwell. © 2002, 2004 by Blackwell Publishing Ltd.).

Thank you to Ricard Solé and Tusquets for permission to reproduce Figures 2.3 and 2.4: "Network types" and "Networks with varying degrees of internal cohesion" (© Ricard Solé, 2009. Published by arrangement with Tusquets Editores, Barcelona, 2009).

Georgetown University Press gives permission to reproduce Figure 5.1, "Series of cup-like objects," from William Labov's "The Boundaries of Words and their Meanings" (in Ralph Fasold, *Variation in the Form and Use of Language*, pp. 29–62. © 1973, 1975, 1977, 1980, 1983 by Georgetown University Press).

Ultimately, I thank *Universidad de Alcalá* (Spain) for permission to reproduce Figure 12.1 included in the book by María Sancho *Integración sociolingüística de los inmigrantes ecuatorianos en Madrid* (Servicio de Publicaciones, 2014).

The final version of these pages has benefited directly from comments faithfully and generously provided to me by six specialists—for whom I hold as much personal regard as professional admiration: Rocío Caravedo, Humberto López Morales, Andrew Lynch, Pedro Martín-Butragueño, Rachel Varra, and Juan Villena Ponsoda. They have made this work more valuable, but cannot be responsible for its limitations, which will now be subjected to the judgment of readers. As noted by Paul Valéry in his *Cahiers*: a man shall be both father and son to his ideas.

INTRODUCTION

The objective of this book is to understand and explain language from a cognitive point of view, which means attending to the linguistic and the social as realities analyzed from the perspective of human cognition. And precisely because the social is an inalienable part of the linguistic, considerable doubt was raised when deciding on the title of this volume. As it turns out, there could have been an alternative title, which might still merit its own volume: *Sociocognitive Linguistics*. Since, when all is said and done, we seek to study language, it would not be in the least bit strange that the noun "linguistics" would be at the core of this volume's title. And, for its part, the adjacent adjective would indicate the centrality of the cognitive, always in relation to the social dimensions of language. The reason, in the end, we finally opted for the formula "Cognitive Sociolinguistics," was, rather, to highlight that we consider language in relation to its social environment to be of central importance, realizing that not everyone agrees that linguistic theory and practice are eminently social. In my opinion, this book is more "linguistics"—being a quest for general knowledge about language—than it is "sociolinguistics"—a quest for knowledge limited to the social use of language—although, as William Labov indicated in 1972, it is probably unnecessary to further discuss what linguistics is or is not at this point.

Networks, Brain and Computer Science

In recent decades the Humanities and the Social Sciences have experienced several prominent trends affecting their various fields of study. Among these, we highlight just four such trends that have had great influence on the social analysis of language. One of them is the development of neuroscience, which has led to a revival of studies on the human brain and unprecedented knowledge of its morphology, processes and functions. Language processing, learning mechanisms (Gallistel 1990) and the way information in the memory is stored and retrieved are pressing issues in current research, with implications for multiple facets of human behavior. Thus far, we know many things about the brain. We know that its average weight is about 1.4 kg, that it contains a hundred billion neurons and that there exist a thousand trillion connections between its cells. We also know that certain human functions such as "learning words," "doing calculations" or "experiencing euphoria" cannot be made by individual nerve cells, but are rather the responsibility of areas of brain tissue containing millions of neurons. These brain areas can self-coordinate their activities as well as coordinate more complex tasks inter-individually, that is between themselves. This has permitted talk about the existence of a "social brain," configured by a network of cerebral areas that are involved in social communication and intersubjective understanding (Dunbar 1988; Blakemore and Frith 2005: 336). The brain has, therefore, a social dimension, which is not incompatible with its biological matter.

In tandem with the advances of neuroscience have been the consolidation and dissemination of cognitive psychology as a reference discipline (De Vega 1984). Cognitive psychology plays a crucial role linking the brain sciences and the field of education. The latter field engages directly with questions about learning processes, among which language development, and the use of language in social communication, enjoys a privileged position. It is well known that Vygotsky (1934) had long highlighted the importance of social interactions for learning, as well as their importance for the relationship between language and thought, and this, despite the fact that the Russian psychologist did not have at his disposal the knowledge of the brain that neuroscience gives us now. Currently, cognitive science has a neural basis and, thus, lots of material to embark on the study of conscious processes, thoughts, emotions, conflicts and social interactions, among which are communicative interactions. From within cognitive psychology, a way of interpreting human realities that has received the generic name of "cognitivism" has begun to influence language studies, first in the grammatical and semantic realms (Rosch and Lloyd 1978; Lakoff 1987; Langacker 1987), then in almost every other realm (Cuenca and Hilferty 1999; Levinson 2003; Pütz, Robinson and Reif 2004). Cognitivism, beyond its specific conceptual proposals, has outlined a way to understand physical and social realities. It is a perspective that is aligned with the Uncertainty Principle of quantum physics and the judgments of numerous thinkers who have (long) been raising concerns about the limitations of rationalism and the importance of subjectivity in the mediation of reality. Ortega y Gasset stated in his *Ideas y Creencias* "Ideas and Beliefs" (1940) that a topographic map is neither more nor less amazing than a landscape by a great painter and that the physical world is not only incomplete, but that is crowded with unresolved problems that are not to be confused with reality itself. Something similar happens with language and linguistics.

A third area of investigation has been developing in recent decades, with the cooperation of disciplines such as sociology, psychology, mathematics and physics and through the proposal of concepts with great explanatory power. Studies in this area examine "complex networks" and are concerned with emerging realities that cannot be explained with respect to the properties of component parts. Rather, these studies reveal patterns of invariance and mechanisms for the exchange of information; the superorganism composed of colonies of termites, the spread of diseases in urban centers or the network of neural connections all demonstrate how (and *how well*) these complex networks function. In the field of communications, semantic or conceptual relationships within language or large social networks created on the Internet also function as complex networks (Solé 2009).

Finally, computer science has put in the palm of our hands not only direct access to knowledge, but the control of information flows. The study of language has benefited from the use of technological tools in a very clear way, not only because they allow examination of the quantitative dimension of language itself but also because we have gained access to information that would otherwise have remained hidden in the gobbledygook of massive data. Nonetheless, the question remains: how is all of this linked with the social reality of language?

The Future of Sociolinguistics

Sociolinguistics has evolved over the past forty years in a way that, rather than converging on a single specific object of study, has led to remarkable diversification. In a process of progressive inclusion, approaches to sociolinguistic research demonstrate a pattern of continuous enrichment, welcoming the exploration of issues using techniques characteristic of the 1970s together with those typical of the 1990s or the first decade of the twenty-first century. The breadth of objectives deriving from a discipline that defines its object of study as language in its social context, or more broadly, as the relationship between language and society, has devoted itself from the very beginning to the treatment of a wide variety of issues. These range from the choice of languages in bilingual communities to the sequencing of conversational turns in professional contexts and include the social history of particular languages. All of these have fallen under the purview of "sociolinguistic" (Mesthrie 2001).

Even focusing on a way to make sociolinguistics more specific, such as with variationist sociolinguistics, which is concerned with the impact of social facts on language variation and change and which is characterized by the use of quantitative techniques, we find the gradual inclusion of different means for understanding the same object of study, of interpreting the socio-communicative reality, or of practicing the discipline (Lieb 1993). Let us take three examples, each of which exemplifies, to a greater or lesser extent, one of the three waves of variationist study as proposed by Penelope Eckert (2012):

1973   Henrietta Cedergren discusses various phonetic phenomena of Spanish in Panama and does so according to the guidelines set by Labov in his investigations during the sixties: starting from a functionalist sociological model, developing rules for sociolinguistic variables and running statistics of probabilities.

1987 Lesley Milroy concludes her investigation of three Belfast neighborhoods, which analyzes different phonic phenomena employing a social networks model, correlating network characteristics with linguistic variants and managing a statistics of inferences.

1993 Richard Cameron published a study on the use of impersonal *tú* in the Spanish of San Juan, Puerto Rico and Madrid, and did so working on two separate sets of informants representing their respective communities by nesting grammatical, semantic, and pragmatic factors and by combining various statistical techniques, among which the probabilistic multiple regression analysis stands out.

As anyone can see, among these three sample studies there is no overlap in the basic sociological model used (1. Functionalism, 2. Marxism, and 3. No sociological model defined), in the linguistic model used (1. Variable rule construction, 2. Sociolinguistic description, and 3. Contrastive pragmatic grammar) nor in the quantitative techniques applied. Nonetheless, it is seems clear from these examples both that the development of computer science has enabled the spread of increasingly complex tests and that the sociolinguistic variationist paradigm espouses a relatively heterogeneous set of methodological approaches. Moreover, the spread of interest into realms beyond those that concerned sociolinguistics during the 1970s, such as variation at the syntactic and discourse levels, stylistic wealth or the management of pragmatic factors, has led us to talk of a post-Labovian sociolinguistics even though Labov himself is alive and active.

The Weaknesses of Variationism

For those of us who have worked within the variationist sociolinguistic paradigm, it is difficult to dismiss how much William Labov has contributed to linguistics (not just to sociolinguistics) and how decisive his contribution has been to the modern development of what is known as the linguistics of speech. In fact, though the disparity of criteria and rationale between Labov's urban sociolinguistics and Chomsky's theoretical linguistics is well-known (Moreno-Fernández 1988), it is striking that many who ascribed to the latter find it extraordinarily easy to claim that Labovian studies are not truly "linguistic," basing their claim on the solid argument that sociolinguistics does not proceed according to the canons of hypothesis-deduction. Such a claim is made as if the linguistics that supposedly does so does not itself daily engage with the management of induction. And it is that much more striking when the most theoretical of linguists have started to recognize the power of the knowledge we have received from corpus linguistics.

Accepting the transcendence of Labov's thought and work, what is certain is that the evolution of sociolinguistics—of *his* sociolinguistics—while it has diversified its areas of interest, has experienced over the years an internal critical review that has highlighted its limitations of substance and form. The books by Norbert Dittmar (1973, 1989) and the collective works of Rajendra Singh (1996) or Carmen Fought (2004) can be taken as proof of this. It is important to know, however, that much of the criticism of variationism has arisen with a positive, constructive spirit, as evidenced by Labov's own involvement in these critical reviews, showing a consistent desire to update methodological techniques and participate in dialectical discussions.

Criticism of Labov's sociolinguistics could be grouped as follows, which, of course, is not the only valid way of so doing (Villena Ponsoda 2008). In the first group would fall criticisms arising from theories that conceive of language differently. The clearest case is generativism, which operates from psychological foundations and disregards (a) supposedly superficial phenomena, such as linguistic variation, and (b) relationships with social and contextual parameters (Moreno-Fernández 1988). The second grouping includes the criticisms of those who, interested in the social dimension of language, understand social reality and, specifically, sociolinguistic reality from a perspective other than the Labovian (Williams 1992). In this group may be included creolists (Bickerton, Bailey) as well as the proposals grounded in Marxian social models (Dittmar 1973; Bourdieu 1982; Milroy 1987) and the work concerned with language as a component of social identity (Gumperz and Hymes 1972, Le Page and Tabouret-Keller 1985). The third category relates to criticisms focusing on methodological and technical aspects, although methodological discrepancies often stem from a disparity of theoretical criteria. These criticisms may refer, for example, to the excessive attention given to phonological, compared with syntactic, investigations (Macaulay 1988), to the lack of appreciation given to analyses of individual speakers (Horvath 1985; Dorian 2010), to how sociolinguistic interviews are conducted (Fought 2004) or to the suitability of certain statistical tests, among other concerns.

This assortment of criticisms of labovianism has included those related to the cognitive dimension of the phenomenon of sociolinguistic variation, even if the criticisms have not emanated from said cognitivist perspectives. Often these criticisms have revolved around the concept of "competence" and how to characterize its nature and constitution. One of the oldest debates, in this sense, has to do with the location of linguistic variation on the abstract level of language: Is variation part of the internal configuration of linguistic competence or are there rather different competences—different grammars—among those that speakers choose from in specific social and contextual circumstances? It is the old dispute between sociolinguists and creolists, between defending monolectal and polilectal grammars, a dispute that has proved largely fictitious, as there is no absolute incompatibility or irreconcilable methodological difference between the two interpretations. In the end, it also has to do with working with theoretical models in which variation would have appropriate space and where quantified and variable data would make sense within a functional structure, essentially making compatible the substantial and the accessory in linguistic communication (Schlieben Lange and Weydt 1981; Villena Ponsoda 1984–1985). We will revisit this issue later (Chapter 1).

Another issue that has been discussed is where quantification fits, if it fits at all, within sociolinguistic competence (Moreno-Fernández 2009: 135–137). If variable rules, as competence rules, include odds of application under certain constraints, does that mean that the speaker "knows" somehow, how much he can use a variant under the right conditions? How can this quantitative knowledge be explained? In this regard, López García (1996) remarks that it is highly unlikely that frequency listings or histograms are part of speakers' mental knowledge. However, it is not impossible to think that, in a certain sense, some knowledge of quantification exists in a speaker's mind. Dennis Preston has proposed a variable competence model consisting of psycholinguistic representations with multiple adjoining grammars. This model is able to combine psychological elements and sociocultural variables in the configuration of variation (Preston 1993). This issue will also occupy our attention.

Given the development of sociolinguistic research as a whole, including both the progress made in its latest contributions and the criticisms of its least convincing aspects, one can speak of the existence of a series of concepts, criteria and methodological elements that have proved useful, although at certain times they pose problems of a theoretical or practical nature. We think of concepts like "speech community" (Romaine 1982), "social class" or "sociolinguistic competence"; we think of the treatment given to the variable units that carry linguistic meaning, of how the number of variables relevant in the explanation of sociolinguistic facts is determined or in how to perceive and identify the variants of a linguistic variable. Many of these concerns can be reduced to more general issues such as the classification and characterization of social and linguistic categories or the treatment of continuous realities by means of discrete classes. At the same time, many of these points also have to do with how sociolinguistic facts are perceived and the space in which speakers "store" their knowledge. Therefore, it seems not only possible but desirable to approach these issues from a cognitivist perspective. In fact, the heterogeneous approach which was earlier mentioned, and some issues of complicated theoretical treatment have for some time been leaving room in variationist sociolinguistics for the inclusion—albeit irregular and sporadic—of elements of a cognitive nature. Among these elements, two that have continually stood out (due to the frequency of their mention and the weight they are given in the interpretation of certain phenomena) are the concepts of "linguistic attitude" and "monitor." At the same time, we have also been able to use cognitive resources for the methodological development of other concepts, such as that of "linguistic market." It seems, then, that the conditions are appropriate to lay the foundations for a stronger cognitive sociolinguistics with greater explanatory power.

The Goals of Cognitive Sociolinguistics

The arguments presented so far imply that it is possible to develop a "cognitive program" for sociolinguistics in two directions. On the one hand, it would consider the type of research questions that could be properly addressed by cognitive sociolinguistics. On the other, it would verify that the foundations of cognitive linguistics can operate within sociolinguistics to account for areas where the application of other theoretical formulations have proven partial or inadequate.

As for the research questions that would be central to a cognitive sociolinguistic endeavor, the following incomplete catalog could be enumerated: What do speakers know about their language? What do they know about communicative interaction? What do speakers know about sociolinguistic variation? Where does that knowledge reside and how is it configured? How does social reality influence the origin and processing of language? How does language use affect the configuration, evolution and variation of language? What do speakers know about their socio-communicative context? How do speakers perceive sociolinguistic reality? What are speakers' attitudes and beliefs regarding linguistic variation? How do speakers detect and respond to the linguistic patterns of their community? How does sociolinguistic perception influence speakers' communicative behavior at all levels? How does language contribute to the construction of identity (Guibernau and Rex 1997, Martin and Mendieta 2003)? It is true that many of the questions included in a sociocognitive program have been addressed for some time, but most of them have not, or at least not always, been convincingly so.

The evidence discussed, along with other proposals that we will be presenting, constitute good ground to bring together criteria and organize the underpinnings of a cognitive sociolinguistics. Fortunately, recent history of linguistics no longer views with suspicion those approaches that do not defend the absolute autonomy of linguistics or that do not limit their object of study to purely linguistic matters. Linguistics has denied theoretical coverage to several manifestations of language for the simple reason that they are manifestations, that is, they are facts that are necessarily occurring or are being produced in a largely non-linguistic environment. Yet, if linguistics is defined as the science that studies language, it should be recognized that theoretical linguistics has shown little appreciation for one glaring reality: the use of language in society.

What we would call "cognitive sociolinguistics" is that which, following the general guidelines of cognitive linguistics, is particularly concerned with the study of cognitive resources involved in processing and contextualizing language use. This cognitive sociolinguistics pays special attention to the knowledge and perception that speakers have of their language in social use, including information about communicative environments, processes of interaction, linguistic variation and change, and to the way these are perceived. A cognitive sociolinguistics is concerned with the environments in which linguistic manifestations are produced, with the way the environment influences these manifestations and with the subjective perception that the speakers themselves have of such environments and the languages they know and use. Graciela Reyes (2002) has spoken from the perspective of pragmatics about reflexivity regarding what is meant and regarding processes of linguistic selection. The phenomenon of language usage must be located in an environment (context) that can be natural or social: a reflection of human duality, the reality of *homo loquens* (Lorenzo and Longa 2003). The natural or physical environment contains the external conditions that act on the language (predisposing factors and negative constraints). The social environment acts as an ideological intermediary and is part of the dynamics of the system. In turn, social consciousness is manifested on two levels: that of the speakers' attributes, as individual actors, including their ability to know and be known (human knowability) (Giddens 1982), and that of collective representations (Durkheim 1893), defined as supra-individual relationships that connect ideas or beliefs.

In terms of beliefs, the importance of cognition to sociolinguistics is again revealed. Speakers' beliefs and perceptions affect their linguistic behavior. If ethnographers claim that an actor is not a fool devoid of judgment, a cognitive sociolinguists would claim that the speaker is not an "idiot interlocutor devoid of linguistic judgment," with all the criticism of generativism or, more generally, to immanentism that such a statement holds. The speaker holds beliefs, be they imposed or self-created, which also affect his capability of perceiving himself as object. This is the basis of the well-known concept of "self" of George Herbert Mead (1934), because the *self* presupposes a social process, that of communication, and emerges along with the development of one's attitudes and social relationships. Communication and language, the speaker's main instrument, are the essence of, the product of and the means of sustaining interpersonal relationships. The characteristics of a language as well as cross-linguistic differences result from context and social interaction. That is, the internal changes that linguistic systems undergo are allowed, cut short or molded by social interaction. There are certainly universals—principles and parameters—but the ones that are manifested and endure are those that social interaction permits.

Furthermore, a cognitive sociolinguistics must explain how categorization processes of social and linguistic objects originate. According to Schütz (1962, 1964), the very use of language involves a typology that speakers build as they interact with it in their community. In any situation of daily life, an action comes about on the basis of types and categories constructed as a result of previous experiences; people routinely typologize and self-typologize from a linguistic point of view. For this reason, as the anthropologist Evans-Pritchard (1961) noted, societies always employ means to help maintain typologies and categorizations. All of this, of course, has points of contact with, but remains far away from, the sociological basis that has inspired variationist sociolinguistics in the United States.

The development of a cognitive sociolinguistics requires concepts such as "prototype," "cognitive category," "centrality," "exemplar" or "construction," among others (Lakoff 1987; Langacker 1987, Cuenca and Hilferty 1999). From this conceptual basis, it would be possible to address theoretical concepts such as "speech community," "class" and "social group" or "variable" and "sociolinguistic variant," using an approach different from that used in more conventional sociolinguistics. Cognitive sociolinguistics presents itself as a metatheory that brings together the proposals of various sociolinguistic theories and draws on a dynamic approach to the use of language. Thus, cognitive sociolinguistics goes beyond the epistemological fragmentation of the discipline (which sought to adapt to each object of study) in order to propose a common denominator to all sociolinguistic analyses. Coulmas (2005) attempted to do the same using the concept of "language choice" as the backbone of his research, but a theory based on a rational choice model is not sufficient for the study of language and communication. It is essential to combine this with criteria such as categorization, perception, accommodation and use, bringing to bear a necessary subjective substance for the understanding of linguistic behavior. In addition, the integrative character that we intend to embed in a cognitive sociolinguistics forces acceptance of, conveniently, a wide variety of objects of interest, ranging from linguistic construction, political discourse, meaning of variation, worldview or sociolinguistic variation to the perception of language varieties. That is our challenge.

Is a Cognitive Sociolinguistics Possible?

In 1970, the creolist David DeCamp wondered: "Is a sociolinguistic theory possible?" Several decades later we reformulate the question and we answer that a cognitive sociolinguistics is indeed possible. It is a sociolinguistics that demands both basic and applied research by linguists and that, in any case, must show itself as "applicable," that is, as leading to a better understanding of language and society. This sociolinguistics does not encounter insurmountable difficulties by accepting that one of its priority concerns *is* the best possible understanding of social life and, ultimately, of the human being, including his tools of communication. To go into this cognitive-sociolinguistics, or socio-cognitive linguistics if you will, we have, in this monograph, chosen to enter by means of the reasoned proposal. We propose that to understand language in its social context, we must explain its subjective components and interpret communication in accord with how language is used to achieve it. And we do this by presenting arguments about the most important areas in which the social dimensions of language are manifested, from the very conception of language as an instrument and linguistic interaction to the application of an appropriate methodology for study. Among the more distant antecedents of this linguistic approach, we shall mention the refreshing ideas of Mikhail Bakhtin and those of Voloshinov (1929), in which not only were the paradoxes created by the struggle between Saussure's structuralist objectivism and Vossler's idealistic subjectivism criticized, but where the relationships between context, interaction and discourse were emphasized (Morris 1994). These will be, as well, the underpinnings of a sociocognitive linguistics.

A Framework for Cognitive Sociolinguistics is articulated through a series of propositions, accompanied by annotations and commentaries that develop, qualify and exemplify these propositions. All of them together offer more than just a sum of general propositions, since they aim to configure a theoretical system that can be subjected to empirical verification in each of its facets. Propositions are generally formulated with respect to the cognitive, the social and the dynamic nature of language reality. By means of these propositions and their annotations, we will highlight aspects that remain, have been, or could be a matter of debate within our field of study. The debates are a way of systematizing the objectives of the different schools of thought that deal with language in its social context and must serve to highlight the issues of greatest interest and complexity. They shall also serve to mark the most frequently found positions and to present where a cognitive sociolinguistics would stand regarding each issue, either to offer alternatives to the debate, or to align with some of the theoretical positions already proffered. This way of presenting theoretical arguments and options is well-suited to the treatment of complex issues, provided it does not fall in Manichaeism.

The internal organization of this book offers an overview of various lines of thinking that affect the study of language from a cultural, social and situational approach. It starts with a presentation of language as a product of and resource in complex social dynamics (Chapter 1), and establishes the theoretical foundations that allow a cognitive interpretation of communication and language variation. Next, we analyze, from a sociocognitive perspective, the social realities that are inserted in language use (Chapter 2), that is, how worldview, society and discourse are interrelated (Chapters 3 and 4). This is followed in Chapters 5, 6 and 7 by a cognitive analysis of the semantic, grammatical and phonic domains of language. This relatively uncommon presentation of linguistic levels is meant to highlight the centrality of meaning in social interaction, given that the study of linguistic meaning constitutes par excellence the foundations of a cognitive approach to language and social use in natural contexts. As any epistemology requires, we then present, in Chapters 8, 9 and 10, the main methodological consequences arising from the application of a cognitive sociolinguistics, paying particular attention to the sociolinguistic interview and its internal dynamics. Finally, in Chapters 11 and 12, we analyze how linguistic varieties and languages in contact situations are perceived, giving primacy to variation over language contact.

In giving clear priority to the cognitive, it could be thought that this work continues the line of inquiry opened by authors like Dirk Geeraerts and Gitte Kristiansen (Kristiansen 2001, 2004, 2008; Geeraerts 2005; Kristiansen and Dirven 2008; Geeraerts, Kristiansem and Peirsman 2010; Geeraerts and Kristiansen 2015). To some extent it does, since it is intended to contribute to a vision of language that coincides largely with what was formulated by these authors, all from the field of cognitivism. But it will accomplish this not by exploring specific sociolinguistic subfields or by analyzing concrete features of language, but by applying a comprehensive and panoramic view of cognitivism to language and its social use. To do this, it has been necessary to adopt, along with cognitivist proposals, other theoretical approaches, such as the model of language as a complex adaptive system, usage-base linguistics, choice theory or the theory of communicative accommodation, in addition to variationism. This is why this cognitive sociolinguistics is presented as a metatheoretical model. In fact, not only will (socio)linguists who seek an overview of work in cognitive linguistics find inspiration in these pages, but cognitive (socio)linguists who are looking for the sociolinguistic research of immediate import to their own work will have a ready reference tool. Scholars and researchers in related disciplines, such as psychology, sociology, anthropology and cultural studies, can also find in this tome abundant linguistic support for research in their fields.

This book's index may resemble that of any sociolinguistics textbook, but its primary aim has been to revisit and re-analyze, in a comprehensive way, every aspect of language's social life from a cognitivist perspective and from an interpretation of languages as complex and adaptive systems. We offer thus a cognitive panorama of sociolinguistics, although we do not deny that anyone could understand it as a sociocognitivist view of linguistics or perhaps just as a "relational linguistics." We do not rule out the possibility that our metatheoretical proposal could be interpreted as an *aggiornamento* of traditional sociolinguistics in order to adapt it to a cognitivist framework; to some extent, that is in part what our metatheory does. Nonetheless, we understand that even though cognitivist arguments have been a latent part of sociolinguistics since the 1970s and have since then increasingly been given attention (Labov 1972; Sankoff 1978; Sankoff and Laberge 1978; Romaine 1982; Lavandera 1984), the cognitive model has only come to fruition in recent years.

References

Blakemore, Sarah-Jayne and Uta Frith, 2005. *Cómo aprende el cerebro. Las claves para la educación*. Barcelona: Ariel.

Bourdieu, Pierre, 1982. *Ce que parler veut dire*. Paris: Librairie Artheme Fayard. Trans. Spa. *Qué significa hablar*. Madrid: Akal, 1985.

Cameron, Richard, 1993. "Ambiguous agreement, functional compensation, and nonspecific tú in the Spanish of San Juan, Puerto Rico, and Madrid, Spain." *Language Variation and Change*, 5: 305–334.

Cedergren, Henrietta, 1973. *The interplay of Social and Linguistic Factors in Panama*. Ithaca, NY: Cornell University.

Coulmas, Florian, 2005. Sociolinguistics. *The study of Speakers' Choices*. Cambridge: Cambridge University Press.

Cuenca, Maria Josep and Joseph Hilferty, 1999. *Introducción a la lingüística cognitiva*. Barcelona: Ariel.

De Vega, Manuel, 1984. *Introducción a la psicología cognitiva*. Madrid: Alianza.

DeCamp, David, 1970. "Is a sociolinguistic theory possible?" In *Report of the 20th Annual Round Table Meeting on Linguistics and Language Studies,* Ed., J. A. Alatis, 157–173. Washington, DC: Georgetown University Press.

Dittmar, Norbert, 1973. *Soziolinguistik. Exemplarische und kritishce Darstellung ihrer Theorie und Anwendung*. Mit kommentierter Bibliographie. Frankfurt: Athenaum Fischer Taschenbuch. Trans. Eng. *A Critical Survey of Sociolinguistics: Theory and Application*. New York: St. Martin's Press, 1977.

Dittmar, Norbert, 1989. *Variatio delectat. Le basi della sociolinguistica*. Galatina: Congedo.

Dorian, Nancy, 2010. *Investigating Variation. The Effects of Social Organization and Social Setting*. Oxford: Oxford University Press.

Dunbar, Robin, 1988. *Primate Social Systems*. London: Chapman & Hall.

Durkheim, Émile, 1893. *De la division du travail social*. Paris. Obtained from: http://classiques.uqac.ca/classiques/Durkheim_emile/division_du_travail/division_travail_1.pdf (accessed 15 December, 2015).

Eckert, Penelope. 2012. "Three Waves of Variation Study: The Emergence of Meaning in the Study of Sociolinguistic Variation." *Annual Review of Anthropology*, 41: 87–100.

Evans-Pritchard, Edward, 1961. *Social Anthropology and Other Essays*. New York: The Free Press.

Fought, Carmen (Ed.), 2004. *Sociolinguistic Variation: Critical Reflections*. Oxford: Oxford University Press.

Gallistel, Randolph, 1990. *The Organization of Learning*. Cambridge: MIT Press.

Geeraerts, Dirk, 2005. "Lectal variation and empirical data in Cognitive Linguistics." In *Cognitive linguistics. Internal Dynamics and Interdisciplinary Interaction*, Eds., F.J. Ruiz de Mendoza and M.S. Peña, 225–244. Berlin—New York: Mouton de Gruyter.

Geeraerts, Dirk and Gitte Kristiansen, 2015. "Variationist linguistics." In *Handbook of Cognitive Linguistics*, Eds., E. Dabrowska and D. Divjak, 365–388. Berlin: De Gruyter Mouton.

Geeraerts, Dirk, Gitte Kristiansen and Yves Peirsman, 2010. *Advances in Cognitive Sociolinguistics*. Berlin—New York: Mouton de Gruyter.

Giddens, Anthony, 1982. *Profiles and Critiques in Social Theory*. Berkeley, CA: University of California Press.

Guibernau, Montserrat and John Rex (Eds.), 1997. *The Ethnicity Reader. Nationalism, Multiculturalism and Migration*. Cambridge: Polity.

Gumperz, John J. and Dell Hymes, 1972. *Directions in Sociolinguistics: The Ethnography of Communication*. New York: Holt, Rinehart & Winston.

Horvath, Barbara, 1985. *Variation in Australian English: The Sociolects of Sidney*. Cambridge: Cambridge University Press.

Kristiansen, Gitte, 2001. "Social and linguistic stereotyping: A cognitive approach to accents." *Estudios Ingleses de la Universidad Complutense*, 9: 129–145.

Kristiansen, Gitte, 2004. *Referencia exofórica y estereotipos lingüísticos: una aproximación sociocognitiva a la variación alofónica libre en el lenguaje natura*. Doctoral thesis. Obtained from: www.ucm.es/BUCM/tesis/fll/ucm-t27033.pdf (accessed 15 December, 2015).

Kristiansen, Gitte, 2008. "Style-shifting and shifting styles: A socio-cognitive approach to lectal variation." In *Cognitive Linguistics. Internal Dynamics and Interdisciplinary Interaction*, Eds., F.J. Ruiz de Mendoza and M.S. Peña, 45–88. Berlin—New York: Mouton de Gruyter.

Kristiansen, Gitte and René Dirven (Eds.), 2008. *Cognitive Sociolinguistics. Language Variation, Cultural Models, Social Systems*. Berlin and New York: Mouton de Gruyter.

Labov, William, 1972. *Sociolinguistic Patterns*. Philadelphia, PA: University of Pennsylvania. Trans. Spa. *Modelos sociolingüísticos*. Madrid: Cátedra. 1983.

Lakoff, George, 1987. *Women, Fire, and Dangerous Things. What Categories Reveals about Mind*. Chicago, IL: The University of Chicago Press.

Langacker, Ronald W., 1987. *Foundations of Cognitive Grammar. Volume I. Theoretical Prerequisites.* Stanford, CA: Stanford University Press.
Lavandera, Beatriz, 1984. *Variación y significado.* Buenos Aires: Hachette.
Le Page, Robert and Andrée Tabouret-Keller, 1985. *Acts of identity: Creole-based Approaches to Language and Ethnicity.* Cambridge: Cambridge University Press.
Levinson, Stephen, 2003. *Space in Language and Cognition.* Cambridge: Cambridge University Press.
Lieb, Hans-Heinrich, 1993. *Linguistic Variables. Towards a unified theory of linguistic variation.* Amsterdam: John Benjamins.
López García, Ángel, 1996. "Teoría de catástrofes y variación lingüística." *Revista Española de Lingüística*, 26: 15–42.
Lorenzo, Guillermo and Víctor Longa, 2003. *Homo loquens. Biología y evolución del lenguaje.* Lugo: Tris Tram.
Macaulay, Ronald, 1988. "What happened to sociolinguistics?" *English World Wide*, 9: 153–169.
Martin Alcoff, Linda and Eduardo Mendieta (Eds.), 2003. *Identities. Race, Class, Gender, and Nationality*, Oxford: Blackwell.
Mead, George Herbert, 1934. *Mind, Self, and Society.* Ed., Charles W. Morris. Chicago, IL: University of Chicago Press.
Mesthrie, Rajend, 2001. *Concise Encyclopedia of Sociolinguistics.* Amsterdam: Pergamon.
Milroy, Lesley, 1987. *Language and Social Networks.* Oxford: Blackwell.
Moreno-Fernández, Francisco, 1988. *Sociolingüística en EE.UU. Guía bibliográfica crítica.* Málaga: Ágora.
Moreno-Fernández, Francisco, 2009. *Principios de sociolingüística y sociología del lenguaje.* 4th ed. Barcelona: Ariel.
Morris, Pam (Ed.), 1994. *The Bakhtin Reader: Selected Writings of Bakhtin, Medvedev, Voloshinov.* London: Arnold.
Ortega y Gasset, José [1940], 1986. *Ideas y creencias.* Madrid: Revista de Occidente.
Preston, Dennis, 1993. "Variationist linguistics and second language acquisition." *Second Language Research*, 9–2: 153–172.
Pütz, Martin, Justyna A. Robinson and Monika Reif (Eds.), 2014. *Cognitive Sociolinguistics: Social and Cultural Variation in Cognition and Language use.* Amsterdam: John Benjamins.
Reyes, Graciela, 2002. *Metapragmática.* Valladolid: Universidad de Valladolid.
Romaine, Suzanne, 1982. *Sociolinguistic Variation in Speech Communities.* London: Arnold.
Rosch, Eleanor and Barbara Lloyd, 1978. *Cognition and Categorization.* Hillsdale NJ: Lawrence Erlbaum Associates.
Sankoff, David (Ed.), 1978. *Linguistic Variation. Models and Methods.* New York: Academic Press.
Sankoff, David and Suzanne Laberge, 1978. "The linguistic market and the statistical explanation of variability." In *Linguistic Variation: Models and Methods*, Ed., D. Sankoff, 239–250. New York: Academic Press.
Schlieben-Lange, Brigitte and Harald Weydt, 1981. "Wie realistisch sind Variationsgrammatiken?." In *Logos Semantikos. Studia Linguistica in Honorem E. Coseriu (vol. V)*, Eds., H. Geckeler et al., 117–145. Madrid—Berlin—New York: Gredos/de Gruyter.
Schütz, Alfred, 1962. *Collected Papers I: The Problem of Social Reality.* The Hague: Martinus Nijhoff.
Schütz, Alfred, 1964. *Collected Papers II: Studies in Social Theory.* The Hague: Martinus Nijhoff.

Singh, Rajendra (Ed.), 1996. *Towards a Critical Sociolinguistics*. Amsterdam: John Benjamins.
Solé, Ricard, 2009. *Redes complejas. Del genoma a Internet*. Barcelona: Tusquets.
Valéry, Paul, 2007. *Cuadernos* (1894–1945) [*Cahiers*]. Barcelona: Galaxia Gutemberg.
Villena Ponsoda, Juan M., 1984–1985. "Variación o sistema. El estudio de la lengua en su contexto social: William Labov." *Analecta Malacitana*, VII-2: 267–295; VIII-1: 3–45.
Villena Ponsoda, Juan M., 2008. "Sociolingüística: corrientes y perspectivas." In *Diccionario Crítico de Ciencias Sociales*, dir. R. Reyes. Obtained from: www.ucm.es/info/eurotheo/diccionario/S/sociolinguistica.htm (accessed 15 December, 2015).
Voloshinov, Valentin N., [M. Bakhtin] [1929]. 1973. *Marxism and the Philosophy of Language*. New York: Seminar Press—Harvard University Press—Academic Press.
Vygotsky, Lev, 1934 [1986]. *Thought and Language*. Cambridge, MA: MIT Press.
Williams, Glyn, 1992. *Sociolinguistics. A Sociological Critique*. London: Routledge.

1
THE DYNAMIC AND COMPLEX NATURE OF LANGUAGE

Conventional definitions of "sociolinguistics" refer to a conceptual spectrum so broad that its study could be approached from almost any perspective. In principle, the study of sociolinguistics requires consideration of realities external to the individual and beyond language itself, allowing the exclusion of elements considered to be part of what generativists call *I-language* as well as entities of a purely psychological nature (Chomsky 1995). This being the case, the concepts of "psycholinguistic processing" and "communicative interaction" could be considered irreconcilable. The same would also be the case for "social organization" and "individual behavior" so that the terms "cognition," "statement," "interaction" or "socialization" could not be combined within a single sociolinguistic analysis. However, several recent linguistic contributions to our common knowledge concerned with the origin of language, brain function, language variation, learning processes and communicative exchanges have opened the door to a sociolinguistics where the individual is projected socially and where cognitive interaction is modeled using contextualized linguistic interaction. This requires recognition of the dynamic nature of language and its interpretation as a complex, adaptive system. This interpretation, which is founded on the concept of "language usage," among others, has direct antecedents in the 1960s (Greenberg 1966), although it has taken a new turn in the twenty-first century (The Five Graces Group 2007; Ellis and Larsen-Freeman 2009).

A. On the Dynamic Nature of Language

Proposition 1.1
Language is a human ability that manifests itself in linguistic varieties and is used in communication for different purposes. Language is exercised collectively and its origin and organization are closely related to social interaction.

Proposition 1.2

Language is a historical phenomenon that emerged with the evolution of the human species by means of the combined effect of thought processes, perceptual-motor skills and cognitive and socio-pragmatic factors, all of which operate reciprocally.

Proposition 1.3

Language is an inherent and fundamental factor in society and culture that enables the progressive development, transfer and reconfiguration of knowledge.

Proposition 1.4

Linguistic usages constitute emerging realities, which are themselves produced and perceived as such.

Proposition 1.4.1

Linguistic usages are essentially variable and simultaneously reflect and determine the shape of a given language.

Proposition 1.4.2

Linguistic usages occur in discourse scenarios; linguistic usages are specific verbal interactions that arise (and help create) cognitive models; they are composed of speech act sequences and are, further, used in specific contexts within a particular social reality.

Proposition 1.5

Language is a *complex adaptive system* of dynamic usage in which the processes of acquisition, usage and linguistic change are not independent of each other, but rather aspects of the same system.

Proposition 1.5.1

The principal characteristics of individual languages as complex, adaptive systems include the multiplicity of agents, the cumulative use of interactions, a combination of factors in a speaker's behavior and the emergence of patterns in interaction, experience, and cognition.

Proposition 1.5.1

Inter-individual communicative cooperation turns language into an emergent phenomenon, with a social life of ever-increasing complexity and an individual existence that rests upon factors of a cognitive psychomotor, perceptual and experiential nature in such a way that variants favored by a particular social language usage end up becoming gradually integrated in an individual's mind.

Scholium 1-A

In 1929, Mikhail Bakhtin—either under this name or as Valentin Voloshinov—skillfully highlighted the importance of *interaction* as a linguistic fundamental and as a way to overcome the "langue/parole" dichotomy (pp. 45–64, 83 ff.). Embedded in his argumentation was the idea that language is an individual capacity built and exercised in an essentially collective and interactive manner within a cultural environment. This environment reflects what, in the long run, societies consider important in their history as well as the biological and social conditions in which the society operates. From this perspective, it is clear that there is a link between the origin, development and use of a language and social interaction in the communities, regardless of the purposes or functions for which the language is used. Ortega y Gasset (1924) stated that our life is a dynamic conversation with our environment, a dialogue established through the psychic function of perception, which conditions the physical and human reality that surrounds us. The environment of the human being, as individual and as collectivity, is shaped by internal and external perceptions, which, although not itself reality, lead us to interpret and "view" things in a particular way. The sounds of language are measurable physical realities, but they are linguistically relevant only to the extent that they are perceived or not perceived by listeners. Words are identifiable linguistic realities in writing and orally. But perceiving them is not always straightforward. An utterance that constitutes a single word for one person may be less than a word or more than a word for another person. Then again, chains of sounds can often be virtually unsegmentable for one who does not know the language or variety to which they belong.

Moreover, while linguistic meanings seem to be socially predetermined, interaction triggers processes of semantic negotiation that respond to how communicative intentions are perceived by interlocutors; and as the interesting realm of misunderstandings reveals, the success of these negotiations is not always guaranteed. Linguistic facts acquire their value when they are considered to be features that are both produced and perceived, since it is precisely in the connection between production and perception that linguistic variability emerges. In turn, language is an articulating element of societies and cultures, a principal means by which knowledge is transmitted and, therefore, is a tool integral to the survival of human collectivities. It becomes part of society through interactions—

be they direct or indirect—that take place in specific, concrete contexts. And its impact on communication not only depends on its morphological characteristics, but also on the way these characteristics are embodied and perceived by speakers. The nature of language is derived from its role in social interaction. If indeed social interactions are not always cooperative, neither do they occur solely in response to conflict; nonetheless, however, they are often characterized by what the philosophers of action have called "cooperative activity" (Bratman 1992).

But there is an interpretation that better explains linguistic phenomena as a whole; it is that which presents language as a complex adaptive system of dynamic use. This implies the obligatory existence of a multiplicity of agents who communicate with each other with respect to a combination of linguistic and extralinguistic factors, which cumulatively causes the emergence of patterns of interaction, experience and cognition, including social cognition. As with other realities, language and culture are emergent phenomena of an increasingly complex social existence (Solé 2009: 20); in contrast to a mechanistic conception of the whole and the parts (clock mechanisms, automata, dynamic stimulus-response), there exists a cooperative dynamic for the creation of organisms of different types. This interpretation of language finds fundamental methodological support in the concept of "linguistic use" and partially overlaps with the vision adopted from the so-called "secular linguistics" (Trudgill 2003) or "realist linguistics," which also conceives of language as a complex dynamic system (Martín-Butragueño 2011).

Communicative use was ignored in the conception of structuralism and omitted from the foundations of generativism; nonetheless, it is fundamental in shaping linguistic systems. Use implies the existence of interactions, frequency, sequences, language variation and change, all of which are themselves constituents of language systems. With the concept of "use," we are not facing a manifestation of these systems, but rather a factor capable of determining the linguistic form itself. In so doing, it both shows a preference for certain variants and not others in certain specific contextual conditions as well as integrates preferred forms into individual competence. From a cognitive perspective, this means that personal preferences make possible the embodiment of linguistic uses in such a way that the variants preferred for social use end up being gradually integrated into the individual mind (Bernárdez 2005). From a sociological perspective, this implies that the variants preferred in usage end up being incorporated into the individual's *habitus*, as formulated by Bourdieu (1982).

Proposing a model of language as a "complex adaptive system" admits that communication is a cooperative activity in which the speaker's intention is recognized by a listener (Grice 1989), thereby activating a fundamental mechanism for the coordination of communication: convention. Convention emerges from the regularity of behavior and functions as a fundamental procedure in construction of human culture. Linguistic cooperation consists of the choices that speakers make with respect to words and grammatical constructions—understood as conventions—with the purpose of communicating something. From here, the language acts on four levels (Clark 1996, The Five Graces Group 2007): the production of utterances, the formulation and identification of propositions, the signaling and recognition of communicative intentions, and the proposal and execution of joint actions. But the choices made by speakers do not occur *ex novo* in each one of their interactions, but rather from the employment of established conventions in similar previous situations. In such cooperative processes, we should not forget the possibility of misunderstanding, a result of faulty and indeterminate communication, which contributes to a state of apparent uncertainty—though not always disordered (Martín-Butragueño 2000)—which promotes linguistic variation and change.

B. On the Perception of Sociolinguistic Reality

Proposition 1.6

Sociolinguistic perception implies an ordering, a categorization and a simplification of reality.

Proposition 1.7

The most relevant sociolinguistic categorization is that which sorts individuals according to communities and sociolinguistic groupings.

Proposition 1.8

Sociolinguistic perception is the foundation of community members' linguistic and sociolinguistic attitudes toward their linguistic varieties and those of others.

Proposition 1.9

The extraction and evaluation of sociolinguistic information from the spoken language occurs through the sociolinguistic monitor.

Proposition 1.9.1

The information stored by the sociolinguistic monitor is independent of purely linguistic information.

Proposition 1.9.2

The function of the sociolinguistic monitor is independent of community members' gender, ethnicity and region of origin.

Scholium 1-B

The concept of "perception" is undoubtedly one of the foundations of cognitive sociolinguistics or, if preferred, of sociocognitive linguistics. From this position, the sociolinguistic facts and processes would be neither prioritatively nor exclusively based on their intrinsic features, more or less objectified, but on the way they are perceived, more or less subjectively by speakers. Thus, just as it neither suffices to characterize sociocultural hierarchies according to professional or academic accomplishments nor to measure the vowel formants produced by those of a certain age to see if the individuals can be characterized in terms of these measurements, it is not enough to count the instances of a morpheme or its alternant in men's or women's discourse, since, ultimately, the import of the variant for speakers can only be substantiated in how it is perceived. Paul Valéry stated in 1926 (2007: 177): "We are at the mercy of what occurs in our field of perception." Perception is a cognitive process and, therefore, the epistemological apparatus of cognitive linguistics is applicable within any of a language's perceptual realms.

The weight of perception in communicative interaction does not deny the importance of linguistic and social realities, quantified and correlated. We have simply to accept that such realities are reality to the extent that they are perceived. Traditional sociolinguistics has endeavored to show that individual behavior includes components that respond to social norms and sociolinguistic analysis provides access to how social realities affect language use. For this reason, it is important to establish objective quantitative limits with respect to factors such as social class, educational level and sex. What is not the result of decisions made by an individual speaker can respond to tendencies within the group to which that individual belongs. In this way, statistical sociolinguistics can detect what a speaker does not perceive. Where, then, do problems arise? They arise at the point where social factors fail to be determinants: that is, when socioeconomic levels, sex or age, neatly and objectively defined, are unable to provide an explanation for a variable linguistic fact. The perception of social factors may also explain the reason for their influence—or lack thereof—over language usage. But a speaker can mistakenly diverge from the social or linguistic behavior of another if he is unable to perceive similarities. The perception or misperception of social and linguistic elements has a major impact on language usage and on the interactive process as a whole; traditional sociolinguistic analysis, in overlooking the role of perception, is not enough to capture it.

One of the cognitive concepts that traditional sociolinguistics put into circulation was that of the "monitor." The monitor theory has been of great importance for the socio-stylistic explanation of variation and it constitutes proof of the long-standing existence of cognitivism in sociolinguistics, even at times when preference was given to the measurement of objective realities. The monitor theory incorporates some basic psychosociological mechanisms that allow speakers to pay attention to and assess both their own linguistic knowledge and their linguistic production, thereby influencing the outcome of communicative interactions. A speaker's monitoring consists of paying attention to their own speech and being able to consciously modify their communicative output. Regarding what interests us the most, the monitor theory—well known in the field of language acquisition (Krashen 1982)—has been very successful for the study of discourse styles. According to William Labov (1966: 60–88), spoken language styles can be arranged along a single parameter—the degree of attention paid by the speaker to his discourse, which allows the construction of a scale of styles with various degrees of formality.

The monitor theory continues to be of central relevance to this day and the recognition of its cognitive underpinnings has increased in response to the increasing scope that cognitivism has had within linguistic research. Proof of this is work by William Labov himself entitled *The Cognitive Capacities of the Sociolinguistic Monitor* (2008), in which he presents some tests intended to determine the sensitivity of listeners to the frequencies of use of the variables -*ing* and /r/ in the English of Philadelphia, South Carolina and Boston/New Hampshire. Labov explores the reactions of adult judges to the frequencies of variants with a greater or lesser degree of deviation from the norm, proving that speakers exhibit less sensitivity toward ongoing sound changes while having a greater awareness of linguistic features that are socially and stylistically well stratified. According to Labov, there are reasons to believe that the sociolinguistic monitor's information is stored independently from lexical and grammatical information and, further, that the features that are least perceived work in a manner incongruent with the dialectal profile, sex and ethnicity of the speaker. However, it has also been observed that such sensitivity develops with age and is correlated with social class.

Sociolinguistic perception involves an ordering and simplification of reality that leads to processes of categorization and classification. Categorization is a basic process of social—and sociolinguistic—perception that implies a simplification of reality while at the same time adapting to a considerable extent to that reality (Bruner 1986; Morales 2007). In communicative interaction, the categorization that most concerns us involves the identification of individuals by sociolinguistic or dialectal groups. On the other hand, the development of cognitive types assumes a perceptual and privative abstraction of each speaker, even though language also includes core components of an intersubjective nature (e.g., forms of address) that imply social consensus (Eco 1997). When it is time to explain personal relationships within society, Alfred Schütz (1962) asserted that he was not interested so much in people's physical interaction, as in the way they achieve reciprocal understanding of each other through intersubjectivity.

C. On the Theoretical Space of a Cognitive Sociolinguistics

Proposition 1.10

Cognitive sociolinguistics is part of the field of experiential cognitive linguistics and shares fundamental principles with theories of communicative interaction, linguistic variation and change and with dynamic sociologies of the situation.

Proposition 1.11

Cognitive sociolinguistics is a metatheory of social and communicative interaction, and of how this interaction contributes to the internal and external configuration of language.

Proposition 1.12

Cognitive sociolinguistics provides a program from which to interpret the origin of language, first and second language acquisition, as well as linguistic history, variation and change.

Proposition 1.13

The preferred objects of study of cognitive sociolinguistics are the use of language in society, language variation and change, linguistic accommodation and choice, as well as the implications and consequences that social structures, social dynamics, social organizations and social contexts have on language

Scholium 1-C

When Hymes (1964) categorized areas of sociolinguistic reality, he distinguished four levels reflecting, on one hand, the totality of the system in contrast to the individuality of features and, on the other, the difference between potential reality and actualized reality. The four levels were that of the *structure* (the system as potential), that of the *dynamics* (the system as actuality), that of the *agents* (the particular facts as well as those that are possible) and that of the *acts* (the facts). If indeed it is true that sociolinguistic subfields (such as variationism or ethnography of communication) are capable of meticulously exploring each of these areas, it is no less feasible that sociolinguistics could integrate of all these levels in its explanatory apparatus. This would not only be a desirable for a given sociolinguistic subfield but would also mean a more powerful and more ambitious epistemological framework than the one that has been implemented so far. A sociolinguistics with theoretical resources to integrate the systems with the acts could successfully address what has been a key issue for sociology: the problem of the theoretical formulation of the relationship between the social system and the individual's personality (Parsons 1937; Simmel 1971).

Cognitive sociolinguistics is a theoretical program broad enough and solid enough to address the integrated treatment of the different levels of sociolinguistic reality because cognitive processes are capable of articulating the relationship between the individual and the social, between the particular and the systematic. Also, let us not assume that the inclusion of cognition in sociolinguistic explanation is a novelty; sociolinguistics has long employed cognitively based concepts. In fact, it could be claimed that to speak of cognitive sociolinguistics is tautological because all of sociolinguistics necessarily has to be cognitive, just as any theory that seeks to explain language in its totality necessarily has to be social. This cognitive sociolinguistics is presented as a metatheory or integrative model, which does not seek to deny the existence nor curb the exercise of other forms of research. That is, a cognitive sociolinguistics is not incompatible with other interpretations of linguistic and social realities of speech communities. Just as interpersonal relationships do not deny the existence of mental processes—but are rather based on them—the linguistics of interaction insistently calls for attention to psycholinguistic processes. In other words, cognitive sociolinguistics aspires to address the socio-interactive and the psycho-sociolinguistic, always in the spirit of being a discipline both theoretical as well as applied or, at least, applicable to concrete social and communicative realities. In this sense, cognitive factors emerge as essential for sociolinguistic explanation.

A sociolinguistics with the characteristics that we are discussing cannot be developed outside of the concerns of cognitive linguistics. Within its conceptual map (Geeraerts 2006: 19), cognitive sociolinguistics would be located in the area of experiential cognitive linguistics, which is concerned on one hand, with the relationship between *langue* and *parole*, employing a model of "usage-based linguistics" (Bybee 2001), "cognitive grammar" (Langacker 1987), or a so-called "construction grammar" (Lakoff 1987; Fillmore 1995). On the other hand, experiential cognitive linguistics is also concerned with the relationship between lexicon and grammar. That is, sociolinguistics would relate to a cognitive linguistics based on experience, as opposed to a cognitive linguistics of perspectives, although it would incorporate concepts from all of them. The experiential perspective implies that words or other significant structures are not objective realities or based on logical rules, but rather supposes that these structures arise in conjunction with the participation of associations and impressions that are part of the speaker's experience (Ungerer and Schmid 1996).

Cognitive sociolinguistics would align itself with those tendencies that do not attempt to define reality by its essence but by its manifestations. In contrast to a linguistics which aspires toward absolute answers to categorical questions such as "what is meaning?" or "what is grammar?" emerges a non essentialist linguistics with two major manifestations, according to Janicki (2006): cognitive linguistics and integral linguistics (Harris 1981). Janicki proposes the application of a guide for a "non-essentialist" conception of language, including statements such as the following, adapted to our current interests:

a. It is not important to make distinctions between disciplines and sub-disciplines because there are no clear boundaries between them (for example, between pragmatics and sociolinguistics). Consequently, we should not discuss disciplinary boundaries because they can be freely crossed.
b. The development of taxonomies should not be the main objective of a study.
c. What is important is what we do instead of what we call what we do.
d. A linguistic investigation should discard expressions such as "typical sociolinguistic study," "sociolinguistics itself," "strictly speaking" or "in the true sense of the word."

Ultimately, what is important in the construction of scientific reasoning is the validity of the arguments that are used for it. We have insisted that cognitive sociolinguistics is presented as a metatheory, which incorporates a variety of perspectives regarding general principles. Such perspectives are not unprecedented; rather, they have been guiding the development of a significant number of investigations under the label of different approaches, theories or models. Of all those who have dealt with and have been concerned with language in its social use, the theoretical models that are most easily integrated into a cognitive sociolinguistics are those of communicative accommodation, the ecolinguistic, the variationist and, naturally, usage-based linguistics. Integration of these models occurs within the theoretical model of general cognitive linguistics and is predicated upon a conception of language as a complex adaptive system.

The *theory of communicative accommodation* is fundamental to cognitive sociolinguistics (Giles 1984; Shepard, Giles and Le Poire 2001). As we know, the communicative accommodation theory is interested in the cognitive processes that occur between the perception of the social context and communicative behavior. It aims to explain the motivations underlying both use of and changes in speech styles as well as the social consequences resulting from them. The basic principles of the theory are those of *convergence* and *divergence*. The former is defined as a communication strategy that speakers follow to adapt to a situation and to their interlocutors' linguistic usage. The latter is defined as a process in which speakers accentuate their differences with respect to other individuals. The goals that determine speakers' convergent behavior are convergent social approval from the listener, the improvement of communication efficiency, and the maintenance of positive social identities. The desire to see the fulfillment of these goals leads speakers to accommodate or adapt their speech under very diverse conditions. Divergent behavior, on the other hand, appears when one wants to maintain social and linguistic distance with respect to individuals belonging to different social groups. Accommodation theory attaches significance not only to listener but also to the communicative interaction between a speaker and his interlocutor in a social context (Nishida 1999).

The *ecolinguistic model* or *an ecology of language* (Haugen 1972; Fill and Mühlhäusler 2001) contains in itself a multitude of ways to understand the life of a language in social and cultural environments. Haugen (1972: 325) defined the ecology of language as the study of interactions between a given language and its environment or environmental surroundings. If cognitive sociolinguistics takes all linguistic actions to constitute situations within a sociocultural environment and within a situational context, it is adopting a perspective similar to that of the ecology of language. This ecological perspective is also essential to the so-called sociolinguistics of complexity (Bastardas 2014; Blommaert 2014).

Variationist sociolinguistics (Labov 1966, 1972) constitutes a cornerstone of cognitive sociolinguistics. Everything that has to do with linguistic variation, with variables and their variants, as well as with language varieties, must be based on the principles and techniques of Labovian sociolinguistics because they have demonstrated an explanatory power superior to that of any other theoretical initiative. This does not, however, prevent the study of language in society from going beyond variation nor from giving attention to usage in its most diverse manifestations.

A *usage-based* theory of linguistics (Langacker 1987; Bybee 2001, 2010; Tomasello 2003) proposes that the cognitive organization of language is based on one's direct experience with language, as well as on the pragmatic and contextual factors that accompany its use (Kristiansen and Geeraerts 2013: 1–4). Usage-based linguistics does not consider it possible to formulate linguistic theories built solely on introspection to the exclusion of actual data, among other reasons, because the context of usage has a direct impact on linguistic structures and representations. The link between this model and cognitivist theories is clear when we concede that language is directly connected to other cognitive systems such as memory or perception. The importance of usage is such that, for an adequate understanding of language, linguistic expressions in speech must be taken to be constantly emerging realities that maintain a dynamic relationship with cognitive representations. Thus, and because probability is a foundation for establishing predictability (Bresnan and Ford 2010), frequency becomes key for understanding both linguistic usage and its evolution over time. Variation, change, learning and acquisition can only be understood from the experience of language usage. Consequently, the methodological projection of this theory requires attention to the corpora of spoken and written language for a proper study of linguistic usage (Barlow and Kremmer 2000; Baker 2010).

Beyond these theoretical proposals, there are several other approaches to language, like Joan Bresnan's and Marilyn Ford's (2010) probabilistic variation grammar, Janet Pierrehumbert's (2001) exemplar theory or Penelope Eckert's (2012) interactional "three waves" sociolinguistics (an interactional, constructivist approach). Each will be considered in due course.

The objectives of a cognitive sociolinguistics are comprehensive and complex. Among them, three broad areas of interest can be identified:

a. that of the social origins of language and linguistic variation (sociolinguistic genesis), as well as that of language usage and its interpretation as a complex adaptive system. We would, therefore, be facing a *phylogenetic sociolinguistics*;
b. that of linguistic differences arising from social and cultural factors that constitute the dynamics of variation (sociolinguistic morphosis). We would, at this point, be facing a *phenotypical sociolinguistics*; and
c. that of communicative interaction in all dimensions of linguistic usage (sociolinguistic praxis), including the psychosocial, the ethnographic or the discursive. This would be an *interactive sociolinguistics*.

Cognitive sociolinguistics recognizes the importance of the social component in both the origin of language and in its form and dynamics. Using cognition as a basis, then, the sociolinguistic is explained in all of its manifestations: from perception to attitudes and from the construction of the grammar to the formation of meaning. Cognitive maps of these areas—with their spaces, paths, edges, nodes and landmarks—are capable of guiding us along the most appropriate routes for a clearer, more logical and meaningful understanding of societal language use.

The preferred objects of study of a cognitive sociolinguistics are societal language usage, language variation and change, linguistic accommodation, and language choice. Such wide objectives are perfectly reflected in the multiplicity of its applications, from sociological realms (multilingual policies, integration of immigration, language pedagogy and education, intra-group communication, professional communication) to realms of the essentially linguistic (language acquisition, child language development, transdialectalization processes, linguistic variation and change, stylistic variation, dialects and jargons, conversational mechanisms, forms of address, language choice and substitution, language attrition and language death, consequences of language contact, interlanguages).

D. On some Fundamental Concepts of Cognitive Sociolinguistics

Proposition 1.14

The concepts from cognitive linguistics that underlie a cognitive sociolinguistics are "perception," "prototype," "schema," "category," "frequency" and "use."

Proposition 1.15

The concepts from theories of communicative interaction that underlie a cognitive sociolinguistics are "accommodation" and "attitude."

Proposition 1.16

The concepts from theories of language variation and change that underlie cognitive sociolinguistics are "variation" and "choice."

Proposition 1.17

The concepts from a dynamic sociology of situations that underlie cognitive sociolinguistics are "context," "network," "communicative interaction," "discourse" and "act."

Scholium 1-D

Within cognitive sociolinguistics, reliance on models of different theoretical origin brings with it the introduction of key concepts from each one of them. These concepts, the metaphorical bricks that allow the construction of our particular sociocognitivist building, include notions like "usage," "interaction," "accommodation," "variation" and "frequency," along with related notions like "convergence" and "divergence," "language change," "context," "network" and "discourse." Because it rarely receives the prominent treatment it deserves, we highlight the essential function that "frequency" serves for the social epistemology of language, being the empirical basis for the categorization of social and linguistic reality that a speaker practices. Some concepts assume part of the conceptual content of several others. This occurs with the concept of "choice" (Coulmas 2005), which possesses great explanatory power with respect to variation, language contact and communicative interaction.

As expected, the battery of tools that cognitive linguistics possesses is also at the disposal of cognitive sociolinguistics. One of these concepts, that of "family resemblance" proposed by Ludwig Wittgenstein (1953), is extremely useful in understanding perceived relationships between a language's manifestations, as would be the case between social and geolectal varieties. The weight of the concepts of "prototype" and "schema," closely linked to the frequency of events, facilitates the management of other notions, such as "use," "corpus" or "quantification." Similarly, the key concept of "categorization" leads to others, such as "centrality" or "periphery" and that of "embodiment," in the sense that our linguistic and conceptual systems are grounded in the physical, cognitive and social, embodiment of facts. Perceived—embodied—realities are the central focus of the experience and the filter that processes reality. Embodiment implies a relationship between language and material reality (versus the independence of generativist language) and, at the same time, requires the existence of a cultural and social environment in which the speaker, social cognition and language itself are always situated (Geeraerts and Cuyckens 2007).

Alongside these essential fundamental concepts, there are other important concepts involved in sociocognitive linguistic explanation which are, nonetheless,

less essential in practice. Although ecolinguistics was previously mentioned as important, it may not be necessary to incorporate notions such as "population," "ecosystem" or "environment" (Hawley 1986) because they can be replaced by closely related sociological concepts such as "community," "culture," "context" and "habitat." Likewise, several concepts fundamental to disciplines like ethnomethodology are already closely aligned with the sociological theories related to cognitive sociolinguistics. Important among them are the concepts of "indexicality" and "reflexivity." Indexicality refers, in the words of Garfinkel (1967), to the fact that the contents of expressions are not invariable; they are not defined once and for all. Their meaning derives from the environment where acts and social experiences take place. As a result, participants in everyday conversations are often required to clarify ambiguities and misunderstandings arising from the use of indexical expressions (Wolf 1982). In terms of reflexivity, ethnomethodology treats social facts as something that people execute through practical reasoning in everyday life. In as much as language use represents a description of the scenes of social interaction, it also constitutes organizing elements of those scenes. Language transmits information and time creates contexts in which information appears (Silverstein, 1976, Wolf, 1982: 132). We shall refer to this explicitly in addressing the cognitive aspects of semantics and the importance of discursive scenarios.

Debate: the Static and the Variable

Throughout its history, linguistics has handled many conceptual dualities that, either complementarily or contradictorily, have attempted to explain the nature or the workings of language. One of those most fundamental dualities is the one that originates in the Aristotelian distinction between *act* and *potency*. It is the opposition between what is done and what is feasible, between what is real and what is possible, between product and production. *Mutatis mutandis*, in linguistics, this is the distinction at the core of Wilhelm von Humboldt's *ergon* and *energeia* duality, or Émile Benveniste's (1967) *énoncé* and *énonciation* duality, or Noam Chomsky's *performance* and *competence* (1995). These concepts, in turn, have a direct correlation with *langue* and *parole*, as advanced by Ferdinand de Saussure (1916): the latter as an individual and concrete phenomenon, the former as a social and abstract entity. Likewise, sociolinguistics also incorporated into its theoretical framework a parallel duality: that of *language*, as variable competence, and *linguistic varieties*, in any of its manifestations (geographical, social, stylistic), called *lects* by Charles-James Bailey (1973).

In a cognitive sociolinguistics, neither facet of this duality should be disregarded. It is not possible to understand *speech* in its concreteness without *language* in its abstraction. It is not possible to understand the product without knowing the production process. A *lect* does not exist independent of a *language* that orders its components, both constant and variable. Just as an analysis of utterances should reveal the enunciation processes that underpin them, so too must competence clearly be able to produce the linguistic behaviors we observe. In this sense, cognitive sociolinguistics does not force us to be biased in favor of one side or the other of this conceptual debate.

Now, when we move from conception to linguistic epistemology, dualities are not always easy to resolve and sometimes become paradoxes. It is indeed true that, with respect to both the elaboration of concepts and epistemological construction, we situate ourselves in metalinguistic space. Nonetheless, while it may sufficiently satisfy our expectations for rigor that proposals, definitions and the treatment of proposed concepts be concrete and consistent, the development of an epistemology requires more. It requires us to reconcile our methodology with our theory. In such reconciliations, not everything is possible because, in the transition from research to social reality, methodology imposes limits. In this state of affairs, sociolinguistics, as an epistemological proposal, finds itself facing two possibilities: either putting more emphasis on the dynamics of sociolinguistic processes and the results of said processes or else facilitating a better understanding of sociolinguistic reality. The former is the main task that guided the work of the Labovian school, which, starting with the analysis of spoken language data —linguistic products—tried to build or explain the mechanism of production of that spoken language. And to accomplish that, it proposed the concepts of "variable competence," "variable rule" and "multilectal competence."

Yet, beyond interest in a sociolinguistic product, its production, or both, the fact is that understanding sociolinguistic reality can be based on phenomena that are either more static or more dynamic in nature. Let us be clear: it is not a matter of constructing a barrier between performance and system, between fact and potential. It is a matter of deciding whether to build with entities conceived of in their static manifestation or from entities conceived of in their dynamic manifestation. A few examples are worth mentioning. When we conceive of a phonological system of structural oppositions and safety margins between phonemes, we accept a static view of the language's phonic level. When we speak of linguistic meanings set in a lexicographic tool (e.g., a dictionary), we are employing a static manifestation of the concept of "meaning." When we use the concept of "social class" as an analytical tool and link it to objective parameters such as income, education or occupation, we adopt a static perspective of social structure. On the other hand, when we do not link the concept of "phoneme" to a limited group of sound options, when we state that word meanings can only be specified in interaction or when we give priority to the psychosocial reality of communicative exchanges in a community over its class structure, we are adopting a vision of language that has a more dynamic nature. All these approaches are tied to precise methodological resources, so simultaneously admitting both views is not easy.

This being the case, in a situation where a dynamic conception of language would come into conflict with a static conception, cognitive sociolinguistics would align with the dynamic. That is, it aligns itself with a conception of language in which communicative action contributes to the construction of sociolinguistic reality, but without denying the existence of static components. We think that, in this way, we can overcome the limitation of reductionist theoretical patterns focused on the relationship between language and speech, between the systematic and the atomistic, between the formal and the factual, which can only be dichotomous (Schlieben, Lange and Weydt 1981; Villena Ponsoda 1992, 2008a, 2008b).

Conclusion

Cognitive sociolinguistics is presented as an integrating and internally heterogeneous model in which different lines of research converge. However, these lines of research are based on a common conception of language, interaction and society. This conception understands language as a complex adaptive system. Cognitive sociolinguistics provides a metatheoretical space for integrating approaches and theories that intersect, creating a model of complex structure.

The starting point of our theoretical proposal is a dynamic view of language, of linguistic communication and of social configuration in which the processes of production and creation, as well as all the mechanisms of perception and understanding of language use, acquire great relevance. Thus, we move from a sociolinguistics of social strata to a sociolinguistics of cognition, perception and accommodation. As we do so, the psychosocial factors that appear alongside the purely sociological and linguistic receive the prominence they deserve. Language has a social dimension, which manifests itself in communication and in the activity of complex networks of speakers. It also offers a psychological dimension, which acknowledges the importance of factors such as frequency, convention and interaction and which carries out cognitive processes essential to the acquisition, variable use and changes of language in society.

References

Bailey, Charles-James N., 1973. *Variation and Linguistic Theory*. Arlington: Center for Applied Linguistics.

Baker, Paul, 2010. *Sociolinguistics and Corpus Linguistics*. Edinburgh: Edinburgh University Press.

Barlow, Michael and Suzanne Kremmer (Eds.), 2000. *Usage-Based Models Of Language*. Stanford, CA: CSIL.

Bastardas, Albert, 2014. "Towards a complex-figurational socio-linguistics: Some contributions from physics, ecology and the sciences of complexity." *History of the Human Sciences*, 27(3), 55–75.

Benveniste, Émile, 1967. *Problèmes de linguistique générale*. Paris: Gallimard.

Bernárdez, Enrique, 2005. "Social cognition: variation, language, and cultura in a cognitive linguistic typology." In *Cognitive Linguistics. Internal Dynamics and Interdisciplinary*

Interaction, Eds., F.J. Ruiz de Mendoza and M.S. Peña, 191–224. Berlin and New York: Mouton De Gruyter.
Blommaert, Jan, 2014. "From mobility to complexity in sociolinguistic theory and method." *Tilburg Papers in Cultural Studies*, 103.
Bourdieu, Pierre, 1982. *Ce que parler veut dire*. Paris: Librairie Artheme Fayard.
Bratman, Michael E., 1992. "Shared cooperative activity." *The Philosophical Review*, 101: 327–341.
Bresnan, Joan and Marilyn Ford, 2010. "Predicting syntax: processing dative constructions in American and Australian varieties of English." *Language*, 86–1: 186–213.
Bruner, Jerome, 1986. *Actual Minds, Possible Worlds*. Cambridge, MA: Harvard University Press.
Bybee, Joan, 2001. *Phonology and Language Use*. Cambridge: Cambridge University Press.
Bybee, Joan, 2010. *Language, Use and Cognition*. Cambridge: Cambridge University Press.
Chomsky, Noam, 1995. *The Minimalist Program*. Cambridge, MA: MIT.
Clark, Herbert H., 1996. *Using Language*. Cambridge: Cambridge University Press.
Coulmas, Florian, 2005. *Sociolinguistics: The Study of Speakers' Choices*. Cambridge: Cambridge University Press.
de Saussure, Ferdinand, 1916. *Cours de linguistique générale*. Paris: Payot.
Eckert, Penelope, 2012. "Three waves of variation study: the emergence of meaning in the study of sociolinguistic variation." *Annual Review of Anthropology*, 41: 87–100.
Eco, Umberto, 1997. *Kant e l'ornitorinco*. Milano: Tascabini-Bompiani.
Ellis, Nick and Diane Larsen-Freeman (Eds.), 2009. *Language as a Complex Adaptative System*. Chichester: Wiley-Blackwell. *Language Learning*, 59: Suppl.1.
Fill, Alwin and Peter Mühlhäusler, 2001. *The Ecolinguistics Reader*. London: Continuum.
Fillmore, Charles J., 1995. *Construction Grammar. Lecture Notes*. Stanford, CA: CSLI.
Garfinkel, Harold, 1967. *Studies in the Ethnomethodology*. Englewood Cliffs, NJ: Prentice-Hall.
Geeraerts, Dirk (Ed.), 2006. *Cognitive Linguistics: Basic Readings*. Berlin/New York: Mouton de Gruyter.
Geeraerts, Dirk and Hubert Cuyckens (Eds.), 2007. *The Oxford Handbook of Cognitive Linguistics*. Oxford: Oxford University Press.
Giles, Howard (Ed.), 1984. "The dynamics of speech accommodation." *International Journal of the Sociology of Language*, 46.
Greenberg, Joseph H., 1966. *Language Universals: With Special Reference to Feature Hierarchies*. The Hague: Mouton.
Grice, H. Paul, 1989. *Studies in the Way of Words*. Cambridge: Harvard University Press.
Harris, Roy, 1981. *The Language Mith*. London: Dockworth.
Haugen, Einar, 1972. *The Ecology of Language*. Stanford, CA: Stanford University.
Hawley, Amos H., 1986. *Human Ecology. A Theoretical Essay*. Madrid: Tecnos.
Humboldt, Wilhelm von, 1991. *Escritos sobre el lenguaje*. Barcelona: Península.
Hymes, Dell, 1964. "A perspective for linguistic anthropology." In *Horizons in Anthropology*, Ed., S. Tax, 92–107. Chicago, IL: Aldine.
Janicki, Karol, 2006. *Language misconceived. Arguing for Applied Cognitive Sociolinguistics*. Mawhah, NJ: Lawrence Erlbaum.
Krashen, Stephen D., 1982. *Principles and Practice in Second Language Acquisition*. Oxford: Pergamon.
Kristiansen, Gitte and Dirk Geeraerts (Eds.), 2013. "Contexts of use in Cognitive Sociolinguistics." Special Issue. *The Journal of Pragmatics*, 52: 1–104.

Labov, William, 1966. *The Social Stratification of English in New York City.* Washington, DC: Center for Applied Linguistics.
Labov, William, 1972. *Sociolinguistic Patterns.* Philadelphia, PA: University of Pennsylvania.
Labov, William, 2008. *The Cognitive Capacities of the Sociolinguistic Monitor.* Obtained from: www.ling.upenn.edu/~wlabov/home.html (accessed, 15 December, 2015).
Lakoff, George, 1987. *Women, Fire, and Dangerous Things. What Categories Reveals about Mind.* Chicago, IL: The University of Chicago Press.
Langacker, Ronald W., 1987. *Foundations of Cognitive Grammar. Volume I. Theoretical Prerequisites.* Stanford, CA: Stanford University.
Martín Butragueño, Pedro (Ed.), 2011. *Realismo en el análisis de corpus orales.* México: El Colegio de México.
Martín Butragueño, Pedro, 2000. "Los malentendidos naturales en el estudio sociolingüístico de la ciudad de México." *Nueva Revista de Filología Hispánica,* 48: 373–391.
Morales Domínguez, José F. (coord.), 2007. *Psicología social.* 3rd ed. Madrid: McGraw-Hill-Interamericana.
Nishida, Hiroko, 1999. "A cognitive approach to intercultural communication base on Schema Theory." *International Journal of International Relations,* 23–5: 753–777.
Ortega y Gasset, José [1924], 1986. "La percepción del prójimo." In *Ideas y creencias,* 123–137. Madrid: Revista de Occidente en Alianza Editorial.
Parsons, Talcott, 1937. *The Structure of Social Action.* New York: McGraw-Hill.
Pierrehumbert, Janet B., 2001. "Exemplar dynamics: Word frequency, lenition, and contrast." In J. L. Bybee and P. Hopper (Eds.), *Frequency and the Emergence of Linguistic Structure,* 137–157. Amsterdam: John Benjamins.
Schlieben-Lange, Brigitte and Harald Weydt, 1981. "Wie realistisch sind Variationsgrammatiken?" In *Logos Semantikos. Studia Linguistica in Honorem E. Coseriu* (vol. V), Eds., H. Geckeler *et alii,* 117–145. Madrid—Berlin—New York: Gredos/de Gruyter.
Schütz, Alfred, 1962. *Collected Papers I: The Problem of Social Reality.* The Hague: Martinus Nijhoff.
Shepard, Carolyn A., H. Giles and Beth A. Le Poire, 2001. "Communication accommodation theory." In *New Handbook of Language and Social Psychology,* Eds., W.P. Robinson and H. Giles, 33–56. Chichester: Wiley.
Silverstein, Michael, 1976. "Shifters, linguistic categories, and cultural description." In *Meaning in Anthropology,* Eds., K.H. Basso and H.B. Selby, 11–55. Albuquerque: University of New Mexico Press.
Simmel, Georg, 1971. *On Individuality and Social Forms.* Chicago, IL: The University of Chicago Press.
Solé, Ricard, 2009. *Redes complejas. Del genoma a Internet.* Barcelona: Tusquets.
The Five Graces Group, 2007. "Language is a complex adaptative system." Santa Fe Institute. Obtained from: www.santafe.edu/media/workingpapers/08–12–047.pdf (accessed 15 December, 2015).
Tomasello, Michael, 2003. *Constructing a Language: A Usage-Based Theory of Language Acquisition.* Cambridge, MA: Harvard University.
Trudgill, Peter, 2003. *A Glossary of Sociolinguistics.* Edinburgh: Edinburgh University Press.
Ungerer, Friedrich and Hans-Jörg Schmid, 1996. *An Introduction to Cognitive Linguistics.* Cambridge: Cambridge University Press.
Valéry, Paul, 2007. *Cuadernos (1894–1945).* Barcelona: Galaxia Gutemberg.
Villena Ponsoda, Juan M., 1992. *Fundamentos del pensamiento social sobre el lenguaje (Constitución y Crítica de la Sociolingüística).* Málaga: Ágora.

Villena Ponsoda, Juan Andrés., 2008a. "Redes sociales y variación lingüística: el giro interpretativo en el variacionismo sociolingüístico." In *Actas del VI Congreso de Lingüística General. Vol. III. Lingüística y variación de las lenguas*, Eds., P. Cano López, I. Fernández, M. González Pereira, G. Prego and M. Souto, 2769–2803. Madrid: Arco/Libros.

Villena Ponsoda, Juan M., 2008b. "Sociolingüística: corrientes y perspectivas." In *Diccionario Crítico de Ciencias Sociales*, dir. R. Reyes. Obtained from: www.ucm.es/info/eurotheo/diccionario/S/sociolinguistica.htm (accessed 15 December, 2015).

Voloshinov, Valentin N. [M. Bakhtin], [1929] 1973. *Marxism and the Philosophy of Language*. New York: Seminar Press—Harvard University Press—Academic Press.

Wittgenstein, Ludwig, 1953. *Philosophical Investigations*. New York: Macmillan.

Wolf, Mauro, 1982. *Sociologías de la vida cotidiana*. Madrid: Cátedra.

2
SOCIAL REALITY AND PERCEPTION

The two great thinkers Ludwig Wittgenstein (1953 [2009]) and Lev Vygotsky (1978) came to agree on the same interpretation: we humans are like fish in the water of culture. That metaphor has permeated the works of other scholars of history, society and cognition (Tomasello 1999). Culture is defined as the environment in which language is used and developed. Of the two, culture is the more general, more durable and has the farthest reach. Language, meanwhile, is a substantial element of culture. It is both an essential part of its nature and its medium of expression. Culture sets the limits within which social life unfolds and where contexts and situations arise for which language is deployed. Culture and society shape language's environment, but always within natural spaces, geophysical frameworks that determine and shape it (Auer and Schmidt 2010). Natural and cultural environments comprise the setting in which language occurs: language that is employed by speakers who live in these settings and perceive them in different, individual ways (Palmer 1996).

In regards to sociocultural reality, Labovian linguistics—like most social-based disciplines developed in the United States during the second half of the twentieth century—has been based on the structural functionalism of Talcott Parsons (1937), Kingsley Davis and Wilbert Moore (1945) and Robert Merton (1949). The discipline incorporates the concept of "consensus" as one of its foundations. Consensus theories consider common norms and values to be fundamental to society and that social order is based on a tacit agreement that causes social changes to be slow and orderly. This consensus also extends to language since linguistic behavior responds to the monitoring of norms that affect all speakers belonging to a community or a group. In contrast to consensus theories, conflict theories— of Marxist roots—stress the predominance of some social groups over others and explain social order as a result of manipulation and control by the dominant over the dominated, which can cause rapid and disorderly social changes. These ideas align with Dahrendorf's (1959) theories of *sociological conflict* and Marx's (Marx and Engels 1844) theory of *radical conflict*.

However, whereas the theories of consensus and conflict, respectively often appear to oppose each other as distinct interpretations of social and sociolinguistic reality, they are still both macro-theories focused on the interpretation of structures and social institutions, which makes them complementary rather than contradictory positions (Bernard 1983). To find radically different approaches to this sociology of structures, one has to turn to symbolic interactionism, phenomenological sociology or ethnomethodology (Ritzer 1996). These turn out ultimately to be dynamic sociologies of situation, of face-to-face interaction, of everyday life, of an individual as its protagonist in all its dimensions, including the social and the cognitive (Azurmendi 2000: 253–260).

A. On the Environments of Linguistic Usage

Proposition 2.1

Languages and their speakers are influenced by the cultural, communal, group and situational environment.

Proposition 2.2

Natural and cultural environments set the stage for language use by the speaker, who dwells in them and perceives them in different ways.

Proposition 2.2.1

Settings and environments have dimensions and duration that condition the relationship that speakers and communities establish with them.

Proposition 2.2.2

Sociocultural settings perceived as geographically larger or which involve a broader community are valued positively by speakers.

Proposition 2.3

Sociocultural settings produce normative values whose acceptance or rejection, tacit or explicit, contribute to shaping the linguistic identity of social groups and communities.

Proposition 2.4

The city constitutes a social environment that is positively perceived by speakers and provides a framework for the production, exchange and consumption of all types of goods, including the linguistic and cultural.

Proposition 2.4.1

The city is the social entity that best embodies the notion of *speech community* as it has been defined by traditional sociolinguistics.

Proposition 2.4.2

In cities, large structures augment social distance by hindering the face-to-face communication, which is characteristic of personal relationships.

Scholium 2-A

When we talk about communicative environments, we often use "sociocultural" as a label to identify them. However, despite the convenience of speaking of a "sociocultural environment," there are clear differences between what are properly called "cultural" elements and those that are considered "social." According to William Labov (2010: 3), cultural factors can be distinguished from the social according to the degree they involve face-to-face communication. Social factors, meanwhile, appear in the linguistic interaction between members of specific groups. Cultural factors mediate the association between linguistic facts and social patterns, which are partially, if not completely, independent from face-to-face interaction. Among the components of cultural environments, we find general dialectal features. On the other hand, social factors produce normative values whose acceptance or rejection contributes to shaping the linguistic identity of social groups or communities. In the sociology of Alfred Schütz (1964), social environments would belong to the realm of directly experienced reality where face-to-face interactions are produced (*Umwelt*) while culture and the major communal structures would be indirectly experienced realities (*Mitwelt*). This does prevent concepts such as that of "gender" or that of "social class" from being useful. Such concepts can be treated as social when they respond to a learning of patterns by means of face-to-face contact or as cultural if they are considered part of the learned cultural construct.

As we are observing, the internal structuring of that general category that we are calling "environment" is complex and includes, along with cultural factors, issues of a more concrete reality such as those of a social and situational nature. Among the social, we have included the "community" and those groups that comprise it. The community is conceptually and analytically prior to the individual since the individual's behavior cannot be understood without knowledge of the community to which he belongs. Traditional sociolinguistics often uses the term "speech community" to refer to the group of speakers who share (at least) a language variety, usage rules, as well as attitudes and appreciation for linguistic forms. From a methodological point of view, the city is the social entity that best corresponds to the notion of "speech community" as we just defined it. Thus, the city constitutes a social environment positively perceived by speakers and provides a setting for the production, exchange and consumption of all types of goods (Weber 1921), including the linguistic and cultural. In cities, the social distances established by large structures make face-to-face interaction between everyone in them impossible. However, such interaction does indeed occur in the area of personal relationships subject to the limits of specific situations (Calvet 1994; Villena Ponsoda 1994; Werlen 1995).

We have established, then, that language and its speakers are influenced by their surroundings at four different levels: the cultural, the communal, the group and the situational. Although this way of conceiving the structuring of the environment would reveal certain parallels with a concentric arrangement of cultural, sociolinguistic, pragmatic and linguistic competences, their real significance lies in presenting a different way to interpret the social factors that influence language and in reinterpreting some factors—such as social class—that have played a pivotal role in traditional sociolinguistics. That is, understanding linguistic behavior in terms of cultural, community, group and situational factors facilitates reinterpretation of notions such as "social class," "social groups" and "social networks," which deserve special attention because of their explanatory power in much sociolinguistic research.

A cognitive sociolinguistics cannot stop at describing the nature of the external factors that determine the language because it also aims to address the way in which those factors are perceived by speakers. Thus, in addition to the "objective environment," we may speak of the existence of a "perceived environment," which ultimately mediates the influence of the external on language. If the objective environment of linguistic communication includes, concentrically arranged, the "culture," the "community," "groups" and "situations," then the perceived environment, as a reflection of the objective environment, would include the same components and, in the same arrangement, with the exception that the degree to which each is perceived may be different.

The natural and sociocultural environments, then, set the stage for the use of language by the speaker, who not only lives in them but who perceives them in different ways. The influence of the environment on the community and its members has an objective existence. But it also has an existence in its recognition and perception (or not) by the community members themselves. These individuals store and recall information about the impact that cultural factors, such as identity or geographical origin, and of social factors, such as age or gender, have on linguistic use. From this perspective, the prototype model offers the possibility of

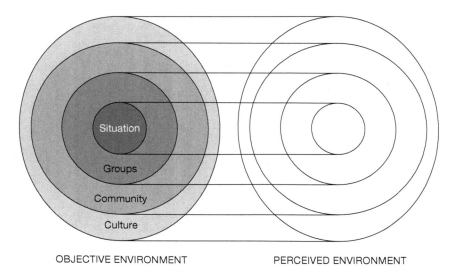

FIGURE 2.1 Social Reality as Objective Environment and Perceived Environment

explaining how the speaker categorizes sociocultural and situational factors associated with language, including factors such as the type of interlocutor or where a communicative interaction occurs.

The way in which environments and linguistic communication interrelate is not easy to explain. One way to account for it is to turn to the concepts of "regulation" and "creation," also utilized to analyze the relationships between social structure and linguistic structure (Moreno-Fernández 2009: 296). If we admit the possibility of distinguishing, in the sociocultural environment, levels corresponding to different degrees of abstraction, one could start by identifying three levels. The first level would be the most abstract and general, corresponding to the culture, macrostructure and power relations of the social organization. On the second level, relationships between organizations and social groups would be located. Finally, the third level, the most concrete, would correspond to relationships between individuals. The relationship between these three levels could be explained by the action of two components, which John Searle introduced in 1969: a *regulatory component* and a *constitutive component*. The *regulatory component* exists independently of behavior and therefore predates any activity. The *constitutive component* "constitutes" and creates an activity that logically depends on it. The *regulatory component* is created from the activity but, once established, it influences the activity itself (Searle, 1976, 1980: 111–134).

The constitutive element can be manipulated by the individual, to a greater or lesser degree, depending on its characteristics; the regulatory component cannot be manipulated by the individual. This sequencing from regulation to

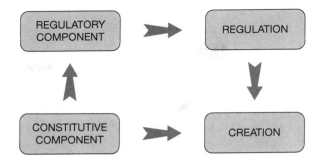

FIGURE 2.2 *Regulatory-Creating* Dynamics

constitution, from what is not manipulable by the individual to what can be manipulated by him, would be located in both the elements of the sociocultural environment and in those of the language.

Finally, the study of communicative environments can be understood as part of the discipline called "ecolinguistics," a field that has been expanding in scope since Einar Haugen started talking about the "ecology of language" in 1972. In general, ecolinguistics is based on the concepts of "interaction" and "diversity" and examines the relationship between social and cultural environments and culture. It constitutes a contextualized view of language, in which the speaker moves within an environment, perceives it, and lets it influence its own linguistic behavior. From here, the possibilities of applying ecological principles to linguistic matters is clear since these principles themselves have already been applied to inquiries on topics ranging from the coexistence of languages (including the disappearance of languages or language planning and linguistic policy) to communicative interactions and discourse analysis (Fill and Mühlhäusler 2001).

B. On Social Relationships and Language Use

Proposition 2.5

Language and the environment are interconnected in such a way that communicative intentions and an expression's meaning can only be completed and properly interpreted in context and with reference to a world in which they interact.

Proposition 2.5.1

Language and its use are influenced by the sociocultural context through the relationships that social groups and their members establish between each other.

Proposition 2.5.2

The influence of the social context is conditioned by the way speakers interpret each other's linguistic profiles, as well as by the way they categorize and perceive social organization and its dynamics, including the communicative.

Proposition 2.6

Societies—communities or cities—are organized into three structural levels: the institutional, the group and the interpersonal.

Proposition 2.6.1

The articulation of the three levels of structural organization of a society is possible thanks to the distribution of speakers in groups, which must reach a critical number for the social system to exist as a unit.

Proposition 2.6.2

Communication is the fundamental process that allows the formation of emerging institutions and groups within a society.

Proposition 2.7

The main types of social associations are social groups and social networks.

Proposition 2.8

The relationships between a society's networks and between members of those networks are based on a dynamic relationship that requires direct contact among speakers, even though not all group members are in direct contact with one another.

Proposition 2.8.1

Networks can be categorized according to their function as "informational" or "social"; both types are fundamental to language usage.

Proposition 2.8.2

Networks present different degrees of density and complexity; they can be interconnected in various ways, depending on the form they take.

Scholium 2-B

The lives of societies or human groups—let's call them "communities" or "cities"—develop within natural and cultural environments and are organized into three structural levels: the institutional, the group and the interpersonal. Such levels, thus sequenced, involve successively greater need for face-to-face interaction between speakers. They also exert two-way vertical influences upon each other. The three levels of structural organization, despite involving different structural types, are interrelated and can be articulated with respect to one another thanks to the distribution of speakers in groups and networks. This articulation is essential because the influence of the sociocultural environment is conditioned by the way speakers interpret one another's linguistic profiles, as well as by how they perceive and categorize social organization and its dynamics, including the communicative.

As established by symbolic interactionism, interwoven patterns of action and interaction allow the constitution of social groups and societies. Therefore, "interaction" is the key element in understanding the relationships between the individual's realization, including his language, and society's abstraction, including its culture. The adequate formulation of the relationships between the social system and the individual's personality was a key issue for the sociology of Talcott Parsons (1937) and a fundamental contribution of Georg Simmel's thought (1971); it has also constituted a concern in several other areas of knowledge, such as ethnography and social psychology. From a communicative perspective, language is influenced by the environment by means of the relationships established between social groups and members of those social groups.

The Old Social Class

Among the social groupings that have interested modern sociolinguistics throughout its not very long history, more ink has probably been spilled and more diatribes provoked by the concept of "social class" than any other (Trudgill 2003). Traditionally, the treatment of class or social strata in sociolinguistics has triggered the proposal of a range of multidimensional factors according to which the concept and its sublevels could be defined. This has been done, it seems, with the recognition that there are no clear boundaries between levels and that, in the end, these levels are no more than categories ordered along a continuum. The result has been that conflict between classes has been unable to achieve more than a minimum theoretical expression. The consensus proposed from the perspective of structural functionalism also reaches language from the moment that linguistic behavior responds to the adherence to norms that affect all speakers belonging to a community or a group. The way in which this consensual dynamics is articulated is linked to a conceptualization of society as being organized in a stratified and vertical manner. According to this conceptualization,

Western societies can be subdivided into groupings of strata or classes ordered from bottom to top, so that there exists a lower and an upper stratum among which one or more intermediate layers are identified. Membership in a stratum or class is recognized by the appearance of indicators among which the linguistic are not those of least importance.

As is known, the configuration of these strata is achieved by developing indices that attend to different factors, such as occupation or income level. When these factors are combined with the level of education or schooling, we obtain "socio-cultural strata." Following these social stratification patterns, William Labov used in his study *The Social Stratification of English in New York City* the social division proposed by John W. Michael in 1962. It is a linear scale of social status classification based on a 9-point socioeconomic index that combines three elements: the level of education, occupation and family income. Each dimension is divided into four degrees or possibilities (0, 1, 2 and 3). Speakers are assigned a score for each of the three dimensions, so that they can receive a maximum of 9 points (3 + 3 + 3) and a minimum of 0. Speakers are subsequently grouped into the following categories or classes: lower class (0–1), working class (2–5), lower middle class (6–8) and upper-middle class (9). This same way of determining social status was adopted by Peter Trudgill (1974) in Norwich (UK), by Shuy, Wolfram and Riley (1968) in Detroit (USA) and by other researchers in different Western cities.

According to Abercrombie, Hill and Turner (1986), the division of the population into three classes—working, middle, and upper—responds to a conventional sociological model of British class structure: manufacturing workers are in the working class; low level non-manufacturing workers (clerical, technical) are situated in the middle class; managers, administrators, and professionals are assigned to the upper class. An overlap of these classes in their linguistic usages has been discovered even with respect to the speakers' cognitive orientation. For example, in 1967, William Bright reflected on the relationship between language, social stratification and cognitive orientation. One of the examples that he proposed as a sign of this relationship is the distinction between "elaborate codes" and "restricted codes," a distinction established by Basil Bernstein in the 1960s that was oriented more toward people than toward statuses and which reflects and perpetuates socio-psychological differences between the middle class and the working class. In addition, the analysis of semantic differences observed between castes in India also revealed, according to Bright, different cognitive orientations between those castes, for which the Brahmins could have internalized caste values identified with conservatism, which would lead to a conservative tendency at the phonological and grammatical levels.

Yet, the limitations that a stratified and vertical interpretation of social distribution supposes are great. This has led to a reformulation of its importance in relation to language and to the analysis of its social use. Labov himself (2001) has explained clearly that the first social distinction that a child perceives is not that related to class stratification; a child rather perceives a difference between degrees of situational formality, which, in time, s/he reinterprets as a social hierarchy. From the point of view of linguistic variation, then, this accounts for the close link—the specular relationship—that endures between social strata and styles (Bell 2001). Grimshaw (1981: 11), meanwhile, defined speech models or styles according to the status of the speaker, as well as the type of audience.

When social classes or strata are correlated with linguistic usage, it has often been done in an attempt to identify objective social and linguistic features of the speakers that would lead to an accurate measurement—supposedly scientific—of such correlation. However, it is known that the possession of an intrinsic common characteristic, such as economic level or geographic origin, by members of a group is not enough to establish a correlation since there must also exist some type of spatiotemporal limits between the groupings. In this way, without employing some other (locally relevant) criteria for making the distinction, regardless of the care taken to measure and understand how certain classes influence certain linguistic uses or behaviors, the results of the investigation cannot be explanatory of the reality. This is because not only is it impossible to implement such an analysis, but also because many of these societies are not vertically stratified in the Western style. Furthermore, even in Western communities, phenomena like urbanization, slums or economic changes render any talk of "classes" per se meaningless. The best way to explain the dynamics of communities in most Latin American, Asian or African countries, for instance, would not be to appeal to the absence or exiguity of the middle classes, but to understand that the social groupings found there are not social classes per se but other types of groups or human associations (Sobrero 1978, Calvet 1994). In some cases, it may be useful to distinguish classes in a specific or local way, as Rickford (1986) did in Cane Walk (Guyana), while in other cases it is worth appealing to different concepts.

Social Groupings

Cognitive sociolinguistics proposes escaping the irresistible attraction of the concept of "social class"—especially when it is described from the perspective of objective features—and working with the generic concept of "social grouping." A "social grouping" would be any ensemble of members of a community, characterized by sharing a number of features and by being perceived as such, both by those who belong to this group and by outsiders. In this way, the concept of "grouping" would, without doubt, possess a universal dimension, which the concept of "class" does not. Furthermore, groupings may also be of two fundamental types: social groups and social networks. Social groups may be perfectly correlated with linguistic traits or usage, resulting in "sociolects," which would cease to be definitively understood as varieties associated with specific "classes" and which would then allow them to be linked to any type of social grouping. Social networks, meanwhile, would also be constituted by grouping members of a given community. The grouping, however, would be based on the frequent and direct contact between individuals rather than by the presence of common objective features. Groups and networks emerge and grow within communities until they reach a minimum critical number that allows a social system to exist as a grouping.

Groups and *networks*, as types of social groupings, show similarities and differences that are reflected in Table 2.1. An initial differentiating characteristic between social groups and social networks is the existence of an external and objective trait that identifies members of the group. Group membership is evidenced by that trait, whereas this is not necessarily the case with social networks. Thus, while social groups are often associated with traits and linguistic features that tend to be unique within the immediate/local context of use, linguistic usages characteristic of a network would not have to be unique to it. The groups constituted by youths, the elderly, men or women, or professionals in certain specialties, often display identifying linguistic traits. Networks, meanwhile, arise where there exists face-to-face contact and interpersonal links between individuals in that network, links that go beyond the sharing of a given social or linguistic trait. Appealing to the six ways of approaching a definition of social groupings proposed by Marvin Shaw (1981), we find the following:

a. in terms of *perception*, both the members of groups and those of networks share a particular collective perception;
b. in terms of *motivation*, both the members of groups and those of networks are associated with one other to satisfy needs or mutually profit from their affiliation;

TABLE 2.1 Characterization of Social Groups and Social Networks

Social Group	Social Network
Differences	
Constituted by qualitative traits	Constituted without qualitative traits
With an identifying linguistic or social characteristic	Without an identifying social or linguistic characteristic
Face-to-face contact among members not necessary	Regular face to face contact between members
Homogeneity	Heterogeneity
Similarities	
Inclusion of members of different groups	
Accommodation of uses	
Existence of leaders	

c. in terms of *interdependence*, the members of groups and those of networks are in some respects interdependent in order to satisfy needs or as part of their dynamics;
d. in terms of *purpose*, groups can form with the purpose of achieving common goals while individuals in a network do not have to be associated by any prior purpose;
e. in terms of *organization*, while the group members are organized and regulated by a system of roles and rules, agreed upon and accepted by the group, individuals in a network may be organized by means of socially received systems (kinship) or in accordance with specific internal dynamics; and
f. in terms of *interaction*, while the network members enter—or can enter—easily in face-to-face interaction, although with varying frequency of contact, social groups do not require contact between all of their members and it is very likely that many of them never get to maintain personal interactions.

Communication is the key process that makes the formation and reinforcement of institutions and emerging groups possible within a society. In fact, in intergroup communication, participants in the interaction attach more importance to their social than to their personal identity, a common occurrence, for instance, among users of mixed varieties, pidgins or creoles. And it is on the *continuum* between social identity and individual identity where language usage is configured (Tajfel 1984; Viladot 2008), where patterns of language use within different groups can be observed and where the diffusion of normative, urban usages by wealthier social groups can be examined. In fact, what Jules Marouzaeau (1944: 96) called "*la manie de copier le bourg*" is a key concept for the emergence of a common language, or *koine*. Furthermore, experience shows that the existence of categorizations based on different factors is possible. Thus, in European Mediterranean communities, it is common to find categorizations made by geolinguistic groups in which language works as an index of dialectal origin, while such type of geolinguistic categorization is not so frequent in the United Kingdom, where priority is given to the identity of sociolinguistic features, especially those linked to social classes or strata.

While the sociolinguistic study of social groups (occupational, gender, youth gangs, elderly) is bearing fruit of great interest for our knowledge of language usage at all levels (from the phonic to the discursive), the proposals emerging from the sociolinguistic study of social networks are also very valuable. A social network according to Lesley Milroy (1987), who pioneered the diffusion of this concept among sociolinguists, is a network of direct relationships among individuals that allows the exchange of goods and services, imposing obligations and granting the rights to which its members are entitled. Networks are characterized by the density, multiplicity and strength of relationships among its members. In sociolinguistic research the characteristics of a network are correlated with those of its members using corresponding linguistic variables. Thus, for example, Juan A. Villena Ponsoda (2001) has found that the density, the multiplicity and the strength of a network especially influence those with less education and that, as he observed in an Andalusian social network, the less educated clearly reject the distinction between the phonemes /s/ and /θ/, which is characteristic of Castilian Spanish and frequent in some social groups in Malaga, Andalusia (Spain).

Social groups and networks offer differentiating features but, nonetheless, share common elements. The nature of groups and networks is such that some members of one may also be members of the other. The organization of the dynamics between groups and networks present challenges in terms of their description. The Milroys' (1985) sociolinguistics has utilized the concept of "life-mode," which would include networks within a more abstract entity. The concept of "life-mode" connects small social networks with larger social structures or groups. Life-modes are part of a model in which social groups are considered internally structured entities related to other groups. In this model, linguistic behavior is due more to networks' power of determination and to the structures in which the speakers interact than to perceived attributes that would be characteristic of certain social groups. The model gives priority to the labor type, the type of family activity and to relationships that speakers maintain with other members of their groups.

For their part, groups are considered to result from fundamental structures of society that divide the population according to substantially different lifestyles. Since the 1990s, Peter Trudgill (2002) has been illustrating how different types of society can affect the manifestation of linguistic variation. Thus, in communities with low degrees of contact between varieties and with dense networks, we find concentrations of vernacular speech in low status groups, whereas when contact between different varieties is frequent, high status groups favor the concentration of elitist usages. Conversely, if networks in a community are loose and there is a high degree of contact, such state of affairs favors the dispersion of the vernacular emanating from middle status groups (Villena Ponsoda 2005, 2008).

Yet, the way in which life styles and other forms of social organization have been treated often brings to mind the weaknesses identified in the concept of "social class." Perhaps because of that, it is worthwhile to propose a double level of articulation for these groups. On one hand, the structures and particular dynamics of groups and networks crisscross within the community. On the other hand, the members of these groups and the groups themselves carry out activities within a linguistic market, understood as the social space in which they develop all kinds of interactions and communicative transactions. We shall return to this point later.

Finally, among the factors common to social groups and social networks, both communicative accommodation as well as the presence of linguistic leaders function to enable the cohesion of both (Labov 2001: part II; Martín-Butragueño 2006: 186ff). Linguistic leaders are individuals who emerge in both larger networks (large-world networks) and in more concrete networks (small-world networks). They are often capable of maintaining contact with many members of the groups or networks and, consequently, have remarkable linguistic influence and an ability to spread variations and changes.

Network Sociolinguistics

The concept of "network" is fundamental to understanding social reality (Wellman and Berkowitz, 1988) as well as sociolinguistic reality. Networks, woven between "nodes" by means of "ties" through which information flows, enable the development of social intelligence and, ultimately, the creation and workings of culture, which José Antonio Marina (2010) redefines as the set of cognitive, affective, normative messages passing through a network.

The dynamics of social networks, however, still possesses secrets that scholars have not yet uncovered. These secrets have to do with their formation and evolution as well as contact between their nodes. It is known that the distance between two unknown members of the same network could be up to six degrees of separation, at the most. However, our everyday personal relationships, those that occur within our immediate social environment, create intricate connections with no more than two degrees of separation between individuals. Consider that the relationships among the networks of a society and the individuals of that network are based on certain dynamics that require direct contact among speakers, although it does not demand mutual contact among all of its members. As Ricard Solé notes (2009) that, within networks, the complex has more to do with the nature of the interactions than with the nature of the objects that interact. The ways in which connections are established among different networks and among members of a network can be very different and may resemble the patterns depicted in A, B or C of Figure 2.3.

In the practice of sociolinguistic communication, networks are predominantly of type B, in which multiple subnetworks of different organization come into contact through shared components. Naturally, below a certain critical number of connections the system would be fragmented or non-existent; to exist as a large-scale system, however, it would be enough to simply exceed that minimum number of relationships between elements (Solé 2009: 37–38).

From a sociolinguistic perspective, fragmented communities would present a network structure similar to that of pattern I (Figure 2.4) whereas more cohesive communities, with a greater degree of contacts among its members, would bear closer resemblance to pattern II. In the latter case, the propagation of social and linguistic signals would be much faster and more intense than in the first.

Network architecture is extremely heterogeneous. It could present as containing a large number of elements that are loosely connected; else, it could contain very few elements with a large number of internal connections between elements. The latter type, classified as a "free scale" network due to its complexity, possesses great potential for propagating changes. In such networks, members of

48 Social Reality and Perception

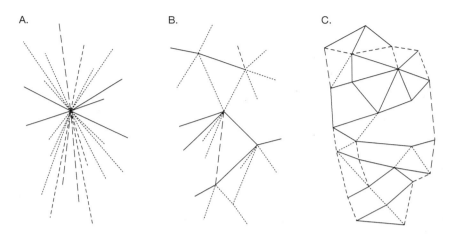

FIGURE 2.3 Network Types: Centralized (A), Decentralized (B), Distributed (C)
Source: Solé (2009: 64)

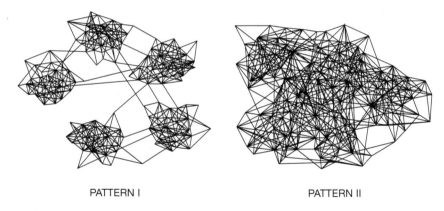

PATTERN I   PATTERN II

FIGURE 2.4 Networks with Varying Degrees of Internal Cohesion
Source: Solé (2009: 187)

a speech community relate in a non-random way, leading to a huge amount of potential triangular relationships that would make their communication possible because, if indeed individual behavior is unpredictable, the behavior of the masses, including their linguistic behavior, allows a statistical treatment that brings us closer to their knowledge (Solé 2009: 27).

The size and shape of networks depend on an individual's social memory as well as social factors. "Social memory," based on basic mechanisms of learning, enables the association of simultaneous elements, such as the use of linguistic features linked to groups and personal relationships with individuals. Personal relationships built up over an individual's life can amount to approximately 3,500. However, many of these are forgotten, resulting in active relationships that include, on average, about 300 people. These 300 individuals are "selected" largely on the basis of non-random social factors such as social position, sex or other social characteristics of the speaker (Molina et al. 2007: 222).

Figure 2.5 clearly shows the difference in the size and shape of the network if a Ghanaian immigrant living in the Catalan town of Vic and the personal network of a young Catalan woman, with higher education, a wealthy social position and a summer residence in Calella. For each of the networks represented in Figure 2.5, the communication patterns of language usage and the acceptance or propagation of linguistic change will work differently according to the external factors that define it.

In terms of their function, networks can be "information networks" or "social networks" and both are critical to language usage, even though the former overlap with the latter to some extent. From a communicative perspective, two types of network can be identified: "small world" networks and "big world" networks. The former are the personal networks of a speech community's members and within them occurs a dynamic of identity, variation and change, which can be tuned to the dynamics of other social networks and other groups. The latter social networks would include media networks, created by major media consortiums, able to reach all members of a community and even to penetrate different natural and sociocultural environments. These large-world networks, which unify language and communication patterns, are spreading and penetrating small networks, producing a conflict between identity and community values with

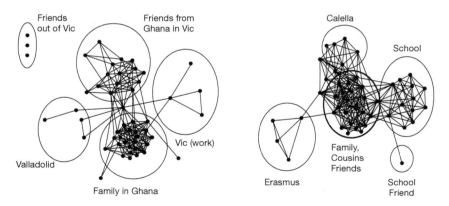

FIGURE 2.5 Social Networks of a Ghanaian Immigrant (Left) and a Young Catalan Lady (Right)

Source: Molina et al. (2007: 227, 228)

various consequences for language. On one hand, it seems that the unified lexicon easily penetrates different communities in which language operates, and on the other hand, phonetic features seem to index similar types of identities across different small networks. Nonetheless, emblematic language usage at any linguistic level can be converted into unambiguous signs of identity. This notwithstanding, linguistic elements that fail to become emblems may be affected by general leveling. In this dynamic, the most marked of features are either acquired or abandoned before the unmarked (Bortoni-Ricardo 1985). In light of these tendencies, it seems clear that a small-world network architecture may favor linguistic fragmentation, as was feared in the Hispanic world during the nineteenth century, whereas large world networks are indubitably beneficial for cohesion, as we have been showing with the universal reach of mass media, especially television.

C. On the Speaker as an Agent of Social Communication

Proposition 2.9

The speaker as an individual is a social agent who, using a system of symbols learned and employed in an environment, interacts with other individuals with specific purposes within a market dynamics.

Proposition 2.10

The individual constructs his identity and comes to perceive himself on the basis of patterns that he acquires by means of his communicative interaction with others and his history of interaction.

Proposition 2.11

The individual speaker is capable of perceiving differentiated language use and has the ability to associate these uses with groups of speakers and their respective characteristics, enabling a process of dialectal, ethno-linguistic, sociolinguistic and stylistic categorization.

Proposition 2.12

The ability to associate linguistic usages with specific speaker groups underlies the manifestation of sociolinguistic attitudes and beliefs.

Proposition 2.13

The individual speaker, whose identity is manifested in his linguistic usage, may himself serve as a model for social reference, thereby influencing other speakers and potentially leading linguistic usage and change.

Scholium 2-C

The interactions of individual speakers, as members of groups and networks, occur within linguistic markets. The concept of "linguistic market" is based on a Marxian principle whereby linguistic behavior is determined with respect to the relationship between speakers and means of production. A linguistic market reflects behaviors dependent upon individuals' socioeconomic activities (Sankoff and Laberge 1978). Within a given linguistic market, speakers in certain occupations tend to make normative use of language, while those in other professions do not need to do so, even if both kinds of speakers share similar socioeconomic profiles. The cognitive component appears when one attempts to link a linguistic variable with those indices of linguistic market integration, that is, with speakers' attributes. In order to assign such indices, we start from the assessment made by various individuals (judges) with respect to each speaker's history of socio-economic life. These assessments are used to "calculate" a speaker's index of market integration. The index is then, in turn, correlated with the linguistic variable studied. From a Marxist sociological position, Rossi Landi (1974: 33) indicated that languages are not creations of individuals, but products of the community and that a speech community is a kind of immense market, where words, expressions and messages circulate as commodities; every word, expression or message is presented as a unit of value, use and exchange.

We believe, however, that when the concept of "market" is presented in such a way, it does not reap all the benefits of its theoretical possibilities. The market is an appropriate environment, for example, to analyze the performance of the sociolinguistic norm or, generally, normative activity within a community (Fernández Marrero 2004). William Labov established (1972: 167 ff.) three classic sociolinguistic behaviors taking place in markets that present a clear cognitive dimension: (a) behavior that is submissive, obedient and that is in accord with institutionalized norms and the individual's linguistic image, (b) behavior that rebukes, subverts and opposes values associated with the institutional prestige norm, and (c) contradictory behavior that evidences both discourse by an individual that conforms to the norms that serve as a model and the individual's actual linguistic practice that neglects those norms, oftentimes falling into hypercorrection phenomena. In the latter situation, the individual configures and represents the world linguistically in line with the normative patterns he acquires from interaction with other individuals (Bruner 1986: 86; Fernández Marrero 2004: 142). Through accumulated interactions that linguistically expose individuals to normative social values, a speaker creates a sense of social belonging to certain groups or networks. In the course of accumulating these interactions, of constructing register and dialect through discursive situational contexts, the speaker experiences a tension between a normative macro-ideal, representing the sociolinguistic variety considered "standard," and a normative micro-ideal configured by the speaker himself. According to Fernández Marrero (2004: 145), in the symbolic order, the main consequence of this tension is the emergence of identity, the congruence/conflict between the "I" and the "other."

Kathryn Woolard (1985), meanwhile, indicated that there is no single language market, but that each variety is evaluated in a given vernacular context. In the Hispanic world, for example, varieties that emerge as a result of massive contemporary migration should be analyzed within their own contexts; logically the analysis is much more accurate when taking into account specific contexts. According to Woolard, this contextualized assessment does not constitute an obstacle to the existence of common patterns for a whole community. However, it is indeed interesting to draw attention to competing norms within communities. One may speak of norms that apply to varieties of low status and low prestige in contrast to norms observed with respect to varieties of high status and great prestige. And, the only best way to understand their opposition of dynamics would be by accessing local communities where the forms of certain varieties are significant. In China, for example, status or political credentials are of little help to compete in the markets of a changing economy. Education, language skills and, above all, the ability to adapt to new market rules, including linguistic and communicative institutions get greater rewards in the form of higher wages and better job opportunities. Just the ability to speak *Putonghua* clearly indicates that the speaker has acquired a good education and social preparation.

Pierre Bourdieu's interpretation of the relationship between language and the market complements what has already been explained. Bourdieu stated on several occasions (1977, 1991) that competence in "legitimate" language constitutes the most valuable linguistic capital in the conventional market. Speakers have to possess and accumulate such linguistic capital if they want to ensure their presence and profit in the market. Bourdieu (1984) establishes a close relationship between linguistic use, style and symbolism. Linguistic differences among speakers are analyzed in terms of the importance of language legitimized in socioeconomic activity. Language constitutes a symbolic capital potentially convertible into economic capital. Linguistic usage and variation owes its social value to the fact that it tends to organize itself into varieties that symbolically reproduce the system of social differences. Thus, "to speak" is to appropriate expressive styles already constituted by and because of use, and the hierarchy of styles available to a speaker reflects the hierarchy of social groups. The properties of the variety considered "legitimate"—called by others "standard language" or *langue légitime*—serve to mark social differences and, therefore, opportunities to access this variety are limited. In this way, the educational system becomes essential to sociolinguistics because the institution possesses a monopoly over the mass production of linguistic competence in the "legitimate" variety as well as reproduces the market on which the social value of linguistic competence and its ability to function as linguistic capital depend (Bourdieu 1982: 38). Likewise, the *habitus* is linked to the market because of both the conditions under which it is acquired and the conditions in which it is used; we do not learn to speak by listening, but by talking. That is, we learn to speak by producing speech in the market, in communicative situations in the bosom of a family that occupies a concrete position in the social space and that offers its younger members sanctions and models more or less distant from legitimate usage (Bourdieu 1982: 69).

For cognitive sociolinguistics, sociolinguistic varieties and styles are linked to agents endowed with perceptual schemas that allow the syncretic recognition of sets of systematic differences. What circulates in the market is stylistically characterized speech, both in terms of production, in the way that each speaker constructs an idiolect based on the common language, as well as in terms of reception, in the way that each listener contributes to the validation of a message by how he receives and evaluates that message (Bourdieu 1984: 13). Thus, it may be said that language is formed from the sum of the physiological activity of our vocal-auditory apparatus, communicative activity and cognitive activity. We can also say that linguistic manifestations offer different symbolic values within the market.

Finally, just as the members of a community are able to perceive social relations and the way these are reflected in language, they can also perceive solidarity within communities and groups through, for example, forms of address (Langacker 1991: 496). Speakers also have at their disposal a receptive competence of lectal schemas and the ability to relate them to social groupings (Kristiansen 2008: 68). Speakers, as their activities within the linguistic market develop, constantly put into practice an array of social and lectal categorization of their interlocutors, which may have different manifestations and consequences. According to Gitte Kristiansen (2008), the speaker-listener locates its interlocutors socially and dialectally based on his or her own model, by means of specific traits or in relation to him or herself. In turn, the speaker-hearer changes code according to interlocutor and style or on the basis of pre-existing models.

From all of the above, we conclude that the speaker-listener is able to perceive differentiated linguistic usage and to associate them to speaker groups with certain characteristics, completing processes of dialectal, ethno-linguistic, sociolinguistic and stylistic categorization. This guides his behavior toward sociolinguistic styles or positions that he considers beneficial to his interests. At the same time, the ability to associate linguistic usage to particular speaker groups makes possible the appearance of sociolinguistic attitudes and beliefs.

Debate: Objective Stratification or Subjective Perception?

The main debate that social reality brings to the table has to do with the manner and degree of its influence on language. In this respect, traditional sociolinguistics has worked from an objectivist perspective, where there are objective social realities external to the language, which, in their various components and to varying degrees, are able to directly influence elements of language. This perspective presupposes the possibility of objectively identifying and defining social realities —class, stratum, level—that are presumed to influence phonetics, grammar or lexicon. A cognitive sociolinguistics is situated in another perspective. For this sociolinguistics, the influence of social realities external to language is conditioned by the subjective way in which such realities are perceived and categorized by speakers and by the groups that these speakers constitute. The debate places stratificational sociolinguistics on one end and on the other the dynamic, cognitive based sociolinguistics of interaction.

Labovian sociolinguistics interprets its analysis as a way to discover differences between speakers. It is evident that certain linguistic usages are more characteristic of some social groups (classes, levels) than others and that sociolinguistic differences increase with increasing social distance between members of a community. Moreover, it is clear that the social distribution of linguistic usage functions as a decisive factor in the development and expansion of linguistic changes (Labov 1994). However, the use of stratification indices and the stratificational model as a whole have some drawbacks that cannot be ignored. Without involving affiliations or fighting tooth and nail to defend schools of thought, the weaknesses that have been identified in the multidimensional model of stratification advocated from the perspective of Anglo Saxon functionalism can be listed as follows:

i. There are communities with a social organization far removed from the Western canons of modern industrial societies. The African or Polynesian tribal organizations and the importance of castes in India indicate that social communication is not necessarily organized in vertical strata (Granda 1994).

ii. The stratification process is subject to seemingly objective factors (income, occupation), which actually suppose an implicit subjectivity in the research process itself: what dimensions are taken into account, how they are subdivided or gradated, how they interrelate. Milroy (1992) revealed this subjectivity regarding the reanalysis of the New York City reality studied by Labov in 1966. Perhaps for this reason, stratification is not always able to effectively reflect how external reality influences language.

iii. All of the indicators or dimensions handled by functionalism do not have the same importance within a community. This inequality can be solved on a case by case basis, assigning each factor a different weight or measure. However, such an approach does not resolve the difficulty of rigorously comparing the strata or classes of disparate communities. Likewise, the simultaneous handling of three, four or more indicators to build classes could hide or blur the particular importance of any one of them while contributing to an intermingling of dimensions that should be treated discriminately. Moreover, there is the difficulty of deciding properly—objectively?—each indicator's relative weight.

iv. The number of individuals that may simultaneously belong to different strata can vary from community to community. This fact, besides making difficult a comparison between communities, can create an image of society that does not reflect its natural tendencies or that ignores a configuration better correlated with linguistic usage. At the same time, class mobility can be very different between communities and this fact is likely to be neglected by a more static model of analysis.

Cognitive sociolinguistics does not ignore the analysis of objective social entities such as networks, groups or markets or even social classes, although all of them are conditioned by the way in which speakers perceive and subjectively categorize them.

Conclusion

It is incumbent upon a cognitive sociolinguistics to explain how the categorization and classification of linguistic and social objects are produced. The very use of language supposes a categorization (Schütz 1962, 1964) and societies always have at their disposal regular elements that help categorizations (Evans-Pritchard 1961). All of that has points of contact with—but it is situated far away from—the sociological base that has inspired variationist sociolinguistics, a base that supported stratification, with an effect on language variation that is not always clear and direct. Social groups correlate with linguistic features and produce "sociolects." Social networks are characterized mainly by direct contact among individuals in the network and provide an architecture that materializes in society and allows the articulation of many linguistic elements. Groups and networks coexist within communities until they reach a critical mass that allows the emergence of a social system. A multi-level interpretation, as has been proposed here, would overcome the artificial opposition between groups and individuals (Villena Ponsoda 2005, 2008).

Finally, regardless of how much impact natural and cultural environments may have on communication, the primary social agent, the engine of dynamic and communicative sociolinguistics is the speaker, as an individual who interacts in a situation and in a context. Norbert Elias (1970: 153) stated that "individual" and "society" are not two objects that exist separately, but two different, inseparable levels of the human universe. The speaker uses a system of symbols learned and employed in a sociocultural environment in order to interact with other individuals within a market dynamics. All of this is integrated with a role for linguistic and social reality that is itself defined by how it is conceived and perceived by speakers.

References

Abercrombie, Nicholas, Stephen Hill, and Bryan Turner, 1986. *Diccionario de sociología*. Madrid: Cátedra.

Auer, Peter and Jürgen E. F., Schmidt (Eds.), 2010. *Language and space. An International Handbook of Linguistic Variation. Vol. 1. Theory and Methods.* Berlin—New York: Mouton De Gruyter.
Azurmendi Ayerbe, María-José, 2000. *Psicosociolingüística.* Bilbao: Universidad del País Vasco.
Bell, Allan, 2001. "Back in style: reworking audience design." In *Style and Sociolinguistic Variation,* Ed., P. Eckert and J.R. Rickford, 139–169. Cambridge: Cambridge University Press.
Bernard, Thomas, 1983. *The Consensus-Conflict Debate: Form and Content in Sociological Theories.* New York: Columbia University Press.
Bortoni-Ricardo, Stella M., 1985. *The Urbanization of Rural Dialect Speakers. A Sociolinguistic Study in Brazil.* Cambridge: Cambridge University Press.
Bourdieu, Pierre, 1977. "The economics of linguistic exchanges." *Social Science Information,* 16: 645–668.
Bourdieu, Pierre, 1982. *Ce que parler veut dire.* Paris: Librairie Artheme Fayard.
Bourdieu, Pierre, 1984. "Capital et marche linguistique." *Linguistische Berichte,* 90: 3–24.
Bourdieu, Pierre, 1991. *Language and Symbolic Power.* Cambridge, MA: Harvard University Press.
Bright, William, 1967. "Language, Social Stratification, and Cognitive Orientation." In *Explorations in Sociolinguistics,* Ed., S. Lieberson. Bloomington: Indiana University – Sociological Inquiry, pp. 185-190.
Bruner, Jerome, 1986. *Actual Minds, Possible Worlds.* Cambridge, MA: Harvard University Press.
Calvet, Louis-Jean, 1994. *Les voix de la ville. Introduction à la sociolinguistique urbaine.* Paris: Payot.
Dahrendorf, Ralf, 1959. *Class and Class Conflict in Industrial Society.* Stanford, CA: Stanford University.
Davis, Kingsley and Wilbert E. Moore, [1945] 1970. "Some principles of stratification." *American Sociological Review,* 10 (2): 242–249.
Elias, Norbert, 1970. *Was ist Soziologie?* München: Juventa.
Evans-Pritchard, Edward, 1961. *Social Anthropology and Other Essays.* New York: The Free Press.
Fernández Marrero, Juan Jorge, 2004. *Actividad normativa y conciencia lingüística. Los problemas de la prescripción idiomática.* Sao Paulo: LGN.
Fill, Alwin and Peter Mühlhäusler, 2001. *The Ecolinguistics Reader.* London: Continuum.
Granda, Germán de, 1994. *Español de América, Español de África y hablas criollas hispánicas.* Madrid: Gredos.
Grimshaw, Allen D., 1981. *Language as Social Resource.* Stanford, CA: Stanford University.
Haugen, Einar, 1972. *The Ecology of Language.* Stanford, CA: Stanford University.
Kristiansen, Gitte, 2008. "Style-shifting and shifting styles: A socio-cognitive approach to lectal variation." In *Cognitive Linguistics. Internal Dynamics and Interdisciplinary Interaction,* Eds., F.J. Ruiz de Mendoza and M.S. Peña, 45–88. Berlin—New York: Mouton de Gruyter.
Labov, William, 1966. *The Social Stratification of English in New York City.* Washington, DC: Center for Applied Linguistics.
Labov, William, 1972. *Sociolinguistic Patterns.* Philadelphia, PA: University of Pennsylvania Press.
Labov, William, 1994. *Principles of Linguistic Change. Vol. I. Internal Factors.* Oxford: Blackwell.

Labov, William, 2001. *Principles of Linguistics Change. Vol. II. Social Factors.* Oxford: Blackwell.
Labov, William, 2010. *Principles of Linguistics Change. Vol. III. Cognitive and Cultural Factors.* Chichester: Wiley-Blackwell.
Langacker, Ronald W., 1991. *Foundations of Cognitive Grammar. Volume II: Descriptive Applications.* Stanford, CA: Stanford University.
Marina, José Antonio, 2010. *Las culturas fracasadas.* Barcelona: Anagrama.
Marouzeau, Jules, 1944. *La linguistique ou science du langage.* 2nd ed. Paris: Libririe Orientaliste Paul Guthner.
Martín Butragueño, Pedro, 2006. *Líderes lingüísticos. Estudios de variación y cambio.* México: El Colegio de México.
Marx, Karl and Friedrich Engels, [1844] 1932. *Gesamtausgabe,* Abt. 1, Bd. 3. Trans. Spa. *Manuscritos económicos y filosóficos.* Madrid: Biblioteca de Autores Socialistas. Obtained from: www.ucm.es/info/bas/es/marx-eng/44mp/ (accessed 15 December, 2015).
Merton, Robert, [1949] 1968. *Social Theory and Social Structure.* New York: The Free Press.
Michael, John W., 1962. "The construction of the social class index." In *Appendix A-1. Codebook, Mobilization for Youth.* New York: Mobilization for Youth.
Milroy, James and Lesley Milroy, 1985. *Authority in Language: Investigating Language Prescription and Standardisation.* London: Routledge & Kegan Paul.
Milroy, Lesley, 1987. *Language and Social Networks.* Oxford: Blackwell.
Milroy, Lesley, 1992. "New perspectives in the analysis of sex differentiation in language." In *Sociolinguistics Today. International Perspectives,* Eds., K. Bolton and H. Kwok. London: Routledge, pp. 162–179.
Molina, José Luis, Chris McCarty, Claudia Aguilar and Laura Rota, 2007. "La estructura social de la memoria." In C. Lozares, *Interacción, redes sociales y ciencias cognitivas,* 219–234. Granada: Comares.
Moreno-Fernández, Francisco, 2009. *Principios de sociolingüística y sociología del lenguaje.* 4th ed. Barcelona: Ariel.
Palmer, Gary, 1996. *Toward a Cultural Linguisitics.* Austin: University of Texas Press.
Parsons, Talcott, 1937. *The Structure of Social Action.* New York: McGraw-Hill.
Rickford, John, 1986. "The need for new approaches to social class analysis in sociolinguistics." *Language and Communication,* 6/3: 215–221.
Ritzer, George, 1996. *Teoría sociológica contemporánea.* Madrid: McGraw-Hill.
Rossi Landi, Ferrucio, 1974. *Ideologías de la relatividad lingüística.* Buenos Aires: Nueva Visión.
Sankoff, David and Suzanne Laberge, 1978. "The linguistic market and the statistical explanation of variability." In *Linguistic Variation: Models and Methods,* Ed., D. Sankoff, 239–250. New York: Academic Press.
Schütz, Alfred, 1962. *Collected Papers I: The Problem of Social Reality.* The Hague: Martinus Nijhoff.
Schütz, Alfred, 1964. *Collected Papers II: Studies in Social Theory.* The Hague: Martinus Nijhoff.
Searle, John, 1976. "The classification of illocutionary acts." *Language in Society,* 5: 1–24.
Searle, John, 1980. *Actos de habla.* Madrid: Cátedra.
Shaw, Marvin E., 1981. *Group Dynamics: The Social Psychology of Small Group Behaviour.* 3rd ed. New York: McGraw Hill.
Shuy, Roger W., Walter A. Wolfram, and William K. Riley. 1968. *Field Techniques in an Urban Language Study.* Washington, DC: Center for Applied Linguistics.

Simmel, Georg, 1971. *On Individuality and Social Forms*. Chicago, IL: The University of Chicago Press.
Sobrero, Alberto, 1978. "Borgo, città, territorio: alcuni problemi di metodo nella dialettologia urbana." *Rivista Italiana di Dialettologia*. II/1: 9–21.
Solé, Ricard, 2009. *Redes complejas. Del genoma a Internet*. Barcelona: Tusquets.
Tajfel, Henri, 1984. *Grupos humanos y categorías sociales*. Barcelona: Herder.
Tomasello, Michael, 1999. *The Cultural Origins of Human Cognition*. Cambridge, MA: Harvard University Press.
Trudgill, Peter, 1974. *Sociolinguistics. An Introduction*, Harmondswoth: Penguin.
Trudgill, Peter, 2002. *Sociolinguistic Variation and Change*. Edinburgh: Edinburgh University Press.
Trudgill, Peter, 2003. *A Glossary of Sociolinguistics*. Edinburgh: Edinburgh University Press.
Viladot i Presas, Maria Àngel, 2008. *Lengua y comunicación intergrupal*. Barcelona: Editorial UOC.
Villena Ponsoda, Juan Andrés, 1994. *La ciudad lingüística. Fundamentos críticos del a sociolingüística urbana*. Granada: Universidad de Granada.
Villena Ponsoda, Juan Andrés, 2005. "How similar are people who speak alike? An interpretive way of using social networks in social dialectology research." In *Dialect Change: Convergence and Divergence in European Languages*, Eds. P. Auer, F. Hinskens and P. Kerswill, 303–334. Cambridge: Cambridge University Press.
Villena Ponsoda, Juan Andrés, 2008. "Redes sociales y variación lingüística: el giro interpretativo en el variacionismo sociolingüístico." In *Actas del VI Congreso de Lingüística General. Vol. III. Lingüística y variación de las lenguas*, Eds., P. Cano López, I. Fernández, M. González Pereira, G. Prego and M. Souto, 2769–2803. Madrid: Arco/Libros.
Villena Ponsoda, Juan M., 2001. *La continuidad del cambio lingüístico*. Granada: Universidad de Granada.
Vygotsky, Lev S., [1978]. *Mind in Society*. Cambridge, MA: Harvard University Press.
Weber, Max, [1921] 1987. *La ciudad*. Madrid: La Piqueta.
Wellman, Barry and Stephen D. Berkowitz (Eds.), 1988. *Social Structures: A Network Approach*. Cambridge: Cambridge University Press.
Werlen, Iwar (Ed.), 1995. *Verbale Kommunikation in der Stadt*. Tübingen: Gunter Narr.
Wittgenstein, Ludwig, 2009. *Obra completa*, Ed. Isidoro Reguera. Madrid: Gredos. Vol. I: *Tractatus logico-philosophicus* [1921]. *Investigaciones filosóficas* [1953]. *Sobre la certeza* [1969].
Woolard, Kathryn A., 1985. "Language variation and cultural hegemony: Toward an integration of linguistic and sociolinguistic theory." *American Ethnologist*, 12: 738–748.

3
WORLDVIEW, DISCOURSE AND SOCIETY

Discourse analysis is typically located on the periphery of sociolinguistics. Its origin is linked, on one hand, to pragmatics, where it contrasts with conversation analysis and, on the other hand, to sociopolitical studies, where it is a primary source of information for the understanding of ideology. Likewise, while considering language and speech to be part of culture and worldview has been common practice in anthropological and philosophical studies (Marcus and Fischer 1986), and more recently of cultural studies, it has not been central to sociolinguistics.

The point of view adopted here is different. The study of the most complex language manifestations—speech acts, speeches and conversation—are seamlessly integrated into the core of cognitive sociolinguistics. And this is so for two main reasons. The first is that everything discourse reflects—worldview, culture, social frameworks—meets cognitivist interpretations of sociolinguistic reality, given that representations of the world and perceptions of social relations are processes of a cognitive order. The second reason is that discourse relies on situations that are of central concern to cognitive sociolinguistics, such as the speaker's response to selection processes, the speaker being object and instrument of communicative accommodation and the speaker's experience of linguistic variation processes.

A. On Speakers and their Representation of the World

Proposition 3.1

The representation of the world is a mental construct that is part of a sociocultural framework and part of the cognitive unconscious.

Proposition 3.2

Linguistic relativity assumes that the representation of the world, the organization of knowledge and sociolinguistic perception are determined in each community by the form and use of the languages concerned.

Proposition 3.2.1

Discourse construction is performed by a selective process that can project a representation of the world.

Proposition 3.2.2

Communicative interaction and experience accumulated through interaction help to configure a representation of the world.

Proposition 3.3

Discourse and social uses of language reflect a speaker's, a group's or a community's representation of the world.

Proposition 3.3.1

Speakers have the ability to build descriptions, arguments, narratives and instructions according to their particular worldview and reality.

Proposition 3.3.2

Social changes and changes in natural and cultural landscape may result in new linguistic forms.

Scholium 3-A

A language and the environment in which it is used are connected so that speakers' communicative intentions and the meanings of their expressions can only be properly realized and interpreted with reference to the world in which they exist. The natural and cultural environment constitute a framework for entering the predominant representation of the world in a speech community. Language, meanwhile, is a tool that allows the individual and the community to establish a relationship with their environment. In this relationship, a language expresses or verbalizes the nature of the environment, but in doing so it builds and categorizes that environment, conditioning the way the environment is perceived. The theory of linguistic relativity, mainly proposed by Benjamin Lee Whorf (1940), argues that worldview, sociolinguistic perception and the organization of knowledge in each community are determined by the shape and the use of the languages used to represent those environments. The most recent studies on the naming of colors seem to confirm the weight of linguistic expression on categorical perception (Roberson 2005; Deutscher 2011). This would justify, in a cognitive linguistics, the existence of hundreds of designations for colors in some languages, such as the Maori of New Zealand, or only a few in others, as the Bassa of Liberia (Gleason 1970).

Another way of understanding the relationship between language, culture and worldview is that proposed by Jerzy Bartmiński and his Polish school, inscribed within a "cognitive ethnolinguistics" whose conceptual apparatus is based on the notions of "linguistic worldview," "stereotype," "perspective" or "profile" of the objects (Bartmiński 2010: 19). For cognitive ethnolinguistics, worldview is a subjective interpretation of reality, a reality relativized through the subject's value system and perspective. Worldview is expressed through a set of judgments linguistically configured and reconstructed from systematic, conventional and textual or discursive information. This worldview includes linguistic stereotypes, that is, images of people, places and events related to facts that are considered normal in a culture.

When we hear others speak of "culture", however, it is not always clear what is being referred to. One acceptable possibility is Goodenough's definition (1957: 167), which considers "culture" what a person must know or believe to function properly among members of a particular group of people and to fulfill a role accepted by them. All that knowledge is acquired through a process of socialization in which language plays a crucial role. But this definition of "culture" is not the only one in which language is involved. Clifford Geertz (1973), for example, presents culture as an essentially discursive construction when he defines it as the set of stories we tell ourselves about the reality around us. Other sociologists, too, have language in mind when they define culture as a collection of knowledge, beliefs, customs or habits (Tylor 1871) or as a behavior learned from a society or group (Mead 1964), in which language figures as an important tool for learning.

Returning to the linguistic, it is important to indicate that language structures the reality in which it becomes embedded through the contextualized construction of discourse. Moreover, communicative interactions lead to an accumulation of experiences that gradually shape both the individual and the collective representation of the world. The usage scenario, the place where the reality of the environment is expressed and at the same time is built, is the sociolinguistic market. For Bourdieu (1984: 13), the market helps to build the symbolic value of language while simultaneously building the meaning of discourse. Thus, speech, to be well understood, is subject to the constraints of the situation and the context in which it appears, as well as to its sociocultural environment. Cognitive sociolinguistics argues, therefore, that neither the language nor the discourse in which it is articulated constitutes passive elements or simple reflections of surroundings. Thus, it does not seem enough to explain the relationship between reality, worldview and language with the metaphor of the "mirror," as if one were a reflection of the other.

An alternative to the mirror metaphor would be the "construction" metaphor whereby discourse constructs versions of the world and the world is being built as we speak, write or discuss it. To understand how discursive constructionism works—that is, how discourse constructs reality and worldview, we could appeal to different theoretical proposals. One of them is made by linguistic anthropology, from the work of Whorf, also closely related to that of Malinowski (1982). A second proposal is that of conversation analysis (Sacks 1992), in which linguistic interactions become the bricks that build worldview and the conceptualization of society. The third would be discourse analysis itself, approached from different schools of thought (Lozano et al. 1989; Schiffrin 1994; Van Dijk 1978, 2011). These three proposals share cognitivist elements and opt for conceiving reality as a social construction (Berger and Luckmann 1966; Potter 1998). The way in which social and cultural factors influence the production and interpretation of a statement would be the object of a *sociocultural pragmatics* and would include, among its interests, the study of conversation, discourse genres and style.

A cognitive interpretation of the relationship between discourse and reality maintains that interaction is essential for the understanding of reality and the construction of a particular worldview. From here, discourse is organized differently according to how we try to accomplish major tasks: *argumentation*, *description*, *narration* or *instruction*. The elaboration of arguments allows the construction of reality through discursive and linguistic selection. To construct arguments, the speaker selects what to use and what not to use, from the semiotic and linguistic standpoint, to create categories, or draft discursive metaphors as shown in the work of George Lakoff (1987, 2004). Metaphorized discourse is capable of achieving ontological manipulation when used frequently and persistently in one perspective.

Descriptive discourse permits not only an explanation of how a reality is but also allows a "construction" of realities, in which facts are combined with the speaker's perspective and where two opposing strategies are put into effect: the *accreditation* of objective categories and the *formulation* of subjective interests. Thus, the speaker organizes descriptive speech in a way that is closely aligned with his interests or distant from them. Accreditation—that is, the use of features that seem to reinforce the veracity of a description—is used in discourse, especially where references are made to what are considered to be factual events. The other tactic, that of formulation—that is, the mention (or reproach) of someone's particular interests—then, is a tool used by both sides to undermine the good credit of the party making those descriptions. In this way, descriptions tend to move between the invocation of interests (formulation) and the presentation of reality (accreditation) with the goal of influencing the interlocutor's perception of reality. When descriptions come from community leaders, they have greater credibility. In any case, descriptions can appeal to the components of a "hierarchy

TABLE 3.1 Hierarchy of Modality

X
X is a fact
I know that X
I contend that X
I believe X
I formulate the hypothesis that X
I think that X
I guess that X
X is possible

Source: Adapted from Potter (1998: 148), according to Latour and Woolgar (1986).

of modality," such as the one proposed by Bruno Latour and Steve Woolgar (1986), which makes it possible to enhance the accuracy, that is, factuality, of a description or dodge a description that can be discredited or undermined. Here is a hierarchy that reflects aspects of epistemic modality.

The work of Bruno Latour and Steve Woolgar (1986) is extremely interesting because they try to show that all reality is a social construct developed through language. That is a fact that can be demonstrated even from within the meticulous and empirical world of scientific research, where mechanical errors are not unusual, with little impact on the ultimate value of research, so long as it is wrapped in an appropriate garb of beliefs and supposed social acceptance. From a position akin to this, the attitude toward scientific descriptions can be expressed in rhetorical terms, either with an offensive rhetoric, using ironic speech or formulations meant to undermine it, or with a defensive rhetoric, using objectified speech to prevent others from undermining our descriptions.

Narrative discourse, which has attracted the attention of linguists, psychologists, ethnographers and sociologists, can build a reality by controlling which accreditation elements become part of the narrative and providing details as required for either the acceptance or the rejection of the interlocutor. From this point of view, an interesting topic is the role of citations in narratives in that they seek consensus and corroboration through the construction of (seemingly) factual discourse. A conversational citation is an oral text in the form of sequences in which something is told. The direct quote, being a selective representation in which the speaker chooses certain actions and how they are represented, serves to build the positive image of the speaker (Brown and Levinson 1978). As noted by Laura Camargo (2004), speakers, through quotes, express their perception of the world and show that language is vital for expressing their points of view about the actions narrated and the universe in which the speakers themselves operate.

Finally, instructional discourse (i.e., the discourse of giving instructions), having received perhaps the least amount of attention in linguistics, evidences an important relationship with reality because it neither narrates reality nor describes it, but rather anticipates it. In a way, instructional discourse is a pre-narrative.

The author—often writer, but not by himself—constructs a reality that can only materialize after the instruction itself; yet, it also requires the existence of a prior reality without which instruction would be decontextualized. Instructional speech only achieves its purpose to the extent that the recipient (reader) is able to envision the actions foreseen by the narrator.

B. On Speech and Social Dimension

Proposition 3.4

Cultural, social and contextual factors determine the production and interpretation of linguistic messages.

Proposition 3.5

Contexts are subjective mental models of social situations.

Proposition 3.5.1

Context models are crucial to the mental processes involved in the production and reception of discourse.

Proposition 3.5.2

Contexts control the variable properties of utterances and conversation, and make possible variation at the discourse level.

Proposition 3.6

Discourse and conversational interactions are the fundamental manifestations of language in social use.

Proposition 3.6.1

Conversational interaction is the fundamental form of spoken language production; it consists of speech acts and all other sociolinguistic uses of language can be attributed to it.

Proposition 3.6.2

Speech acts are spoken language manifestations that perform activities of a social nature, that place the speaker with respect to his interlocutors, and that influence their behavior.

Proposition 3.6.3

Discourse is a complex linguistic construction intended to meet specific social and communicative functions.

Proposition 3.6.4

The genre of a discourse—argumentative, descriptive, narrative and instructional—is determined by the speaker and his social context.

Proposition 3.7

Speech acts and discourses may be subject to semantic or conceptual transformations without there being a desire to transmit differentiated meanings or references.

Proposition 3.8

Styles are configured by systematic feature sets that can be seized and syncretically perceived as belonging to a speaker or a social context.

Scholium 3-B

Just as cognitive sociolinguistics recognizes the decisive action of discourse in the construction of the representation of reality and worldview that a speaker, a group or a community has, it also maintains that the production and interpretation of discourse is determined by cultural, social and contextual factors. We have already made reference to the influence of cultural factors on these linguistic manifestations, but we have not yet insisted on the relevance of context.

For Teun van Dijk (2011), contexts should also be understood from a cognitive perspective. Contexts are subjective mental models of social situations and these models are crucial in the processes of speech production and reception. However, the implementation of context models in the production of speech (texts) and conversations is not only a form of cognitive processing but also a practice based on interaction strategies. In this practice, contexts are able to influence discourse thereby triggering discourse variation and the control of variables acting on the discourse itself and on conversation. At the same time, shared sociocultural knowledge is the basis for the formation of both context models and the production and interpretation of discourse. Such processes are the main objective of a research line called *sociology of context* (Van Dijk 2011: 223–225).

After the decisive action of context models on discourse construction—including its variations—it is interesting to dwell on the components of discourse and the concrete forms it takes. The distinction between discourse and conversational interaction, though blurred, is essential. We say blurred because it is not a matter of two stagnant manifestations; conversational interactions may include different types of discourse just as discourse can reproduce dialogues or interactions. However, the distinction is clearer if we focus on their internal dynamics.

Conversational interaction is the fundamental form of spoken language production in an immediate sociosituational context (Calsamiglia and Tusón 2007: 20–35). It is an in-person interlocution, that is a dynamic and cooperative face-to-face interaction. Beyond specific phonic and grammatical characteristics (Briz 1996), a conversational interaction, whether colloquial or not, is sensitive to the interlocutors' perceptions and to the "social pressures" to which they are subjected. Dialogue can also take different configurations according to the goals being pursued: argumentative dialogue, narrative, debate. In argumentative dialogue, for example, there must be a clear intentionality in which the speaker's perspective predominates. His judgments will respond to his attitude and to certain fundamental intentions: an observation, an evaluation or a prescription. From this point on, the agreement or disagreement between interlocutors about what has been observed and about a set of basic criteria will determine the type of dialogue that is built. According Gilbert Dispaux (1984), argumentative dialogues can be of four types: *strategists dialogue* (with agreement on a defined set of observations and on a set of essential rules or criteria); *experts dialogue* (with disagreement on the observed and agreement on the criteria); *ideologues dialogue* (with agreement on the observations and disagreement on the criteria) and *deaf dialogue* (with disagreement on both the observed and the basic criteria).

Interactions are composed of speech acts, which are statements that perform actions of a social nature, that position the speaker with respect to their interlocutors and that influence their behavior. Among the different speech act typologies, perhaps the best known is that which John Searle proposed in 1976, in which he distinguished representative, directive, commisive, expressive and declarative acts.

When discourses, conversations or speech acts are inserted in a given context and respond to precise situational conditions, we speak of "styles," which are configured by systematic feature sets that can be seized and perceived syncretically as belonging to a speaker or a social context. As Bourdieu (1982) indicates, what appears in the market is simply stylistically characterized speech, both in terms of its production, to the extent that each speaker constructs his idiolect from the common language, as well as in terms of reception, to the extent that each listener contributes to reproducing the message that he receives and evaluates.

As for discourse itself, it can be argued that it consists of complex linguistic constructions intended to serve specific social and communicative functions (Van Dijk 1978). However, discourses are not static entities with respect to either how they are constructed or how speakers reproduce them. Discourse undergoes semantic or conceptual transformations influenced by communicative factors such as the speaker's momentary intention. It is also influenced by non-linguistic factors such as short- and long-term memory. This production instability has a parallel in reception, so it is not surprising that misunderstandings occur. Baudelaire said, in his *Mon coeur mis à nu* diaries (1864), that the world works because of misunderstandings. Moreover, William Labov himself attaches importance to misunderstandings for the explanation of sound changes (2010). In the transformations or variations that occur between speeches or within speech, we recognize processes that affect semantic, syntactic, lexical and phonetic structures (Van Dijk 1978: 211–223).

The transformations or variations that a discourse undergoes during construction or replication include omissions, adjunctions, permutations, substitutions and recombinations (Coulthard 1977). These transformations can preserve both the meaning and reference of speech, that is its truth-value. In the latter case, the discursive result would be, from the semantic point of view, strictly equivalent to the original and would respond to "correct" transformations. When improper information is added, information is omitted or recombined and permutated inappropriately, we speak of "incorrect" transformations.

Finally, discursive variation may respond to the need to adapt to a concrete social and communicative situation, with all that this implies regarding the modification of meanings or referents. But it can also respond to factors of an individual, group or communicative-linguistic nature without the intention of transmitting different information with different meanings or referents. In either type of variation, the language displays a rich repertoire of discursive transformations that allows the expression of different ways to say different things or the same things in different ways.

C. On the Position of the Individual in Society

Proposition 3.9

Individual linguistic activity contributes to the configuration of identity and allows integration of the speaker into the macro-social structures by opposing of the individual's discourse to that of other individuals.

Proposition 3.10

The speaker's integration into society is accompanied by processes of communicative accommodation in which both convergence and divergence appear.

Proposition 3.11

Socially and contextually determined discourse is the basis of the normative meta-language policy and of the ideology underlying metalanguage policy.

Proposition 3.12

Linguistic attitudes and beliefs condition the process of communicative accommodation of some speakers toward others and of some social groups toward others.

Proposition 3.13

Communicative interaction has among its main functions the molding of interpersonal relationships, which takes place through linguistic choices.

Proposition 3.14

Communicative behavior is socially appropriate when it conforms to general principles and specific norms that characterize politeness and are consistent with the social environment.

Proposition 3.15

Forms of address constitute an essential component of politeness and reflect the perception of power and solidarity between speakers as well as the judgment on their respective status.

Scholium 3-C

Verbal communication is not limited to the exchange of information but includes, as one of its main functions, the modeling of relationships. Individual linguistic activity allows the integration of the subject in complex macro-social structures by contrasting his own speech to that of other individuals. Moreover, speakers develop these integration or opposition processes through their linguistic choices. Furthermore, let us not forget that the social dimension of discourse includes the way in which the speaker approaches discourse construction. Cognitive sociolinguistics is very aware of this and gives great importance to two dynamics: (a) that of *communicative accommodation* mainly deployed in processes of convergence and divergence, and (b) that of *sociolinguistic attitude*, closely linked to beliefs. Likewise, attitudes and beliefs are crucial in the process of communicative accommodation from some speakers to others and from some social groups to others.

The speaker's position with respect to his immediate social environment can be located with respect to two levels of singular relevance to the contextualized use of language: the level of politeness and the level of ideology. The level of politeness permeates uses of language where social constraints are most readily observable. Behavior is socially appropriate when individuals observe general principles and specific norms included in the concept of "politeness" (Coulmas 2005: 84). Between speaker and interlocutor rests a set of perceptions that is crucial to the functioning of politeness, solidarity and the formation of judgments about the statuses of the speakers, which affects important aspects of communicative interaction, such as address forms (Langacker 1991: 496). Address forms constitute an essential component of politeness and reflect how speakers perceive their power, solidarity and statuses with respect to one another.

It is also important to recognize the impact of ideology on the identity construction of speakers, that is, of social subjects in a specific cultural context. Ideologies provide identities to people and carry associated forms of behavior, including linguistic habits. Thus, identity, defined ideologically, manifests itself through speech. In turn, every culture incorporates identities defined by ideologies that interpret reality and reflect a worldview. However, it must be said that the relationships between discourse, identity, ideology and culture can be interpreted in different ways, according to the theoretical position that is adopted (Althusser 1971; Laclau 2006). Be this as it may, at this juncture we are interested in simply highlighting the existence of close links between such notions.

On the other hand, ideology is crucial for following norms of correctness, ownership and appropriateness in language use. But the interesting thing is not so much that speakers have an ideology that favors or disfavors abiding by externally established rules—defined by the language academies for example—for language production, but that sociolinguistic usage itself also contributes to the development of the normative metalanguage and the ideology that sustains the normative metalanguage thus allowing for categorization and relationships between different types of speakers to be established with respect to the norm. Linguistic praxis is the basis of the normative metalanguage as well as its underlying ideology so that discourse itself becomes a means of explaining normativity (Fernández Marrero 2004: 147).

In sum, cognitive sociolinguistics explains the speaker's position within his social environment by examining what happens in processes of perception: perception of others' discourse, perception of how others handle politeness, perception of others' ideological convictions—all of this according to his own contextual models.

Debate: Language and Reality

One of the oldest debates, not just in linguistics itself, but also in the philosophy of language, is that of the relationship between language and worldview, as well as between language and the perception of reality. Does the world determine language or is language what conditions how you view external reality, including social reality? It seems evident that the natural and cultural environment can influence the architecture of language, especially with respect to the lexicon. Likewise, however, lexical systems can influence the organization of reality. For example, a language's kinship lexicon can influence how family relationships are interpreted, both with respect to how individual terms relate to each other and as a whole. So where is the preeminence?

The interrelationships between language, social organization and worldview constitute some of sociolinguistics' main interests (Casado 1988). This interest is not new, as its modern origins can be traced back to Wilhelm von Humboldt, for whom language shapes thought, at the same time that it perfectly expresses the national spirit of a people, their ideology, their way of life and their worldview. For Humboldt, however, language had an *inner form*. This *inner form* originates prior to any articulation and always communicates the ideology of the users of that language. This sustains the argument that to different languages can be attributed different mentalities. In his philosophy of language, Wilhelm von Humboldt reformulates some of the main ideas of Herder, Kant and Hegel, respectively. From Herder he takes the principle that each language is a different way of seeing the world. From Kant he assumes the apriorism of the individual and language; that is, thought is language itself and it is not possible to think without the prior existence of language. Von Humboldt takes from Hegel the idea that differences in semantic and syntactic structures make it possible for some languages to be more suitable than others for the transmission of certain sciences or knowledge. This interpretation was consolidated in the twentieth century when Ludwig Wittgenstein stated in the *Tractatus Logico-Philosophicus* (1921 [2009]) that the boundaries of his world coincided with the limits of his language.

American linguistic anthropology, through such prominent thinkers as Edward Sapir and Benjamin Lee Whorf, formulated the principles of *linguistic determinism* and *linguistic relativity*. The principle of *determinism* establishes that language has the capacity to determine thought, proven by *linguistic relativity*: the world offers a complex set of images that the minds of individuals perceive and organize using patterns that are useful for a whole speech community and that are codified in the structure of their language. Thus, the organization of knowledge is determined directly by linguistic structure (Rossi Landi 1974). Different languages show very striking structural differences. They do not have the same grammatical categories nor do they formally express them in the same way. Some languages have many words to describe realities that in other languages receive a single name. All these differences contribute to making worldview and the organization of knowledge different from one culture to the next.

From a different perspective, Bartmiński's cognitive ethnolinguistics grants preeminence to worldview over language, coinciding with Wierzbicka's (1991) proposals since it accepts that within a community of speakers of the same language different worldviews can coexist. This is an ethnolinguistics of cultural orientation for which any language is capable of expressing any content and in which there is no experience that cannot be verbalized in any language. This theoretical approach argues that the *Sapir-Whorf hypothesis* was not formulated to defend the preeminence of language over worldview or thought and that one must distinguish between what a linguistic form usually expresses and what it is capable of expressing (Bartmiński 2010: 4).

On the other hand, psycholinguistics is proving that language exerts a great influence when perceiving or remembering. It is always easier to distinguish two concepts if they are associated with different words, just as one often remembers something more easily if it is linked to a particular linguistic element. Adam Schaff (1962) also explained that language is conceived as a product of a social praxis that determines a society's worldview: language reflects a reality while creating an image of that reality. This proposal is known as *reflex theory*. From that perspective, it is true, as pointed out by Humboldt, that humans think just as they speak and they speak just as they think. According to Schaff (1962), humans think in some language, so their thought is always spoken, and the way they think depends on the experiences that society has transmitted to them through a spoken educational process.

Now, for cognitive psycholinguistics, the prototypes around which words are organized for speakers as different languages are usually closer to each other than the meanings associated with those words in the respective languages. By this, we mean that it is relatively easy for languages to share prototypes rather to share linguistic meanings: languages and cultures may be less different than it seems, thus considered (Palmer 1996). Based on these ideas, Richard Hudson said in 1980 that the *theory of prototypes* provides the sociolinguist and anthropologist several attractions, one of them being that it allows an easier understanding of how people learn some concepts on the basis of others in relation to some specifically determined prototypes; a concept based on a prototype can be learned from the knowledge of a very small number of cases and without any previous mental definition of the concept. Another attractive aspect of prototype theory is that it leaves room for particular interpretations of reality since the boundaries between real life concepts or objects are fuzzy; individuals or social groups exercise some freedom in applying and interpreting concepts in a particular way. Besides, the prototype model offers sociolinguists the possibility of explaining how people categorize the social factors that relate to language differently. Such factors include the type of interlocutor or the situation that develops in a communicative interaction.

In the debate that we have formulated, cognitive sociolinguistics insists on the formative function that language has on social reality and its structure as well as on worldview, but thought, that is, cognition, establishes bridges between language and reality that allow us to easily go from point A to point B.

Conclusion

Speech, conversation, speech acts and style are integral parts of sociolinguistic reality as it is interpreted from a cognitive perspective. All these manifestations of language condition worldview, the representation of the world and the relationships established within a society. Linguistic manifestations operate therefore as conditioning elements, but also as a reflection of the deep structures that support a representation of the world. In this conditioning and reflection process, communicative interaction is essential and speech becomes a key element in the approximation to social and linguistic reality.

Linguistic manifestations constitute tacitly and by consensus a view of a culture and the world by means of mechanisms that govern the social use of language. Particularly important among these are linguistic or discursive language choice and communicative accommodation. In social communication, conversational interaction constitutes the basic form of linguistic production, as much as we may find embedded in it other key types of events such as speech acts or discourses of various types. These linguistic manifestations respond to social dynamics and may be subject to the phenomena of variation and change. The cognitive sociolinguistics of discourse can be both ideological and sociological and serves the social use of language, including how speakers locate themselves with respect to their interlocutors.

References

Althusser, Louis, 1971. *Lenin and Philosophy and Other Essays*. New York: New Left Books.
Bartmiński, Jerzy, 2010. *Aspects of Cognitive Ethnolinguistics*. London: Equinox.
Baudelaire, Charles, [1864] 1961. *Mi corazón al desnudo*. México: Aguilar.
Berger, Peter and Thomas Luckmann, 1966. *The Social Construction of Reality. A Treatise of the Sociology of Knowledge*. New York: Anchor Books.
Bourdieu, Pierre, 1982. *Ce que parler veut dire*. Paris: Librairie Artheme Fayard.
Bourdieu, Pierre, 1984. "Capital et marche linguistique." *Linguistische Berichte*, 90: 3–24.
Briz, Antonio, 1996. *El español coloquial: situación y uso*. Madrid: Arco/Libros.
Brown, Penelope and S. Levinson, [1978] 1987. *Politeness. Some Universal in Language Use*. Cambridge: Cambridge University Press.
Calsamiglia Blancafort, Helena and Amparo Tusón Valls, 2007. *Las cosas del decir. Manual de análisis del discurso*. 2nd. ed. Barcelona: Ariel.
Camargo, Laura, 2004. *La representación del discurso en la narración oral conversacional. Estudio sociopragmático*. Alcalá de Henares: Universidad de Alcalá. PhD. Thesis.
Casado, Manuel, 1988. *Lenguaje y cultura. La etnolingüística*. Madrid: Síntesis.
Coulmas, Florian, 2005. *Sociolinguistics. The Study of Speakers' Choices*. Cambridge: Cambridge University Press.
Coulthard, Malcolm, 1977. *An Introduction to Discourse Analysis*. London: Longman.
Deutscher, Guy, 2011. *Through the Language Glass. Why the World Looks Different in Other Languages*. New York: Henry Holt.
Dispaux; Gilbert, 1984. *La logique et le quotidien*. Paris: Editions de Minuit.
Fernández Marrero, Juan Jorge, 2004. *Actividad normativa y conciencia lingüística. Los problemas de la prescripción idiomática*. Sao Paulo: LGN.
Geertz, Clifford, 1973. *The Interpretation of Cultures: Selected Essays*. New York: Basic.
Gleason, Henry A., 1970. *Introducción a la lingüística descriptiva*. Madrid: Gredos.
Goodenough, Ward H., 1957. "Cultural anthropology and linguistics." In *Report of the Seventh Annual Round Table Meeting on Linguistics and Language Study*, Ed., P. Garvin, 167–173. Washington, DC: Georgetown University Press.

Humboldt, Wilhelm von, 1991. *Escritos sobre el lenguaje*. Barcelona: Península.
Labov, William, 2010. *Principles of Linguistics Change. Vol. III. Cognitive and Cultural Factors*. Chichester: Wiley-Blackwell.
Laclau, Ernesto, 2006. "Ideology and post-Marxism." *Journal of Political Ideologies*, 11–2: 103–114.
Lakoff, George, 1987. *Women, Fire, and Dangerous Things. What Categories Reveals about Mind*. Chicago, IL: The University of Chicago Press.
Lakoff, George, 2004. *Don't Think of an Elephant! Know Your Values and Frame the Debate*. White River Junction, VT: Chelsea Green.
Langacker, Ronald W., 1991. *Foundations of Cognitive Grammar. Volume II: Descriptive Applications*. Stanford, CA: Stanford University Press.
Latour, Bruno and Steve Woolgar. 1986. *Laboratory Life: the Construction of Scientific Facts*. 2nd ed. Princeton: Princeton University Press.
Lozano, Jorge, Cristina Peña-Marín and Gonzalo Abril, 1989. *Análisis del discurso. Hacia una semiótica de la interacción textual*. 3rd ed. Madrid: Cátedra.
Malinowski, Bronislaw, 1982. *Estudios de psicología primitiva: el complejo de Edipo*. Barcelona: Paidós.
Marcus, George and Michael Fischer, 1986. *Anthropology as Cultural Critique: An Experimental Moment in ten Human Sciences*. Chicago, IL: University of Chicago Press.
Mead, Margaret, [1964] 1972. *Continuities in Cultural Evolution*. New Haven, CT: Yale University Press.
Palmer, Gary, 1996. *Toward a Cultural Linguistics*. Austin, TX: Texas University.
Potter, Jonathan, 1998. *Representing Reality. Discourse, Rethoric and Social Construction*. London: Sage.
Roberson, Debi, 2005. "Color categories are culturally diverse in cognition as well as in language." *Cross-Cultural Research*, 39: 56–71.
Rossi Landi, Ferrucio, 1974. *Ideologías de la relatividad lingüística*. Buenos Aires: Nueva Visión.
Sacks, Harvey, 1992. *Lectures on Conversation*, Ed., G. Jefferson. Oxford: Basil Blackwell.
Schaff, Adam, 1962. *Introduction to Semantics*. New York: Pergamon.
Schiffrin, Deborah, 1994. *Approaches to Discourse*. Oxford: Blackwell.
Searle, John, 1976. "The classification of illocutionary acts." *Language in Society*, 5: 1–24.
Tylor, Edward, [1871] 1995. "La ciencia de la cultura." In J.S. Kahn (comp.) *El concepto de cultura*, 29–46. Barcelona: Anagrama.
Van Dijk, Teun A., 1978. *La ciencia del texto*. Barcelona: Paidós.
Van Dijk, Teun A., 2011. *Sociedad y discurso. Cómo influyen los contextos sociales sobre el texto y la conversación*. Barcelona: Gedisa.
Whorf, Benjamin Lee, 1940. "Science and linguistics." *Technology Review*. 40: 229–231; 247–248. In *Language, Thought and Reality: Selected Writings of Benjamin Lee Whorf*, Ed., J.B. Carrol. New York: Wiley. 1956. Trans. Spa. *Lenguaje, pensamiento y realidad*. Barcelona: Barral. 1971.
Wierzbicka, Anna, 1991. *Cross-cultural Pragmatics. The Semantics of Human Interaction*. Berlin—New York: Mouton de Gruyter.
Wittgenstein, Ludwig, 2009. *Obra completa*, Ed., Isidoro Reguera. Madrid: Gredos. Vol. I: *Tractatus logico-philosophicus* [1921]. *Investigaciones filosóficas* [1953]. *Sobre la certeza* [1969].

4

COGNITIVE FOUNDATIONS OF LINGUISTIC VARIATION

Cognitive sociolinguistics is concerned with speaker's knowledge and perception of linguistic variation. It incorporates information regarding communicative environments, interactional processes and the way in which they are both perceived. A cognitive sociolinguistics investigates the variable production of linguistic manifestations and the perception that the speakers themselves have of variability. Since this is a realm that involves principles and concepts from cognitive linguistics, such as "prototype" or "schema" for instance, cognitive sociolinguistics imposes upon itself the obligation of explaining, in a way different from that of conventional sociolinguistics, many of its fundamental elements, including linguistic variables and variants. At the same time, cognitive sociolinguistics formulates research questions such as: *What does the speaker know about sociolinguistic variation? Where does such knowledge reside, and how is it organized? How do speakers detect their community's patterns of linguistic variation, and how do they respond to these patterns?*

A. On the Concept of Variation

Proposition 4.1

Variation is an essential part of language; no language lacks variable elements.

Proposition 4.1.1

Variation is manifested in the configuration and historical evolution of language, as well as in acquisition, communicative interaction and linguistic change.

Proposition 4.1.2

Cognitive processes involved in sociolinguistic variation presuppose the ability to perceive general patterns in a speech community's linguistic usage and to respond to them.

Proposition 4.1.3

Subjective perception is a fundamental mechanism in the acquisition of linguistic variation.

Proposition 4.2

Language's variable and invariable realities are perfectly compatible within a cognitive framework.

Proposition 4.3

Linguistic usage, which occurs through interaction in a communicative environment, involves the replication of preexisting linguistic elements and allows for variation.

Proposition 4.4

Linguistic variation is produced homosemically and heterosemically. Both of these means of producing variation can involve social factors.

Proposition 4.4.1

Homosemic variation requires both the existence of different utterances or traits with equivalent content and a desire to mean the same thing on the part of the speaker.

Proposition 4.4.2

Homosemic variation occurs at all linguistic levels: the formal phonetic and morphosyntactic, the semantic-referential and the enunciative-discursive.

Proposition 4.4.3

Heterosemic variation manifests itself in the form of utterances or in different linguistic features to transmit different messages or content.

Proposition 4.5

Linguistic variation can take three basic forms: geo-linguistic, sociolinguistic and stylistic.

Proposition 4.5.1

Geo-linguistic or dialectal variation implies that each geolectal variety corresponds to a geographical domain.

Proposition 4.5.2

Sociolinguistic variation implies that linguistic facts have social significance and may characterize the speakers of a given variety.

Proposition 4.5.3

Stylistic variation implies that a linguistic feature is used by speakers of a particular social group seeking interaction adequacy according to the speaker's linguistic environment, situation and profile.

Proposition 4.6

Sociolinguistic variation occurs in specific communicative environments and reflects the existence of normative patterns that the speaker acquires through his systematic interaction with other individuals, through learning and through systematized socialization at school.

Scholium 4-A

In communicative interaction, linguistic structures—sounds, words, constructions—are replicated in our utterances. This replication occurs when speakers place the language at the service of the joint actions of the community members. Further, the replication of linguistic structures is variably realized, due in part to uncertainty arising from the opposition between communicative efficiency, the effort needed to construct the replication and linguistic articulation (Labov 2010: 371). Thus, variation is a natural part of linguistic production and replication.

Variation is also influenced by subjective perception, especially during processes of acquisition, since the capacity to reproduce or replicate depends on the operation of a selective perception mechanism that focuses on certain elements while downplaying others (Batstone 2010). Subjective perception tends to weaken in stable sociolinguistic situations when the apprehension of a specific linguistic system within a familiar context has taken place. However, when situations are less stable, or when infrequent events come up, perception starts a selective abstraction process that can lead to a subsequent reorganization of the vernacular (Labov 2001). Newly perceived items may cause social reinterpretations that an individual develops over the variation system received from his elders. Furthermore, perception involves memorization and selective activity depending largely on the frequencies of the received elements. Once the language acquisition process has been completed, perception ceases to be functional as a cognitive resource, and it will only be reactivated in subsequent processes of systematized learning at school (The Five Graces Group 2007). Once an optimal perception period has closed, a communicative routine for linguistic production is established and the role of perception in everyday communicative functions is maximally reduced. This status quo remains until new circumstances arise that alter the sociolinguistic stability, as occurs in migratory contexts (Caravedo 2010).

The learning process systematized at school is capable of activating perceptual mechanisms that have been dormant after the completion of the language acquisition process. In that regard, the importance of normed linguistic behavior should be highlighted (Fernández Marrero 2004: 109; Milroy 2001). In academic discourse, the norm is fixed through explicit statements and implicit assumptions. In the former, explicit statements, the most common pattern is that "there are two types of linguistic usage: a good one and a bad one," where the assertion/negation duality is obvious. With respect to the latter, implicit assumptions, the discursive pattern that usually arises is that "such (and such) use is correct (elegant, acceptable educated)," which leads to the tacit understanding that other uses are incorrect, inelegant, unacceptable, uneducated, and so on. The normative meta-language always expresses a polarization and contrast that arise as objects of perception on the speakers' part.

In the realm of "comprehending" linguistic variation, the proposals made by Angel López García (1994, 1996) are worth highlighting. This linguist's intention is to create a model that would make invariable and variable linguistic realities compatible. Additionally, for López García, linguistics and sociology could converge into a common science in which neither would hold more sway than the other. The model that would make this possible would be that of "topological space," parallel to prototype theory. From this perspective, human language consists of a set of concrete elements that are used in social situations that constitute its "context." Social factors may be responsible for a speaker's consciousness of the existence of a particular realization of a given variable, such as for example, [in] or [iŋ] for verbal -*ing* forms in English or the [h] or [Ø] realizations of a final consonant in Spanish. Moreover, since variation can take three basic forms—geolinguistic, sociolinguistic or stylistic—it would be possible to characterize each of these types of variation as topological spaces of different natures. Geographic or dialectal variation would imply *normal spaces*, in which closed sets A and B (dialects) would correspond to open sets U and V (territorial areas), so that A is included in U and B included in V. Sociolinguistic variation would imply *compact spaces*, in which linguistic facts have social significance and may characterize those who use them as speakers of a particular sociolinguistic variety. A linguistic element may be typical of a social group X, but that would not mean that it may be unknown by another social group. And, finally, stylistic variation would imply *regular spaces*, in which for each phenomenon *x* and for each set of phenomena A that did not include *x*, there would be a set of expressions U that would include *x* and that would not have anything in common with the set V that surrounds A. This would mean, for example, that a pronunciation of ['ao] given to Spanish participles ending in *–ado* in Spain may be characteristic of an informal or careless speech style when it is used by upper class speakers or it appears within a careful style when it is used by speakers with a lower sociocultural level; in English the deletion of [ð] in intervocalic contexts (as in *mother, brother*), where it occurs, could, in one context, be indicative of casual conversation and, in another, signal a speaker's lower social level; in English also, the reduction of the periphrasis "going to" to schwa ([ə]) (as in: *I'ma* [ajmə] *check on that*) could, in one context, be indicative of casual conversation or interpersonal solidarity and, in another, signal a speaker's lower social standing. Therefore, it cannot be said that, in itself, a particular variant belongs to one style or another; it can only be ascribed to a group U or V when the speaker's linguistic environment, situation and profile have been defined. Thus, stylistic variation supposes that a linguistic feature may be characteristic of a style when it is used by speakers of a particular social group, or of a different style when it is used by speakers of another social group, so that a feature belonging to one style or another could only be attached to one group or another when the speaker's linguistic environment, situation and profile have been defined.

Finally, it is worth emphasizing the existence of a cognitive process involved in sociolinguistic variation that allows us to detect and respond to a speech community's general patterns: the "monitor." Speakers have at their disposal a sociolinguistic monitor that extracts and evaluates social information from speech production as it relates to their community's patterns. These patterns utilize as references the manner and frequency in which semantic relations between variable elements are established. If the monitor is understood as an individual ability or capacity, it would not be surprising to again raise the question of whether variation occurs between individual grammars or within the same general grammar; this issue has also been revisited in the adaptation of Optimality Theory to variation (Anttila 2002). Consistent with the cognitivist argument that we have been describing, variation can only be understood as alternatives among different individuals or collective grammars. This explains why particular variables appear in some varieties and not in others.

B. On Variation and its Properties

Proposition 4.7

Linguistic variation follows a general process of selection among the linguistic alternatives that exist in a language variety and the communicative alternatives in an environment. Speakers participate in this process either voluntarily or involuntarily.

Proposition 4.8

Lects are linguistic varieties with specific phonic, grammatical, lexical and discursive traits stemming from specific constraints established within certain geographic domains, social profiles or specific communicative situations and contexts.

Proposition 4.9

Speakers store and categorize (i.e., "internalize") replicated linguistic uses (i.e., "habits") through a generalization process that creates sets of exemplars called "schemas."

Proposition 4.10

The uses or exemplars of a language, whether perceived or not by speakers, constitute samples that reveal both possibilities for variation and the factors conditioning variation.

Proposition 4.11

Exemplars perceived with reference to the same category can be considered variants of a single variable.

Proposition 4.11.1

The replication of linguistic exemplars occurs with a given frequency; frequency is understood as a property of variants belonging to the same category.

Proposition 4.11.2

Linguistic habits are stored as mental objects based on a probabilistic pattern.

Proposition 4.11.3

Stored linguistic habits acquire, according to their frequency, emergent properties that can turn them into structural elements.

Scholium 4-B

Florian Coulmas (2005) formulated a sociolinguistic proposal around the concept of "linguistic choice" that falls squarely within the realm of a cognitive sociolinguistics. Indeed, linguistic variation arises largely out of a process of choice among the linguistic possibilities within a language variety and the communicative possibilities of an environment, especially for reasons of style and social adjustment. From this perspective, sociolinguistics is basically a linguistics of choice and, only for this reason, it is necessary to consider realities such as free will, human behavior and language. Here we do not understand, then, the choice as simple voluntary individual action of a dual or stylistic nature. Choice is a process that presupposes the existence of an agent, not an automaton, because choice is a central component of the human condition, which does not require full control or absolute predictability (Coulmas 2005: 9). This understanding of the process of speaking is not completely original since Popper and Eccles already indicated in 1977 (p. 13) that the exercise of choice exerts a pressure under which the human mind and a consciousness of self emerge. In any case, choice is also a key notion for sociolinguistics.

To understand the phenomenon of variation, it is essential to pay attention to linguistic manifestations, whether they may be *habits, features, exemplars, elements, facts* or *utterances*, and consider their frequency. From there, the observation of linguistic manifestations in their social context, we may then gather information in order to formulate general statements such as the following (Langacker 1987):

a. The variable units and expressions of a language are not interpreted the same way by all speakers; some of them even go unnoticed.
b. The units of a language can be considered exemplars that reflect possibilities for (allophonic, allomorphic, allolexic) variation.
c. Linguistic variants may come to form part of more complex entities through processes of categorization.
d. Complex categories can be sorted internally at various levels of abstraction according to the concepts of "prototype" and "schema."

Linguistic habits, then, lead to the creation of perception schema. A schema is a static set of items stored and categorized based on a process of generalization of linguistic units. This storage is organized through a system of lexical connections based on phonic and semantic features. In turn, when groups of words establish frequent semantic and phonic connections, relationships can also become morphological or grammatical. Thus, when we speak of schemas, we do not refer to items created by linguists but to psycholinguistic representations, avoiding, then, the dangerous confusion between reality and the realm of theoretical models, a confusion pointed out by Schlieben-Lange and Weydt (1981), and Stehl (1988), among others.

A schema provides less information than would be provided by the specific cases that materialize it, and so is compatible with a wide range of elaborations. As a result, schemas may be ordered in a hierarchy of schematicity. The difference between schemas and prototypes is that schemas refer to all the typical examples (i.e., exemplars) of a particular category, against which other elements are compared in order to decide whether those elements are similar enough to be included in the general category; prototypes are sets of central exemplars. We would be before a *group category* and not before a *class category*, as understood from an Aristotelian view of reality (Gutiérrez Ordóñez 2002). Schemas and prototypes are realities connected from the perspective of a perceived reality. This connection is established as follows. An element X of linguistic reality (exemplar) can be assimilated into a category defined by prototype, so that the full adaptation of X to prototype's specifications would allow it to be recognized as a core or prototypical sample of the category. If there were no conflicts in this process, the prototype could be interpreted as a projection of a schema to which the element X would also adjust because there would be a similarity between X and prototype.

All schemas and prototypes depend on how we perceive the linguistic variables and variants that are part of a particular variety or "lect" (a term suggested by Charles-James Bailey (1973) to refer to any type of variety). Moreover, part of what is perceived is the frequency of these variants. Consequently, frequency affects the formation of "types" or "classes" of linguistic elements and can lead to the creation of schemas built from a large number of cases involving a given pattern or model. According to Pierrehumbert (2001: 118), an individual's phonological system appears to be constructed from the bottom-up on the basis of the statistical propeties of the speech stream available in his/his environment.

The above arguments are well understood in the framework of a usage-based linguistics. Based on Joan Bybee's (2001) phonological analyses, we could develop the following list of clear principles.

1. Experience influences the representation of linguistic phenomena in speakers' memories.
2. Mental representations of linguistic objects have the same properties as mental representations of other objects.

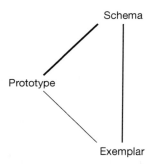

FIGURE 4.1 The Relationship Between Schema, Prototype and Linguistic Exemplar

3. Categorizations are based on concepts of identity and similarity, and make possible the storage of linguistic perceptions.
4. Generalizations are not independent from stored representations but arise from them.
5. Linguistic organization and storage presuppose the existence of generalizations and segmentations of various degrees of abstraction.
6. Linguistic knowledge is procedural knowledge: a language is learned by using it.

Three theoretical models underlie this interpretation of language based on usage. The first is psychologist Eleanor Rosch's *theories of natural categorization*. These maintain that the categorization of reality is not always produced using discrete categories defined by the absence or presence of features, but by comparing elements to a reality considered to be central. Another model, the *computational model*, helps explain mental storage processes and is based on the existence of probabilistic behavior. Finally, *theories of complex systems* and their emergent properties argue that a reiterated application of certain properties can make them structural. The latter theories hold that the use and substance—both phonic and semantic—interact to create structures, that phonetic substance fully affects the realm of phonology.

Using these approaches as a starting point, it is possible to find interpretations of linguistic structure in which the phonic is connected to the grammatical, the discursive to the social and wherein the diachronic and the synchronic can be integrated. In regard to the likelihood of occurrence of linguistic elements, usage-based linguistics accepts the conclusions of psycholinguists who argue that the most frequent words are more accessible to the speaker than those occurring less frequently. This would explain why forms which apparently fall outside the regular patterns of the system, such as those typically labeled as irregular, tend also to be words of high frequency. Linguistic structures are created and consolidated through processes of repetition, whether individual or collective. Repetition or replication, on the other hand, can give rise to blurred meanings and relaxed categories as a result of greater or lesser frequency of use.

C. On Linguistic Change

Proposition 4.12

Linguistic changes should be interpreted as part of a community's evolutionary cultural processes involving social and cognitive factors.

Proposition 4.13

Linguistic changes may be due, on one hand, to a search for articulatory economy and the maintenance of the relationship between form and meaning and, on the other hand, to a search for iconicity, in order to rescue the relationship between form and meaning.

Proposition 4.14

Linguistic changes occur in two related levels: replication and selection.

Proposition 4.14.1

Replication involves the accumulation of elements and mutated linguistic habits, which give rise to variation and, in turn, can lead to change.

Proposition 4.14.2

Selection allows some linguistic uses to be replicated more than others, promoting the stability of the former and the disappearance of the latter.

Proposition 4.15

Linguistic changes occur faster when the mutating traits have a higher frequency although that same frequency may favor the retention of some instantiations of the change over others.

Proposition 4.16

The origin and dissemination of linguistic change is affected principally by social dimensions of language use. The origin of change is especially affected by processes involving social groups; dissemination is especially influence by processes involving social networks.

Proposition 4.17

Linguistic changes can occur either abruptly, in terms of qualitative leaps along an evolutionary line, or gradually, through continuous successions of evolutionary stages.

Scholium 4-C

One of the main conclusions that can be derived from the work of William Labov dedicated to the principles of linguistic change (2010) is that change should be taken as an integral part of a community's evolutionary cultural processes, which involve linguistic, social and cognitive factors. The importance of social factors stems from the fact that the speech community itself participates in the evolution of a language (Ellis and Larsen-Freeman 2009) and influences it. Peter Trudgill (2002) established correlations among different types of communities, analyzing characteristics such as the breadth of the phonological inventory, grammatical redundancy and simplification of the deictic system. He, as well as Labov, found that the older a speech community is, the more difficult it is to find uniform patterns of linguistic change (Labov 2010: 368).

Linguistic evolution and change possess characteristics that immediately reveal their complexity. On one hand, "The Five Graces Group" (2007) and Ellis and Larsen-Freeman (2009) assume that evolutionary processes occur at two levels: replication and selection. Replication includes accumulated errors, resulting from the mutation and recombination of elements, thereby causing variation. "Replicator selection," in turn, is a process by which agents of an interaction produce differentiated replicas. On the other hand, a community's linguistic evolution can follow a natural drift, as when foreign or novel elements are evident. Linguistic evolution and change would occur, then, in two stages: the first would correspond to the generation of variation by means of replicas, which is usually effective in the initial stages. In the second stage, speakers select variants according to selection mechanisms. There are two mechanisms of selection:

I.   a neutral mechanism of evolution, based on genetic drift, which leads to the diffusion of the strongest variant as determined by frequency, and
II. a mechanism of choice based on adaptation.

In the first case, where the speaker has a neutral role, it is common to find a great deal of variability in linguistic habits, corresponding to the early stages of new dialect formation, as well as a significant influence of the community's social network on the ongoing changes. In the second case, the prestige of speakers plays a significant role. Change occurs if there is a clear disparity between the linguistic habits of prestigious speakers and those of other community members.

Linguistic changes typically come about through one of the two general mechanisms: sound change and lexical diffusion. As Labov has explained, sound change is regular, gradual, phonetically motivated and is not usually subject to grammatical or social constraints. This occurs in Spanish with respect to the elision of consonants in syllable-final position (-C > Ø, as in *verdad* > *verdá* 'truth'; *los toros* > *lo toros* 'the bulls') or in English with respect to the elision of [r] in the same position (as in *car* or *four*). Change by lexical diffusion, however, is abrupt, and takes place in all the words where certain phonological elements occur. It often responds to grammatical and social constraints, as occurs in Spanish with the loss of the voiced dental stop in certain suffixes (-d- > Ø, as in *matado* > *matao* 'killed,' and *bebido* > *bebío* 'drunk'); in English /ʊ/ tends to remain after labials, as in *put, bull, full, wool*; elsewhere it unrounds and lowers into /ʌ/, as in *cut, dull, tuck, thumb* (however, *but, bus*); another example in English could be the loss/vocalization of preconsonantal /al/ as in *talk, walk, balm, psalm*. The gradual or abrupt manner in which linguistic changes can occur appears to reflect general perspectives of genetic evolution, such as the gradualist model and that of punctuated equilibrium. Labov himself has spoken of a "Darwinian paradox" according to which evolving forms in linguistics and biology are very similar although the functional goal of natural selection may not appear in linguistic change (Labov 2010: 371). Linguistic changes occur faster when concrete mutation traits have a higher frequency even though the same high frequency may also favor the retention of some intermediate-stage mutation trait; hence the importance of quantitative analysis (Hruschka et al. 2009). Linguistic changes, finally, are a consequence of two opposing trends, economy and iconicity (Company 2003: 23–24). This tension or confrontation may manifest itself in different ways: a tendency toward isomorphic transparency (one form—one meaning) vs. a tendency toward polysemy and homonymy; a tendency toward formalism vs. a tendency toward pragmatics; a preference for unmarked order vs. a preference for marking informative focus; a weight of paradigm vs. the weight of words; a propensity for social conservatism vs. a propensity for social innovation.

Nevertheless, linguistic change and the variation which gives rise to it have been the object of other theoretical interpretations. López García has worked with a mathematical model that tries to explain language variation and change from the perspective of catastrophe theory. This theory examines the transitions between two states and seeks to explain the changes, gradual or abrupt, occurring in evolution. López García (1996) contends that, if one assumes that the speaker knows his linguistic system, he can also know the schemas that determine possibilities for variation within that linguistic system, be they continuous or abrupt ("catastrophic") and, furthermore, that schemas are incorporated as part of basic cognitive processes. The concept of catastrophe has been acquired as a tool for simulating variations, abrupt and gradual. In this way, the concept has allowed the creation of a model of how variations are incorporated into the speaker's symbolic apparatus in the internalized linguistic code. From this perspective, systematic and variable linguistic processes can be treated at the same level of cognition.

Finally, the social factors are absolutely critical to the process of linguistic change, mainly with respect to the origin and diffusion of change. The social dimension of change manifests itself through its component elements: that is, social groups and social networks. Groups constitute a breeding ground for the origin of linguistic change and for initiating the dissemination of change while social networks play a key role in diffusion. In particular, if networks have a "scale-free" form, the action of subjects placed at primary nodes is crucial for the dissemination of changes, especially if those subjects have acquired the status of linguistic leaders. Thus, the complex network theories constitute a good model for understanding the mechanism by which a language trait is propagated within a community.

Debate: Origin and Place of Linguistic Variation

Variation is a characteristic of language that affects its basic structure and its core behavior. It manifests itself at all levels of linguistic usage penetrating language's most fundamental nature. The relationship between external manifestations of language and internal organization is so intimate that usage itself contributes to the configuration of form and content of a linguistic system. Yet, there remain many details of linguistic variation that have not been completely resolved. This, of course, generates a good amount of disagreement with respect to issues such as the origin of variation and the role it places in the configuration of the linguistic system.

Controversy regarding the origin of the variation continues to be significant enough that, at this juncture, it would be unwise to dismiss either internal or external factors as a source of variation. In fact, we could probably go so far as to say that any perspective that dismisses one type of explanation for the other could be considered to be false or at least baseless. Linguistic variation exists not only because the system supports it but also because the speaker's competence tolerates it, leaving room for the possibility that both internal and external factors, both linguistic and social or contextual factors, operate on language. This, of course, does not rule out the possibility of discovering that some factors may play more or less decisive roles in language variation. From this perspective, linguistic usage becomes a key concept for explaining variation since, on the one hand, it can direct and reflect internal variability and, on the other, it is sensitive to external factors that condition and constrain it.

A more interesting debate concerns how variation coexists in the language system with other, more invariant components. The debate has been presented in the following terms: Should we posit the existence of a collective sociolinguistic competence that includes a statistical apparatus that governs the appearance of stable and variable elements of language in each utterance and context? Alternatively, should we posit the existence of a complex collective entity that emerges from the sum or the juxtaposition of particular individual contributions? Cognitive sociolinguistics tends to favors the latter model, a model where particular instances of usage, defined by their frequencies, forms and conditions, lead to the construction of general schemas and categories that are integrated into emergent trends. This relies, in a sense, on a blurring of the boundaries between competence and performance along the lines indicated by Jay Jackendoff (2002: 9–34), as well as a decisive role for a mechanism by which speakers monitor frequencies. From the sociocognitive perspective, sociolinguistic competence is interpreted collectively and includes speakers' individual perceptions of repeated stimuli. As a result, probabilistic storage, as conceived by Cedergren and Sankoff in 1974, would only be of interest as a theoretical model and could not be understood to reflect the psycholinguistic reality of speakers.

Conclusion

Variation, based on speakers' selection of some variants or others among the possibilities offered by their linguistic instrument, their communicative environment and their social context, is an essential linguistic process. It comes about through repeated uses of linguistic features in contexts of interaction and communicative cooperation. These uses occur with particular frequencies that affect both mental representations and formal configurations of language.

The nature of linguistic variation is excellently reflected in the concepts and theoretical machinery of a "usage-based linguistics." On the one hand, the presence or absence of features that are variably manifested is neatly framed within a perspective that demonstrates that linguistic reality can be categorized with respect to either discrete or non-discrete elements and that these elements are in turn compared with references considered central or prototypical. On the other hand, the perspective has been able to show that variability, a probabilistic behavior, directly determines the central storage processes and, in turn, the structural characteristics of that system. In all this, the phonological is connected to the grammatical, and the discursive with the social, contributing to an integration of the diachronic with the synchronic. This facilitates modeling of the close relationship between variation and change as well as between these processes and sociolinguistic cognition.

References

Anttila, Arto, 2002. "Variation and phonological theory." In *Handbook of Language Variation and Change*, Eds., J. Chambers, P. Trudgill and N. Schilling-Estes, 206–243. Oxford: Blackwell.

Bailey, Charles-James N., 1973. *Variation and Linguistic Theory*. Arlington: Center for Applied Linguistics.

Batstone, Rob, 2010. *Sociocognitive Perspectives on Language Use and Language Learning*. Oxford: Oxford University Press.

Bybee, Joan, 2001. *Phonology and Language Use*. Cambridge: Cambridge University Press.

Caravedo, Rocío, 2010. "La dimensión subjetiva en el contacto lingüístico." *Lengua y migración/Language & Migration*, 2-2: 9–26.

Cedergren, Henrietta and David Sankoff, 1974. "Variables rules: performance as a statistical reflection of competence." *Language*, 50: 333–355.

Company, Concepción, 2003. "¿Qué es un cambio lingüístico?" In *Cambio lingüístico y normatividad*, coord. F. Colombo Airoldi and M.A. Soler Arechalde, 13–32. México: UNAM.

Coulmas, Florian, 2005. *Sociolinguistics. The Study of Speakers' Choices*. Cambridge: Cambridge University Press.

Ellis, Nick and Diane Larsen-Freeman (Eds.), 2009. *Language as a Complex Adaptive System*. Chichester: Wiley-Blackwell. *Language Learning*, 59: Suppl.1.

Fernández Marrero, Juan Jorge, 2004. *Actividad normativa y conciencia lingüística. Los problemas de la prescripción idiomática*. Sao Paulo: LGN.

Gutiérrez Ordóñez, Salvador, 2002. "¿Clases o tipos?" *De pragmática y semántica*, 353–394. Madrid: Arco/Libros.
Hudson, Richard A., 1980. *Sociolinguistics*. Cambridge: Cambridge University Press.
Hruschka, Daniel, Morten Christiansen, Richard Blythe, William Croft, Paul Heggarty, Salikoko Mufwene, Janet Pierrehumbert and Shana Poplack, 2009. "Building social cognitive models of language change." *Trends in Cognitive Science*, 13–11: 464–469.
Jackendoff, Ray, 2002. *Foundations of Language. Brain, Meaning, Grammar, Evolution*. Oxford: Oxford University Press.
Labov, William, 2001. *Principles of Linguistics Change. Vol. II. Social Factors*. Oxford: Blackwell.
Labov, William, 2010. *Principles of Linguistics Change. Vol. III. Cognitive and Cultural Factors*. Chichester: Wiley-Blackwell.
Langacker, Ronald W., 1987. *Foundations of Cognitive Grammar. Volume I. Theoretical Prerequisites*. Standord: Stanford University Press.
López García, Ángel, 1994. "Topological linguistics and the study of linguistic variation." In *Current Issues in Mathematical Linguistics*, Ed., C. Martín Vide, 69–77. Elsevier: North-Hollan.
López García, Ángel, 1996. "Teoría de catástrofes y variación lingüística." *Revista Española de Lingüística*, 26: 15–42.
Milroy, James, 2001. "Language ideologies and the consequences of standardization." *Journal of Sociolinguistics*, 5–4: 530–555.
Pierrehumbert, Janet B., 2001. "Exemplar dynamics: Word frequency, lenition, and contrast." In *Frequency and the Emergence of Linguistic Structure*, Eds., J. L. Bybee and P. Hopper, 137–157. Amsterdam: John Benjamins.
Popper, Karl and John Eccles, 1977. *The Self and its Brain*. Berlin: Springer. Trans. Spa. *El yo y su cerebro*. Barcelona: Labor. 1980.
Rosch, Eleanor, 1975. "Cognitive representations of semantic categories." *Journal of Experimental Psychology*, 104: 192–233.
Schlieben-Lange, Brigitte and Harald Weydt, 1981. "Wie realistisch sind Variationsgrammatiken?" In *Logos Semantikos. Studia Linguistica in Honorem E. Coseriu* (vol. V), Eds., H. Geckeler *et alii*, 117–145. Madrid—Berlin—New York: Gredos/de Gruyter.
Stehl, Thomas, 1988. "Les concepts de continuum et de gradatum dans la linguistique variationnelle." In *Actes du XVIIIe Congrès International de Linguistique et de Philologie Romanes*. Vol. V, Ed., D. Kremer, 28–40. Tübingen: Niemeyer.
The Five Graces Group, 2007. "Language is a Complex Adaptative System." Santa Fe Institute. Disponible en línea. Obtained from: www.santafe.edu/media/workingpapers/08-12-047.pdf (accessed 15 December, 2015).
Trudgill, Peter, 2002. *Sociolinguistic Variation and Change*. Edinburgh: Edinburgh University Press.

5

SOCIOSEMANTICS AND COGNITION

Meaning is a fundamental component of cognitive sociolinguistics. This statement could be made more vigorously, but certainly not more accurately. Social differences manifested in language during oral interactions are based on the meanings of linguistic forms. At the same time, the meaning of structures cannot be constructed or reconstructed independently of the meanings that arise from the context of their use.

For Labovian sociolinguistics, linguistic variation requires the variants of a linguistic variable to have equivalent meanings, whether those variables be phonic, grammatical, lexical or discursive. If sociolinguistics has considered variation to be its central object of study, it has only been possible because of the extent to which semantic equivalence has been elevated as an issue of fundamental importance. Indeed, if such equivalence did not exist, "variation" in the way that sociolinguistics has conceived it since the 1960s could not endure. For this reason, the possibility or impossibility of equivalence between variable forms, be it pragmatic or semantic equivalence, has been debated by those supporting the existence of syntactic variation and discourse analysts, who denied variation (Moreno-Fernández 1988). Nowadays things are discussed differently. Sociolinguistics has strengthened three positions with respect to meaning: the existence of lexico-semantic synonymy, the possibility of semantic equivalence between elements of speech, and the presence of semantic variation at the discourse level. Controversy that remains lies primarily in explaining how all these positions are articulated and manifested.

Cognitive sociolinguistics states that variation of meaning is as important as meaning of variation (Geeraerts, Kristiansen and Peirsman 2010: 6). In maintaining that meaning can be negotiated and shaped during interaction and in response to speakers' social positions, congnitive sociolinguistics introduces new elements for discussion. It starts from the idea that, if the meanings of lexical units are not absolutely preset, synonymy or semantic identicality between variants is virtually impossible. In fact, for scholars like Janicki (2006), synonymy loses its essential *raison d'être* in a cognitive semantics in which there are no predetermined meanings. Sociolinguistics, however, which focuses on the workings of communication in society, cannot afford to completely dismiss the concept of "synonymy." This gives rise to a paradox: the "paradox of contextual meaning." On the one hand, it means that there do not exist stable meanings upon which semantic equivalences can be established and, on the other, that such equivalences are continuously being constructed during interactions.

For cognitive sociolinguistics, it is possible to distinguish the variation that affects signifiers from that which affects meanings. Regarding the former, there is no conflict in being able to negotiate meaning in discourse while maintaining the existence of semantic equivalence between signifiers. What makes it possible, in fact, is that the meaning is the end result of an interactive negotiation in which two forms, which might not *a priori* be considered equivalent, can be understood as equivalent because of that interactive negotiation. Bakhtin already stated in 1929 that true understanding is dialogic by nature and that meaning is the effect of the interaction between a speaker and a listener (Morris 1994: 35).

For this to be possible, it is essential to distinguish between "identicality" and "equivalence." It is the latter that allows significant variability in signifiers as well as sociolinguistic and sociostylistic variation. Such equivalence could be termed *homosemics*, and in that concept could be included both the identicality of meanings (*synonymy*)—which would be necessary for communication—and the similarity of meanings (*parosemics*) (Casas 1999). As for variation in the meaning of signifiers, discourse is the natural space in which such variation exists and is the ground for its development. This type of semantic variation, linked to *polysemy*, but distinct from it, may be determined by both sociolinguistic and discursive factors, and it is what finally gives rise to semantic change.

A. On the Nature of Linguistic Meaning

Proposition 5.1

Linguistic meaning is partially emergent. That is, it is not completely set before linguistic production, but negotiated during interaction and may be expressed using different forms in specific contexts.

Proposition 5.2

Elements of language are associated with central, socially shared linguistic meaning. They also possess a communicative meaning that is variable and negotiable. Both contribute to creating a contextualized meaning for elements of language.

Proposition 5.3

The semantic extension of an utterance, construction or lexical unit arises based on the perception of the similarity between its central meaning and its communicative or figurative meaning.

Proposition 5.4

The specificity and the generality of meaning are linked to usage frequency. More generic meanings are generally expressed using units, constructions or utterances of higher frequency.

Proposition 5.5

Lexical units can exhibit relationships of semantic equivalence or *homonymy*, of semantic identicality or *synonymy* and of semantic similarity or *paronymy*.

Proposition 5.6

The word is the basic linguistic storage unit because it is the smallest phonologically and semantically complete unit, and it can be used in isolation.

Proposition 5.7

Lexical items are not stored as lists (as in dictionaries) but in networks of elements multiply linked through associations of a semantic or formal nature.

Proposition 5.8

Lexicon, grammar and phonology are tightly linked in discourse. Lexical units, consisting of phonological elements, are framed within grammatical constructions that may limit or condition their meaning.

Principle 5.8.1

Lexical units offer various degrees of complexity ranging from those smaller than grammatical words (suffixes) to multilexic units governed by grammatical rules.

Principle 5.8.2

Phonological variation is typically associated with morphology and the lexicon while morphological variation does not usually affect phonological processes.

Scholium 5-A

Labovian sociolinguistics has given ample attention to semantic issues. Let us recall that two linguistic elements have traditionally been considered variants of the same variable when their alternation does not involve a change in meaning.

- Sociolinguistics used to state that the speaker must *say* the same using a different form.

This was later broadened to:

- The speaker *must mean* the same thing in order for variation to be posited.

Yet, how can it be demonstrated that someone is saying the same thing? Or, still more difficult, how can it be demonstrated that someone *wants* to say the same thing? This was a central concern for sociolinguists in the 1970s and 1980s (Romaine 1982; Lavandera 1984; Sankoff 1988). In truth, the contents of the brain's black box are more difficult to recover than the contents of an actual black box. But this is not the appropriate time to linger on cynicism, since sociolinguistics has already demonstrated in numerous works that it is possible to work with linguistic variation at all levels, including the grammatical.

Nevertheless, cognitive sociolinguistics opens other avenues for interpretation and other analytical approaches worth exploring. The starting point is that the meanings of acts, utterances, speech or conversational exchanges are not completely fixed prior to linguistic production but negotiated during interaction in specific contexts. Fundamentally, this supposes that communication operates primarily with emergent meanings, partial meanings, if you will, that also affect the form of the linguistic production itself. As Paul Valéry indicated in 1910, "speech means what it intends to mean only in an ex-cep-cio-nal way" (Valéry 2007: 125).

One of the earliest sociolinguistic studies that addressed the complicated matter of linguistic meaning was "The Boundaries of Words and Their Meanings," published in 1973 by William Labov. It questions the validity of a "categorical view" of linguistic units, and proposes that lexical meanings, while maintaining an invariant core, have blurred boundaries and space for variability; their categorization depends on the way in which a number of accompanying characteristic features appear across contexts of use. To measure that zone of vagueness in meaning, Labov conducted an experiment in which informants were presented with drawings of containers (e.g., *cups, bowls, cups, glasses, pitchers, vases*) of different widths and depths, different materials (china, glass, paper, metal) and relating them to different uses (for coffee, for potatoes, for flowers, or neutral). This allowed, for example, the identification of objects that were called *cups* by virtually all informants and other objects whose denomination became dependent

FIGURE 5.1 Series of Cup-Like Objects
Source: Labov (1973: 43)

on the ratio of their height and width or on having a handle. The results revealed that a thing is not necessarily categorized with respect to its intrinsic characteristics but also with respect to the way in which certain characteristics vary in relationship to each other.

The claim that the lexico-semantic knowledge of reality is inaccurate has been verified with neurobiological experiments, also using "containers," such as the one carried out by Steven Small (1997). This position has also served as the foundation of cognitive semantics, which has demonstrated that (i) things can be considered members of a category to the extent that they share attributes with a prototype (Rosch 1975; Kleiber 1995), (ii) that family resemblance is important for determining the degree to which something is said to belong to a category (Armstrong, Gleitman and Gleitman 1983) and (iii) that members of a category may be considered more or less representative of the category itself (Geeraerts, 1989). These are the lines of investigation that have been taken up by many of the most influential cognitive semanticists (Jakendoff 1983; Lakoff 1987; Taylor 1995).

At this point, we can ask ourselves: Is it possible to build communication on "unstable" meanings? Gottlob Frege argued in 1892 that words can have meaning without reference to anything, and Willard Van Orman Quine (1960) introduced the concept of a "stimulation module" to refer to a nonverbal stimulus that makes linguistic uses converge and that constitutes the basis of processes such as translation or equivalences between dialectal varieties. A stimulation is a repeated event; an affirmative stimulus meaning is a meaning that is accepted, thereby giving terms the necessary stability for communication (Quine 1960: 34, 48, 56). As we have already seen, ethnomethodology used to refer to the "indexicality" of contents. Meanwhile, a basic tenet of symbolic interactionism was that people are able to modify meanings depending on how they interpret a situation, permitting them to discuss possible courses of action and evaluate advantages and disadvantages before acting (Rock 1979). In turn, Karl Popper (1972) made it clear that concepts, as well as meanings, are vague, and that the world can be divided into three: the physical, the mental and that of ideas. All this seems to lead us to the acceptance of cognitivist approaches to meaning. In fact, Manfred Bierwisch (1970), another one of the predecessors of sociosemantic cognitivism, stated that semantic features do not represent external physical properties but psychological conditions under which human beings process their physical and social environments. Semantics, therefore, leads us to those internal mechanisms through which we perceive and conceptualize real world phenomena.

The linguistics that calls itself "non-essentialist"—following Popper's line of thought—has propelled questions of meaning to the forefront of current inquiry (Janicki 2006). Within the non-essentialist framework, it is argued that meaning is not found in words and that words are not mere semantic containers. At the same time, since words do not have a fixed, essential meaning, meaning cannot be conceived of as moving along a communicative channel in its transmission from speaker to hearer. Rather, meaning is assigned by each language user.

In this same line of reasoning, we should avoid the "etymological fallacy," whereby the original meaning of a word or expression must always be the appropriate or correct one. In reality, any deviation from an original meaning is equally legitimate (Janicki 2006: 176).

The theoretical overview that has just been reviewed reaffirms the suitability of a cognitive sociolinguistics that has at its disposal a variety of conceptualizations of meaning, including central, intersubjective and constant meanings (etymological or not) as well as socially shared and conventional meanings. It has recourse to communicative, variable and negotiable meanings. The former set are conceptualizations of meaning that tend to be included in lexicographic sources. The latter are those that emerge or take shape within discourse itself in specific contexts. Both of them, together, shape the "contextualized meaning" of utterances, constructions or lexical units and come into play when relationships among the meanings of different units are established. The latent semantic analyses of Landauer and Dumais (1997), which apply statistical computations to large corpora of text, have allowed the contextual usage of words to be extracted and modeled. Given the dynamic and complex nature of meaning, it not only stands to reason, but has been shown, that the meanings of lexical units in speech can vary, to the point of being involved in semantic transformations without the intention of transmitting differentiated meanings or references (Palmer 1996: 61). And, at the same time, lexical units may demonstrate relationships of semantic equivalence or homonymy, of semantic identicality or synonymy, and of semantic similarity or paronymy in accord with the conditions of the context.

Given this semantic reality, the question becomes: How do the dynamics of meaning within lexical units, statements and discourse work? It turns out that, within this dynamic, *frequency*, as it relates to semantic specificity, is decisive since the more generic a meaning is, the higher the frequency of the units, constructions or utterances that convey that meaning. Also essential is the *word*, considered the basic unit of linguistic storage because it is the smallest phonologically and semantically complete unit, and it can be used in isolation.

In the mind, words or lexical units are arranged as networks of elements multiply associated via links of a formal or semantic nature. A sample of the reticular formation that the lexicon can adopt is obtained from the lexical and semantic fields in which lexical units are available. This network of "available" lexical units is modeled using data from questionnaires in which respondents write down words related to a topic or field (i.e., a "lexico-semantic area") which come to their mind. Hernandez Muñoz (2006) has used this technique to analyze the cognitive foundations of lexical availability as well as the psychological processes that support them. The lexico-semantic areas work like associative fields, consisting of natural categories (of the type X *is* Y), of well-defined categories (closed lists), of radial categories (X *has some kind of relationship with* Y) or of *ad hoc* categories (elements associated via links of any sort). By examining available lexicon within a field, we can discover relationships between the words that are within that field.

These relationships can be graphically arranged according to the number of times they appear contiguously on completed questionnaires (Echevarría, Vargas, Urzúa and Ferreira 2008). Such graphical representations (*grafos*) reflect in network fashion the relationship between various lexical units of a speaker's mental lexicon (Figure 5.2).

Finally, speakers' knowledge of grammar and the lexicon includes knowledge about which words typically appear in which constructions. This leads to a conceptualization of lexicon and grammar in which they are interconnected (Langacker 1987; Bybee 2001). Words that are used together often can be processed as units, as it is easier to retain a larger chunk of language than a part of an expression linked morpheme by morpheme or word by word. At the same time, semantically weaker words (particles, conjunctions) constitute the main connectors of adult speakers' lexical networks (Solé 2009: 212). Thus, the dynamics of meaning is conditioned by the semantic weight of words in relation to their frequency in discourse, by their presence in certain grammatical constructions, and by the influence of the context on how all of these factors interact.

B. On the Relationship between the Lexicon and Reality

Proposition 5.9

Lexical units associated with a particular lifestyle may demonstrate an increase in use, transformation or abandonment depending on communicative situations and needs.

Proposition 5.10

Lexical units that are less prototypical tend not to be common domain. Access to technical, scientific or cultural realms is typically available only to a portion of a speech community's members.

Proposition 5.11

The link between lexical units and the realities designated by them is arbitrary and, therefore, subject to homosemic variation and to negotiation during interactions so that denotative meaning is sociolinguistically multivocal or polysemic.

Proposition 5.12

The boundaries between the general lexicon and the scientific-encyclopedic lexicon are diffuse in the same way as that the boundaries between nomenclature and the scientific-encyclopedic lexicon are.

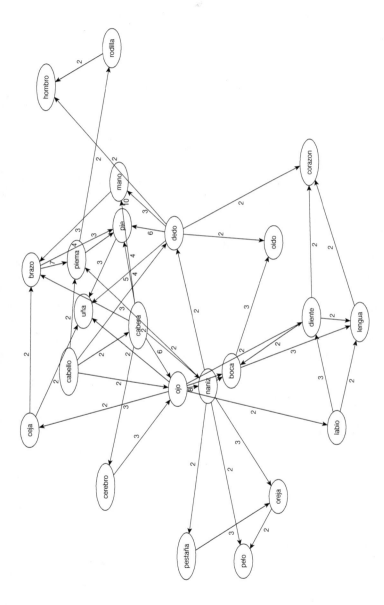

FIGURE 5.2 Lexico-Semantic Network of "Human Body," obtained from 48 Chicago Spanish Speakers (from Moreno-Fernández 2007)

(Translation: *cabeza* 'head'; *ojo* 'eye'; *nariz* 'nose'; *boca* 'mouth'; *dedo* 'finger'; *pie* 'foot'; *pierna* 'leg'; *mano* 'hand'; *uña* 'nail'; *cabello* 'hair'; *brazo* 'arm'; *ceja* 'eyebrow'; *cerebro* 'brain'; *pestaña* 'eyelash'; *pelo* 'hair'; *oreja* 'ear'; *labio* 'lip'; *diente* 'tooth'; *lengua* 'tongue'; *corazón* 'heart'; *oído* 'inner ear'; *rodilla* 'knee'; *hombro* 'shoulder')

Proposition 5.13

Lexical units can associate their use to formal or informal situations, resulting in stylistic meanings.

Proposition 5.14

The use of dialectal lexical units or else general—standard—units in discourse operates to create differences of a stylistic nature.

Scholium 5-B

The lexical meaning of words is established in two fundamental ways: first, by designation or denotation, which establishes a connection between the words themselves, understood as signs or symbols, and reality or designated reference; and second, by discursive construction, which causes the appearance of emerging meanings (Bierwisch 1987; Escoriza 2009).

One of the most obvious ways in which language relates to reality is the association of lexical units to realities linked to a particular lifestyle in a given time, culture, environment or context (Casas Gómez 1999). Due to this association with a particular reality, denotative lexicon experiences changes in frequency of use, transformations or altogether abandonment in accord with the changes present in the lifestyle. That is, new realities can lead to the emergence of new terms, as has happened with the international word *viagra* (coined in 1996) or with Spanish words like *globalifóbico* 'globalyphobic' (coined in 2004) and *vuvuzela* 'lepatata Mambu' (coined in 2010). Similarly, lifestyle changes may lead to the abandonment of words and structures associated with unused components of that lifestyle (Parodi 2007). The academic *Diccionario de la lengua española* (23rd ed., 2014) still includes such words as *alahílca* 'a tapestry used to decorate walls,' *aríolo* 'guess by omens,' *banir* 'proclaim someone for a crime' and *buchín* 'executioner' which nobody uses and whose referents have been completely lost. In the English *Merriam-Webster Dictionary*, we find similar cases, like those of *araba* 'car,' and *scriptitation* 'continuous writing.' In other cases, the realities have ceased to be part of everyday life although the referent has not been completely lost; for instance, *arcabuz* 'harquebus,' *bacía* 'barber's bowl' and *rodela* 'chainmail,' in Spanish and *bascinet, chainmail* and *sibyl* in English.

But denotative words are not the only ones to be abandoned. There are plenty of adverbial, grammatical and discursive elements that come to be unused or antiquated. In Spanish we have *abés* 'difficult,' *ad* 'toward,' *adefuera* 'outside,' *adieso* 'instantly,' *ahe* 'voilà,' *cabe* 'next to.' In this category we also have multilexic sequences such as *entrar a bureo* 'to get together to address something;' in English, *thou* 'you' *dost* 'do (aux.)', *aught* 'something,' *apace* 'quickly,' *yore* 'years ago.' However, the circumstances of the latter do not depend so much on lifestyles, as on cultural conventions and on the frequencies of discourse constructions. Bourdieu recalled, with Bakhtin (1981), that in revolutionary situations of sociopolitical change common words acquired opposite meanings (Bourdieu 1984: 15). Quite simply, the language evolves to survive in a given environment, and it does not take a long time to perceive how abandonments and transformations occur. In a study by Orlando Alba (2011), which compares the lexicon available in the Dominican Republic in 1990 and 2008, the author explains that the 1990 lexicon included words such as *coconete* 'flour and coconut sweet,' *jaguar* 'edible fruit tree,' and *patilla* 'watermelon,' which had disappeared completely in 2008. Concurrently, other words emerged in 2008—*capuchino, cheeseburger, churrasco, enchilada, celular, chatear, game boy, tetris*—that were absent in the 1990 lexicon. And we can verify how gradual lexical mobility occurs, as words like *hot dog, hamburger* or *taco* show in 2008 a much higher availability rate in Dominican Spanish than in 1990 (Alba 2011).

However, despite links to real-world referents, the denotative meaning of lexical units is sociolinguistically polysemic because those links continue to be arbitrary and, therefore, are subject to homosemic variation and interactive negotiation. Among general lexical units and those comprising the scientific and technical-encyclopedic lexicon, in which a non-homonymic denotation would seem obligatory, there is a fuzzy boundary, as diffuse as that separating the encyclopedic lexicon from pure nomenclatures. Concerning the use of such units, access to what is encyclopedic, be it scientific-technical or humanistic, will be available only to a part of the speech community's members. That is, the less prototypical the lexical unit, regardless of the field, the more likely that the lexical unit will be limited to certain groups of speakers.

Nevertheless, as has been mentioned, meanings can also result from communicative situations, independently of their links to an objective and referential reality. Interlocutors' social identities and the social contexts of interaction can trigger the appearance and also the abandonment of linguistic forms associated with particular social values, so that, as proposed by phenomenological sociology, the construction of meaning is also sensitive to what is social (Schütz 1964). Contexts and co-texts are crucial in that construction process since they enable at all times the emergence as well as the relevance and establishment of appropriate meanings. Joseph Vendryès noted (1950: 50) that, if words always communicated all of their meanings simultaneously, speech would be a constant play on words. From a more philosophical perspective, Stalnaker (1999) indicated that context influences the way in which language expresses thought. He emphasized the importance of the external environment for revealing the contents of our thoughts. Against the general assumption that language is prior to mental representation, Stalnaker argued that language has a distorting influence on our understanding and that the interaction of contexts and form can explain linguistic phenomena related to presupposition, assertion or attribution of beliefs. According to this "externalist" conception of meaning, our thoughts have the contents they have due to how they are situated in the world. From a sociological perspective, the close relationship between meanings and their environment leads to the appearance of keywords that can function as brands of a community or social group. Besides, this interpretation of meaning connects to the emergence of meaning proposed by Penelope Eckert (2012) as a third wave of variation study. According to this proposal, variation constitutes a robust social semiotic system and does not simply reflects, but also constructs social meaning. This is the reason why Geeraerts, Kristiansen and Peirsman (2010) are interested in the "meaning of variation."

Finally, context enables the appearance of another type of meaning that is not denotative: stylistic meaning (Geeraerts 2005). "Stylistic meaning" is produced via the use of either neutral or else informal words. The variable use of such lexical units is also known as lectal variation, a familiar manifestation of which is the differentiation made between standard and dialectal forms of a language. The point is that lexical units may become associated with formal or informal situations, producing stylistic meanings (Lavandera 1984; Serrano and Aijón 2014).

C. On the Social Nature of Meaning

Proposition 5.15

Linguistic communities are not homogeneous in terms of lexico-semantic knowledge; lexico-semantic knowledge is unevenly distributed among community members.

Proposition 5.16

The central and communicative meanings of lexical units can be variably distributed among the groupings and networks of a community.

Proposition 5.17

A community's virtual lexicon is principally organized in the form of decentralized networks around a core of words that are very frequent for all speakers. This core of words is continuously updated in each center of interest.

Proposition 5.18

Around the core of a network's most frequent lexical units are arranged areas of progressively less frequent, less shared, and less frequently updated lexical units. This produces for each field of expertise lexical subsets that are prototypical and familiar to most speakers.

Proposition 5.19

Lexical richness appears as a symptom or as a variable predictor of a speaker's social position, and it is strongly linked to their education level and experience.

Proposition 5.20

The strength of social ties among speakers directly influences the social group's lexical capacity, reflecting the effect of education.

Proposition 5.21

Sex and age have little influence on the acquisition, knowledge and distribution of lexical units.

Scholium 5-C

Sociolinguistic diversity manifests itself in accordance with the type of units that language and society put into play at each moment. Just as phonetic or grammatical differences correlate with speakers' social characteristics, sociolinguistic differences also exist on the level of lexico-semantic knowledge and in the use of the "meanings" practiced by speakers, as Julien Greimas (1976) anticipated.

The relationships between semantics and society are established and manifested in four main ways:

a. through communicative interaction, which makes it possible for members of a speech community to participate in the creation and development of the meanings of words;
b. through the association of different signs (meanings and signifiers) with groups of speakers with different social profiles (socially determined lexicon);
c. through variation in the meaning of given signifiers due either to sociogeographical (geo-synonymy, socio-synonymy) factors or to stylistic or discursive factors; and
d. through the equivalence of meanings (synonymy and parosemy) between forms with different signifiers associated with certain social factors. This is the scope of traditional variationist sociolinguistics.

The first type of relationship between society and meanings has to do with the composition of the linguistic sign. As already discussed, words—signs—include core and intersubjective content established by social consensus. Alongside this content or meaning, lexical units possess a communicative meaning that is negotiable in interaction. We could still speak of a peripheral meaning that could vary in its distribution among groups in a community. It could also perfectly match the negotiated part of meaning (Kristiansen and Dirven 2008). These semantic areas of the word are, thus, social products and, as such, objects of interest for cognitive sociolinguistics. According to Geeraerts (2008: 28), each word has a central reading and certain peripheral meanings or subconcepts that can vary in their distribution among a community's groups.

Hilary Putnam (1975) proposed a theory that characterized to the degree to which meaning is dependent on discourse-external factors. She called her theory "semantic externalism." This theory proposes four types of configurations according to the flexibility of the designations and the sociosemantic differences involved. These types would depend on the meaning's level of externalism (its link with an external referent) and on the differences in meaning between words according to speakers' educational level. The first factor distinguishes the existence or absence of semantic externalism in words. The second indicates the extent to which differences in meaning appear in small and prestigious social groups. There would be no such differences in egalitarian societies with similar educational levels or in theoretically homogenous societies constituted by ideal speakers-listeners. For Putnam, to know the meaning of an expression (its intention) supposes a psychological state that allows specifying its referent (its extension). However, social factors may also come into play here, as certain meanings are exclusively accessible to certain community groups or networks.

The second type of relationship between semantics and society associates the usage of certain lexical forms—signs, ultimately—with speakers of certain social profiles. This supposes that lexico-semantic knowledge is unevenly distributed among members of the speech community and that linguistic communities are not homogeneous in this respect either. The use of certain lexical forms by a group or network—their virtual lexicon—is demonstrated by Putnam to be an indication or predictor of the speakers' social positions. It is strongly linked to their education, although not so with respect to sex and age, which seem to have a lesser impact on the acquisition, knowledge and social distribution of lexical units. Moreover, the strength of social ties among speakers directly influences the lexical capacity of social groupings, relativizing the effect of each individual's education (Avila and Villena 2010: 284).

The utilization of the lexicon in the social life of a community or social group would be a consequence of the availability of its own virtual lexicon. A community's virtual lexicon would be organized as sociolexical networks, with cores of words that are very frequent for all speakers. Updates in each realm or communicative environment that related to cores of the network would be ongoing. Around the cores corresponding to the most frequent lexical units, we would find consecutive areas of units that are successively less frequent, less shared and more slowly updated. Less prototypical lexicon are associated with concepts

TABLE 5.1 Basic Types of Sociosemantic Differences

+ Semantic externalism	− Semantic difference
− Semantic externalism	+ Semantic difference
− Semantic externalism	− Semantic difference
+ Semantic externalism	+ Semantic difference

Source: Adapted from Putnam (1975)

different from those that constitute common domain. Concurrently, access to technical, scientific or humanistic realms is available to only subgroups of the community's speakers (Avila and Villena 2010: 282). In addition, the social stratification of the community's speakers would determine each individual's degree of centrality in a model of this type. Social networks would firmly set and connect the *insiders* by means of intense reciprocal connectors and would favor the creation of consensus regarding internal norms as well as the isolation of the local culture (Avila and Villena 2010: 284). Ultimately, the sociolinguistics of the lexicon provides us with a network architecture of lexical units, which would link the uses of different groups in a community. The lower social strata would have at their disposal an architecture of lexical units with more general content and tighter connections to each other. Among the higher educational levels, there would be a greater number of words with unique or very specific links within the lexical network (Solé 2009: 202–204). Although these conclusions seem close to those of Basil Bernstein's deficit theory (1964; Dittmar 1973), the epistemologies on which they are based are substantially different.

Rocío Caravedo (2011, 2014) has specifically called attention to a third type of relationship between semantics and society: one that is established within discourse and has as a consequence the semantic change of certain signifiers, even within the same discourse. We would, then, be outside the Labovian framework since we would be handling variability rather than semantic equivalence. The origin of this variation may be purely discursive since discourse is the realm where the semantic interpretation of variants is elucidated. Once variation in meaning has been acknowledged, it would be possible to use variants to identify the geographical or social profiles of speakers. Caravedo ultimately proposes a theory of polysemy in which certain semantic variables relate to cognitive systems, so that one can think of the existence of a variable component of cognition itself, in relation to meaning and correlated with the social order (Caravedo 2011: 301). According to this theory, linguistic units—lexical, of course, but also grammatical—could offer a space of semantic variability more or less wide depending on the types of discourse used by groups of speakers or on a language's territory. These units would have primary values, probably general to the whole community, and some secondary values, sensitive to stylistic, social and geographical factors. For example, the Spanish word *escuchar* 'to listen' is undergoing semantic shift leading to the neutralization of the meanings of *oír* 'hear' and *escuchar* 'listen,' although speakers of certain dialects, territories or educational groups, neutralization may be completed or blocked.

Lexical examples of this type of polysemy associated with external factors could be words such as *necio* 'ignorant/stubborn' in Colombia and *molesto* 'angry' in Central America; *cabrón* 'bad/angry/self-confident/intelligent person;' *jíbaro* 'unpleasant/rebel' in Cuba and 'amorous' in the Dominican Republic. For English, we can offer examples like the words *lead* 'guide'/'cable' in the UK and 'clue, trace' in the United States or *lush* which may be used especially by women in the UK to mean 'sexually attractive,' or which may be applied in the U.S. especially to women to mean 'drunkard.' Thus, when it comes to certain signifiers that can show different meanings within the same discourse, we refer to 'extensive polysemy,' which also correlates with geography or society. Alongside this, when it comes to synonymous words whose territories are in complementary distribution, we speak of 'geo-synonymy' (in Spanish, *coche* 'automovile' in Spain but *auto* in the American Southern Cone; in English, *lorry* in the UK and *truck* in the United States, Canada, Australia and New Zealand). When it comes to the same signifiers showing different meanings in different geographical areas, we speak of 'geo-polysemy' or 'diatopic polysemy' e.g., Spanish, *prolijo* 'long' in Spain, but 'neat, careful' in Argentina; *conejo* 'biceps' in Mexico and Colombia, 'vulva' in Spain, 'accumulation of fat in women's thighs' in Colombia, 'sound produced by the joints' in Peru, and which refers to a type of fish in Puerto Rico (Asociación de Academias de la Lengua Española, 2010). In English we find *deadbeat*, which means 'exhausted' in the UK or 'delinquent' in the United States; *to table* meaning 'schedule, consider' in the UK and 'dismiss, suspend, postpone' in the United States) (Bauer 2002). In these cases their distinction from the previous type of polysemy may become complicated.

The fourth area of relation between semantics and society is that of sociolinguistic variation, as understood from the Labovian perspective. The most basic difficulty formulated here is demonstrating the existence of semantic equivalences between different forms. We discuss the relationship between semantics and society in the following debate, which starts off with the recognition that a cognitive sociolinguistics, in many ways, circumvents the semantic difficulties traditionally associated with variationist sociolinguistics.

Debate: Is Semantic Equivalence Possible?

Given the perspectives thus far presented, the debate over semantic equivalence, that is whether in a language there can exist units that are semantically equivalent, is one that involves not only lexicon, but more specifically meaning. Those that oppose the proposition of semantic equivalence in language assert that full—logical—identicality between two units is impossible. Such positions rest on several principles proposed to underlie human communication. For instance, *the principle of communicative efficiency* prevents two units with the exact same semantic value from existing (since this state of affairs would be, in fact, inefficient). Likewise, the *principle of semantic identicality*, whereby a word or a text can only be equal to itself, and the *principle of semantic anteriority* (Trujillo 1996), according to which a word predates the thing, support a position opposing the possibility of semantic equivalence. If these principles hold true at the lexical-semantic level, their operation at the grammatical and discursive levels, where elements are semantically more complex, would seem yet more relevant.

On the other hand, those that support the possibility of semantic equivalence in language might insist on refining and disentangling notions such as "identicality" and "equivalence" on the one side, and "logic" and "pragmatics," on the other. Cognitive sociolinguistics, for example, espouses this position and, in particular, the possibility of pragmatic or discursive equivalence, an equivalence of *meaning the same thing*. Such *meaning* is also linked to a *meaning not to say* (e.g., silence, omissions), which itself may occupy a variation space (Ducrot 1982). Trujillo accuses sociolinguistics of reducing the semantic to the referential and of giving priority to referential equivalence, despite the fact that the realm of the referential falls outside the purview of the linguistic (i.e., the structural), properly speaking. This may be true. Nonetheless, such concerns may not be directly relevant for cognitive sociolinguistics, whose focus lies precisely at the level where speakers perceive and assess meanings, adjusting them in response to their interlocutors. A cognitive sociolinguistics, thus, leaves room for semantic equivalence where a more strict linguistics makes it unviable: not only at the referential, but also, and primarily, at the communicative or discursive level.

Conclusion

Cognitive sociolinguistics grants absolute preeminence to usage and subordinates semantic processes to both communicative interaction and social context. It is precisely from the latter that emergent meanings originate. This occurs as a result of negotiations that allow us to complete, specify or modify socially accepted semantic substances. Concomitantly, the meaning of lexical units does not exist prior to language production but is a consequence of it. Also, it is in production that we are able to identify meaning equivalences, the foundation for demonstrating variation, which are possible at both the grammatical and the discursive level. These would be the terms of a *principle of semantic posteriority*, contrary to what has been proposed by Ramón Trujillo in 1996.

The lexicon is organized in decentralized networks of multiple associations and concentrically into subsets of prototypical lexical units. More frequent and common lexical units are located at the cores of each of these sets; around them, we find successive areas of less frequent and less common units. This cognitive arrangement is relevant to the lexicon's social dimension since the more peripheral the lexical space, the less common and available its units become for the members of a speech community. The least prototypical lexicon is typically controlled by only certain groups of speakers. Thus, it could be said that lexico-semantic knowledge is unevenly distributed within a community.

In another vein, a community's (virtual) lexicon consists of units that reflect the reality and the lifestyle in which the lexicon is employed. As a result, those units whose meaning is linked to components of that lifestyle that are susceptible to change, replacement or abandonment typically face the same fate as the components themselves; those units linked to more general, common and stable components of reality rarely undergo mutations. Even so, the relationship between reality and lexicon is of a relatively unstable nature, and denotation does not exempt lexical units from variation or polysemy. For Langacker himself (1987: 154–155), the distinction between semantics and pragmatics, between linguistic knowledge and extralinguistic knowledge is a thorny one. Consequently, he advocates a linguistic semantics of an encyclopedic nature, in which any element that contributes to meaning, be it semantic or part of an external reality, can become a focal element in interaction and can produce an emergent meaning.

Finally, it is worth insisting that the lexicon's semantic dimension shares essential features with those of other linguistic levels, such as the grammatical and the discursive. All of them are affected by processes of variation and meaning negotiation and become associated with specific social groups or stylistic varieties.

References

Alba, Orlando, 2011. *Observación del cambio lingüístico en tiempo real*. Santiago de los Caballeros: Pontificia Universedad Católica Madrid y Maestra.

Armstrong, Sharon L., Lila R. Gleitman, and Henry Gleitman, 1983. "What some concepts might not be." *Cognition* 13: 263–308.

Asociación de Academias de la Lengua Española, 2010. *Diccionario de americanismos*. Madrid: Santillana.

Ávila Muñoz, Antonio M. and Juan A. Villena Ponsoda (Eds.), 2010. *Variación social del léxico disponible en la ciudad de Málaga*. Sevilla: Sarriá.

Bakhtin, Mikhail. 1981. *The Dialogic Imagination*. Austin, TX: University of Texas Press.

Bauer, Laurie, 2002. *An Introduction to International Varieties of English*. Edinburgh: Edinburgh University Press.

Bernstein, Basil, 1964. "Elaborated and restricted codes: their social origins and some consequences." In *The Ethnography of Communication, American Anthropologist*, Eds., J. J. Gumperz and D. Hymes, 66: 99–116.

Bierwisch, Manfred, 1970. "Semantics." In *New Horizons in Linguistics*, Ed., J. Lyons, 166–184. Harmondsworth: Penguin.

Bierwisch, Manfred, 1987. "Linguistics as Cognitive Science: Notes of a research program." *Journal of German Studies* 8: 645-667.

Bourdieu, Pierre, 1984. "Capital et marche linguistique." *Linguistische Berichte* 90: 3–24.

Bybee, Joan, 2001. *Phonology and Language Use*. Cambridge: Cambridge University Press.

Caravedo, Rocío, 2011. "La variación de significado en el corpus." In *Realismo en el análisis de corpus orales*, Ed., P. Martín Butragueño, 281–306. México: El Colegio de México.

Caravedo, Rocío, 2014. *Percepción y variación lingüística. Enfoque sociocognitivo*. Madrid-Frankfurt: Iberoamericana-Vervuert.

Casas Gómez, Miguel, 1999. *Las relaciones léxicas*. Tübingen: Max Niemeyer.

Dittmar, Norbert, 1973. *Soziolinguistik. Exemplarische und kritishce Darstellung ihrer Theorie und Anwendung. Mit kommentierter Bibliographie*. Frankfurt, Athenaum Fischer Taschenbuch. Trans. Eng. *A Critical Survey of Sociolinguistics: Theory and Application*. New York: St. Martin's, 1977.

Ducrot, Oswald, 1982. *Decir y no decir*. Barcelona: Anagrama.
Echevarría, Max, Roberto Vargas, Paula Urzúa and Roberto Ferreira, 2008. "Dispografo: una nueva herramienta computacional para el análisis de relaciones semánticas en el léxico disponible." *Revista de Lingüística Teórica y Aplicada*, 46–1: 81–91.
Eckert, Penelope, 2012. "Three Waves of Variation Study: The Emergence of Meaning in the Study of Sociolinguistic Variation." *Variation Review of Anthropology*, 41: 87–100.
Escoriza, Luis, 2009. "Consideraciones sobre el estudio de la variación léxica." In *La lingüística como reto epistemológico y como acción social*, M. Veyrat Rigat and E. Serra Alegre, 785–796. Madrid: Arco/Libros.
Frege, Gottlob, [1962] 1984. *Estudios de semántica*. Barcelona: Orbis.
Geeraerts, Dirk, 1989. "Introduction: Prospects and Problems of Prototype Theory." *Linguistics*, 27: 587–612.
Geeraerts, Dirk, 2005. "Lectal variation and empirical data in Cognitive Linguistics." In *Cognitive linguistics. Internal Dynamics and Interdisciplinary Interaction*, Eds., F.J. Ruiz de Mendoza and M.S. Peña, 225–244. Berlin—New York: Mouton de Gruyter.
Geeraerts, Dirk, 2008. "Prototypes, stereotypes, and semantic norms." In *Cognitive Sociolinguistics. Language Variation, Cultural Models, Social Systems*, Eds., G. Kristiansen and R. Dirven, 21–43. Berlin: Mouton de Gruyter.
Greimas, Algirdas Julien, 1976. *Sémiotique et sciences sociales*. Paris: Éditions du Seuil.
Hernández Muñoz, Natividad, 2006. *Hacia una teoría cognitiva integrada de la disponibilidad léxica. El léxico disponible de los estudiantes castellanos-manchegos*. Salamanca: Universidad de Salamanca.
Jackendoff, Ray, 1983. *Semantics and Cognition*. Cambridge: MIT Press.
Janicki, Karol, 2006. *Language misconceived. Arguing for Applied Cognitive Sociolinguistics*. Mawhah, NJ: Lawrence Erlbaum.
Kleiber, Georges, 1995. *La Semántica de los prototipos*. Madrid: Visor.
Kristiansen, Gitte and René Dirven (Eds.), 2008. *Cognitive Sociolinguistics. Language Variation, Cultural Models, Social Systems*. Berlin—New York: Mouton de Gruyter.
Labov, William, 1973. "The Boundaries of Words and Their Meanings." In *Variation in the Form and Use of Language: A Sociolinguistics Reader*, Ed., Ralph Fasold, 29–62. Washington, DC: Georgetown University Press.
Lakoff, George, 1987. *Women, Fire, and Dangerous Things. What Categories Reveals about Mind*. Chicago, IL: The University of Chicago Press.
Landauer, Thomas K. and Dumais, Susan T., 1997. "A solution to Plato's problem: the Latent Semantic Analysis theory of acquisition, induction and representation of knowledge," *Psychological Review*, 104–2: 211–240.
Langacker, Ronald W., 1987. *Foundations of Cognitive Grammar. Volume I. Theoretical Prerequisites*. Stanford, CA: Stanford University Press.
Lavandera, Beatriz, 1984. *Variación y significado*. Buenos Aires: Hachette.
Moreno-Fernández, Francisco, 1988. *Sociolingüística en EE.UU. Guía bibliográfica crítica*. Málaga: Ágora.
Moreno-Fernández, Francisco, 2007. "Anglicismos en el léxico disponible de los adolescentes hispanos de Chicago." In *Spanish in Contact*, Eds., K. Potowski and R. Cameron, 41–58. Amsterdam: John Benjamins.
Morris, Pam (Ed.), 1994. *The Bakhtin Reader: Selected Writings of Bakhtin, Medvedev, Voloshinov*. London: Arnold.
Palmer, Gary, 1996. *Toward a Cultural Linguistics*. Austin, TX: University of Texas Press.

Parodi, Claudia, 2007. "La semántica cultural y la indianización en América: un análisis del contacto lingüístico." In *Actas del XV Congreso de la Asociación Internacional de Hispanistas*, Eds., B. Mariscal and T. Miaja, 211–224. México: Fondo de Cultura Económica.

Popper, Karl, 1972. *Objective Knowledge: An Evolutionary Approach*. Oxford: Clarendon.

Putnam, Hilary, 1975. "The meaning of meaning." In *Language, Mind and Knowledge*, Ed. K. Gunderson, 131–193. Minnesota, MN: University of Minnesota.

Quine, Willard Van Orman, 1960. *Word and Object*. Cambridge: MIT Press.

Real Academia Española, Asociación de Academias de la Lengua Española, 2014. *Diccionario de la lengua española*. 23rd ed. Madrid: Espasa.

Rock, Paul Elliott, 1979. *The Making of Symbolic Interactionism*. London: Macmillan.

Romaine, Suzanne, 1982. *Sociolinguistic Variation in Speech Communities*. London: Arnold.

Rosch, Eleanor, 1975. "Cognitive representations of semantic categories." *Journal of Experimental Psychology*, 104: 192–233.

Sankoff, David, 1988. "Sociolinguistics and syntactic variation." In *Linguistics: The Cambridge survey, vol. IV. The sociocultural context*, Ed., F. J. Newmeyer, 140–161. New York: Academic Press.

Schütz, Alfred, 1964. *Collected Papers II: Studies in Social Theory*, The Hague: Martinus Nijhoff.

Serrano, María José and Miguel Ángel Aijón Oliva, 2014. "Discourse objetivization, social variation and style in the use of Spanish 'tú'," *Folia Linguistica*, 48-1: 225-254.

Small, Steven L., 1997. "Semantic Category Imprecision: A Connectionist Study of the Boundaries of Word Meanings." *Brain and Language*, 57: 181-194.

Solé, Ricard, 2009. *Redes complejas. Del genoma a Internet*. Barcelona: Tusquets.

Stalnaker, Robert C., 1999. *Context and Content*. Oxford: Oxford University Press.

Taylor, John R., 1995. *Linguistic Categorization. Prototypes in Linguistic Theory*. 2nd ed. Oxford: Oxford University Press.

Trujillo, Ramón, 1996. *Principios de semántica textual. Los fundamentos semánticos del análisis lingüístico*. Madrid: Arco/Libros.

Valéry, Paul, 2007. *Cuadernos (1894–1945)*. Barcelona: Galaxia Gutemberg.

Vendryès, Joseph, 1950. *Le langage*. Paris: Albin Michel.

6
SOCIOGRAMMAR AND COGNITION

Formalist theories have approached the study of grammar from the perspective of its structure independently of contextualized meaning and communication. From this same perspective, generative grammar has made a fundamental assumption: that the combinatory power of the language's units originates its syntactic structure. However, such syntactic-centered conceptions of language, understandably, have not been unanimously accepted. Indeed, it has been argued that the main consequence of the theoretical ascendency of formalist theories has been that phonologic and semantic theorists have systematically ignored grammar in proposing their own independent models (Jackendoff 2002; Clark, Yallop and Fletcher 2007).

Cognitive linguistics does not subscribe to a model of language organized around syntax, but rather prefers a model that captures the interrelationship between all levels of language—forms and meanings—in the context of communication. That model accounts for how contextualized and dynamic language use is able to influence the internal configuration of language (Langacker 1987). That is, it prefers a conceptualization of language where grammar cannot be understood without reference to discourse and context or without assessing the speaker's experience and perceptions. According to Kristiansen and Geeraerts (2013), grammatical phenomena must of necessity be enriched by lectal and contextual factors. Given this, cognitive grammar could rightly also be characterized as a sociocognitive grammar.

Along the same cognitivist line would be situated a so-called "grammar of constructions." The "constructionist" model consists of a family of grammatical theories for which the concept of "construction" features as fundamental and crucial. The main referents for this type of grammar are the works of Charles J. Fillmore and George Lakoff (Gras Manzano 2010). George Lakoff (1987), for example, proposes a cognitive grammar, understood as a network of related grammatical constructions. In response to more traditional or more formalist models of grammar, constructional grammars are concerned with the mechanisms that permit speakers to establish generalizations and connections between the concrete patterns of the language usage and other more general (cognitive) patterns (Lakoff 1987: 46–468; Gras Manzano 2010). Such models square well with the theoretic model of usage-based grammar (Bybee and Hopper 2001; Bybee 2010), as well as other models that present language as a complex adaptive system (The Five Graces Group 2007). Besides, the constructionist model has been useful for a comparative sociolinguistics (Tagliamonte 2002; Claes 2014; Szmrecsanyi, Grafmiller, Heller and Röthliberger 2013).

A. On the Configuration of Grammar

Proposition 6.1

The grammar of a language is manifested through conventional linguistic units that are created by means of categorized samples of language use.

Proposition 6.2

Constructions constitute the basic units of grammar.

Proposition 6.2.1

Constructions are form-meaning pairings that can be more specific (words or phrases) or more general (e.g., passive construction, ditransitive construction), and include units of all sizes, from small units (words with affixes) to larger ones (clauses, discourse units).

Proposition 6.2.2

A grammatical construction is a symbolic structure of integrated components that involves the syntagmatic combination of morphemes and more complex units so that there is no fundamental distinction between morphological and syntactic constructions.

Proposition 6.3

Grammar is built from a categorization of constructions that is based both on their meaning in context as well as their linguistic form.

Proposition 6.4

Grammar is not fixed and static but has the ability to change in accord with experience. That is, the meaning and form of constructions can be modified in response to linguistic use.

Proposition 6.5

The relationship between grammar and the lexicon can be modified or reinforced depending on linguistic use. Grammar includes information about the lexical units that normally participate in certain constructions.

Proposition 6.6

Emerging relationships between words is based on both their phonetic and semantic similarity; this relationship is facilitated by morphology.

Proposition 6.7

Syntax emerges from a network of relationships among words, which results in sequences of adjacent units linked to each other with different degrees of intensity.

Scholium 6-A

As an alternative to generativism's syntax-centric approach, Ray Jackendoff (2002) proposed a tripartite theory of parallel architecture, in which language offers several options of combinatory power and where different types of structures are created. In this parallel architecture, phonological structures are linked by an interface to the syntactic structures and these, through another interface, connect to conceptual structures that are linked to the first by a specific interface.

Cognitive linguistics proposes a view of language both as similar to these approaches as different from the formalism of generative grammar. For cognitivism, grammar includes a set of cognitive representations of the speakers' linguistic conventions. "Cognition," "representation" and "convention" are key concepts for its proper interpretation, along with the notion of "construction," referring as it does to the basic unit of analysis in this model (Goldberg 2006). Such concepts are, as mentioned, comfortably couched within theories such as cognitive grammar (Langacker 1987) and construction grammar (Lakoff 1987; Fillmore 1988, 1995).

While the present work does not attempt to serve as an introduction to cognitive grammar (there already being an available literature treating its foundations, objects of study and methodology), it nonetheless serves our interests here to discuss those elements of the framework that buttress central proposals of the present work: namely, those regarding the importance of usage, social action and communicative interaction for language. From those enumerated by Langacker in 2005 (p. 102), we highlight the following ideas that are basic to a cognitive grammar:

a. Constructions (rather than *rules*) are the primary objects of grammatical description.
b. The lexicon and grammar are not different components but form a *continuum* of constructions.
c. Constructions are pairings of form and meaning (*sets of symbolic structures*).
d. The information structure of constructions also communicates meaning.
e. Constructions are linked by inherited networks (*categorization*).
f. Regularities in grammar take the form of schematic constructions linked to specific linguistic expressions.
g. Linguistic knowledge comprises a great number of constructions. A large portion of normal grammatical production patterns are idiosyncratic.

With these general ideas as the foundation, construction grammars work with clear objectives: (1) To demonstrate the relevance and theoretical necessity of the concept of "grammatical construction" to analyze key aspects of the grammar (*core grammar*); (2) To apply the general principles of categorization to grammatical analysis; and (3) To achieve descriptive and explanatory adequacy for constructivist analysis (Goldberg 2006: 214; Gras Manzano 2010: 149). Regarding the crucial concept of "construction," various constructionist proposals agree that constructions are grammatical units par excellence and they are formally and semantically interrelated symbolic entities (Croft 2007; Croft and Cruse 2004) whose extensive definition is that proposed by Adele Goldberg in 1995:

> C is a CONSTRUCTION *iff* C is a form-meaning pairing <F_i, M_i>, such that some aspect of F_i or some aspect of M_i is not strictly predictable from the components of C or from other previously established constructions.

According to this definition, a construction's symbolic structure, as it is understood by Croft and Cruse (2004: 258) or Lakoff (1987: 467), includes a conventionalized form and meaning. The form consists of phonological, morphological and syntactic features whereas the meaning consists of semantic, pragmatic and discursive features. Constructions may limit or condition the meaning and form of discourse components, whether they be phonological or lexical. Furthermore, cognitivist grammatical theories interpret constructions as "exemplar" cognitive representations. The "construction" is particularly appropriate in an exemplar theory or model since concrete expressions are associated with categories. That is, categories arise from generalizations formed on the basis of the concrete use of constructions (Pierrehumbert 2003: 132). As regards constructions, the pairings of forms and meanings have no intermediate representations and may, because of this, be related to exemplars associated with cognitive "schemas" (Langacker 2005: 103 ff.).

Without losing sight of these cognitive and constructionist principles, a sociocognitive grammar is constructed on the basis of interaction and is configured in accord with social convention. The theoretical perspective from which it operates is, therefore, a theory of grammar based on usage. Said differently, the cognitive nature of language is based on accumulated experience. The grammar's architecture, so conceived, would be neither that of an abstract system of rules nor that of a formal structure that produces linguistic habits. Instead, its architecture is that of a network of representations woven with categorized samples of use, that is with uses that are conventionally associated with constructions of varying complexity (The Five Graces Group 2007). Bybee's work on grammar (2001, 2010) provides grammatical explanations in which social interaction and communication are authentic cornerstones.

Cognitive representations underlying language use are made by categorizing expressions and building models or groups of models on the basis of linguistic forms, their meaning and the context in which they have appeared (Bybee and Hopper 2001). Because categorizations and grammatical constructions depend on how language is used, we cannot think of grammar as something fixed or static, but rather as something that emerges. Contextualized language usage leads to the integration of two or more structural components, be they phonological, lexico-semantic or morphosyntactic, to form a composite structure in which components demonstrate valence relationships (Langacker 1987: 156–157) and different levels of interdependency.

In short, cognitive sociolinguistics approaches grammar by taking into account two fundamental principles, formulated by Friedrich Ungerer and Hans-Jörg Schmid (1996), that link the process of categorization and the dynamics of grammatical constructions to the speakers. The *experiential principle* makes the speaker's experience (his associations and perceptions) necessary for constructions to exist. The *principle of preeminence* explains how differences in perception are linked to grammatical differences. In terms of grammatical meaning, this means that we bear in mind that meaning emerges from both negotiation in context and from the frequency of units in the interaction.

B. On Grammatical Dynamics

Proposition 6.8

Grammatical categorization, grammaticalization and analogy are the basic grammatical processes that arise from language use.

Proposition 6.8.1

Grammatical categorization is the process of creating a category, which is produced from the comparison between a schema and a concrete expression, based on numerous instances of use.

Proposition 6.8.2

Grammaticalization is a process by which the specific meaning of a lexical unit or expression may change or disappear as a consequence of high frequency of use.

Proposition 6.8.3

Analogy is based on a speaker's recognition of similarities among constructions. Constructions are often sequences learned as a whole, by analogy with the form in which they have previously appeared.

Proposition 6.9

Lexical items that are used together can often get processed as grammatical units.

Proposition 6.10

Frequency is a fundamental factor in grammatical configuration and, consequently, grammar, being based on usage, includes registers of the probabilities of occurrences and co-occurrences.

Proposition 6.11

The formation, acquisition and use of grammatical constructions proceed on the basis of the memorization of discourse characteristics or segments.

Proposition 6.12

Grammar supposes an online construction process during which we utilize computational intelligence, while lexical units are stored in our long-term memory.

Proposition 6.13

Lexical force is a diachronic tendency displayed by inflected lexical units whereby the most frequent forms of a paradigm resist regularizing change, be that change morphological or analogical. They also refuse to serve as a basis for change.

Scholium 6-B

The dynamics of a sociocognitive grammar is based on two fundamental concepts: convention and frequency. These dynamic mechanisms affect the three basic grammatical processes arising from the use of language, which are categorization, grammaticalization and analogy. Categorization is the farthest-reaching of these processes since it affects all levels of language, a conclusion derived from our treatment of sociosemantics and sociophonology.

Categorization is a procedure that organizes the diverse information obtained from reality by simplifying it through generalization or discrimination. At the grammatical level, units are also organized around constructions that share a set of features. These constructions are themselves organized according to degree of centrality (prototypes and schemas) or abstraction and specificity (Cuenca and Hilferty 1999: 31 ff.). According to Givon (1984, 1986), peripheral members of these categories have fuzzy boundaries with respect to other categories. Within the supercategory of the sentence, one can differentiate three types of constructions: the sentence, the clause, and the segment or group. The first is characterized for having a "subject + predicate" structure, distributional autonomy, and prosodic, semantic and communicative unity. Clauses and sentences are similar in that they share the structural arrangement. Segments may share with the sentence other aforementioned traits, but not structure.

Grammaticalization is a process that has long occupied linguists, who have presented it, along with analogy, as a major source of creating grammatical forms (Meillet 1921; Company 2003). In essence, it is the process whereby a lexical element acquires a grammatical value. Bybee (2010) speaks of evolutionary stages, when a unit moves from the lexical to the grammatical level, according to a grammaticalization scale. On this scale, the original form is fuller, freer and less complex than the resulting one. Schematically, the process could be represented as follows (Hopper and Traugott 1993: 7).

lexical item> grammatical word> clitic> inflectional morpheme

It may be further pointed out that the transformation from lexical element into a grammatical one takes into account the morphological, syntactic and discursive conditions under which the element occurs. The importance of conditions of use in grammaticalization is demonstrated by analyzing its causes. In the hypotheses that have been formulated regarding those causes (Cuenca and Hilferty 1999: 160 ff.), communicative interaction always appears as relevant. If we accept that the process begins in discourse and concludes at the grammatical level—*the emergent grammar hypothesis* (Givon 1979)—we are conceiving of grammatical units as emerging from discourse built on linguistic usage. If we accept that the motivation for the process is the interlocutor's tendency to subjectivize messages –*the subjectivation hypothesis* (Traugott 1995)—we are acknowledging the importance of a particular factor of communication: the speaker. According to Traugott, grammaticalization tends to transform lexical elements into elements that structure the text. It also reveals the speaker's position in a discursive situation; for example, in English temporal *while* developed into the concessive *while* in the sense of 'although' (Traugott and König 1991). The evolution of the Latin form *Locus* 'place' into the contemporary Spanish form *luego* 'later, afterwards' (an example of a "noun > adverb > consecutive conjunction" evolution), resulted from changes in how speakers discursively located themselves, moving from a spatial domain to a temporal domain to a notional domain (Traugott 1995: 40–45).

Analogy, also widely studied in other fields such as history of the language, is a process in which forms of a paradigm are modified in order to regularize the paradigm. The operation of this process depends on the human ability to perceive similarities and generalize patterns. Its operation contrasts with production arising from a sequence of rules because it resorts to the similarity of preexisting forms rather than to more general symbolic rules (Bybee 2010). The development and acceptability of a new form, that is, a construction, occurs gradually, making larger or smaller adjustments to previous uses of the construction. Therefore, previous usage and experience are critical in the process of analogy. An example of how analogy operates in syntax is the way in which Spanish verbs such as *ponerse* 'get, become', *volverse* 'turn, become' or *quedarse* 'stay, remain' combine with various adjectives and prepositional phrases. They create very productive paradigms, including constructions such as *ponerse nervioso* 'get nervous,' *ponerse pálido* 'turn pale,' *ponerse furioso* 'get angry'; *volverse loco* 'go crazy'; *quedarse solo* 'stay, remain alone,' *quedarse a solas* 'stay alone,' *quedarse soltero* 'remain single.' Similar productivity may be observed in the English construction "get X" (*get lit, get in on it, get with it, get wasted, get crazy, get hyper*) and in words with suffix *-en* meaning also 'become' or 'make,' as in *whiten, lighten* or *darken*. The most frequent and conventionalized forms serve as the analogical basis for the formation of new expressions.

The basic processes that affect grammatical constructions and govern their origin, use, variation and evolution are often impacted by cognitive mechanisms such as fragmentation or chunking. When certain words repeatedly appear together in the discourse chain, they may form fixed discursive fragments called *chunks*. It has been proven that the most common phrases and constructions eventually come to behave just like words, in a form that the phonological processes that take place within a word also often apply internally to chunked fragments. This discourse segmentation, therefore, is caused primarily by repetition in use and itself underlies the emergence of periphrases and idiomatic expressions such as *pick and choose, take a break* and *break the ice* in English. Some examples of the result of this process in Spanish include *tirar la toalla* 'give up' (lit. 'throw the towel'), *estirar las piernas* 'go for a walk' or *poner una pica en Flandes* 'reach a milestone' (lit. 'put a pike in Flanders'). In fact, all conventional multiword expressions, from utterances to fixed phrases, can be considered *chunks* for the purposes of processing and analysis. Their existence and behavior is crucial for modeling grammar because they show that longer sequences can be stored in memory and processed independently. Unlike other grammatical units such as morphemes, chunks function as the cognitive basis of morphosyntax and its hierarchical organization. Most sentences are constructed as memorized parts, by analogy with the way in which these parts have previously appeared in other sentences that may have been learned as a whole (Quine 1960: 9). And this, a perspective that understands grammar to operate on the basis of processes and organizational principles in which lexicon, morphology and syntax participate, is precisely the way that a usage-based framework approaches grammar (Bybee 2001: 136).

Finally, we return, not for the last time, to the central role of frequency. The frequencies of forms that appear in context are not merely quantitative information from which grammaticality or acceptability judgments derive. Non-occurrence of a unit does not imply ungrammaticality or the prohibition of its use, while high frequency of occurrence does not imply grammaticality; countless ungrammatical forms appear as part of everyday interaction and spontaneous speech. If grammar is based on usage, grammar should include innumerable cases of co-occurrence and record the probabilities of such occurrences. Thus mastering a language also implies managing a stochastic component (Henry 2002). Speakers are aware of the constructions that are conventional and of the relationship between a structure and its frequency. Frequency directly affects the speed with which speakers access units. It also impacts the *priming* of the morpho-phonological properties of high and low frequency words as well as grammaticalization processes (Bybee 2001; Ellis 2002). The frequency with which speakers encounter syntactic difference between varieties of the same language is, according to Bresnan and Ford (2010), a major consideration in accounting for their probabilistic production. The weight of the quantitative can be seen in facts such as the following:

a. Higher-frequency patterns are more productive than low-frequency patterns.
b. Specific members of grammatical categories occur less frequently than nonspecific ones.
c. More frequent grammaticalizing elements and those with a more general meaning in the construction may lose the ability to function as main verbs.
d. Constructions with high-frequency units have weaker connections with other forms. They are more frequently independent and contribute less frequently to the formation of productive classes.
e. Items with high frequency have greater lexical strength; they are more resistant to morphological and analogical change, serve as the basis for change, and have a great deal of autonomy.

Let us recall that the "lexical strength" is the tendency of the most common forms of a paradigm to resist regularizing changes. High-frequency paradigms maintain their irregularities while low-frequency paradigms tends to be regularized. Conversely, the greater the lexical strength of a form, the weaker its connections to other forms (Bybee 2010: 124). Other principles also capture the nature of the formation of morphological categories and classes on the basis of semantic and formal factors. For example, associations by meaning precede associations on the basis of form, and the morphological classes that share schemas eventually become structurally similar. In syntax, high frequency of a construction can lead to the loss of compositionality and analyzability or to the eventual and gradual creation of new constructions (Bybee 2010: 32).

C. On Grammar and its Social Dimension

Proposition 6.14

Grammars are representations emerging from the communicative interactions of a community's speakers who interpret socially established, accepted and shared linguistic conventions.

Proposition 6.15

Speakers are aware of constructions that are conventional and of the impact that frequency of use has on grammatical structures.

Proposition 6.15.1

Constructions can have varying degrees of grammaticality depending on their correspondence with socially established use conventions.

Proposition 6.15.2

Two constructions that have the same level of grammaticality may differ in the degree of their acceptability, which is also socially established.

Proposition 6.16

The complexity, dynamics and change of grammatical constructions and processes can be determined by the social characteristics and groups that speakers belong to; educational level is especially informative in this regard.

Proposition 6.17

Grammatical variation is established on the basis of communicative equivalence between constructions; the frequency of use of these constructions may be correlated with social, contextual and stylistic factors although they are often only conditioned by other linguistic factors.

Proposition 6.17.1

The occurrence of *abrupt* or *discontinuous stratification* in the social distribution of a construction is relatively common in the realm of grammar.

Proposition 6.17.2

Generally, identifying and defining of the envelope of variation for grammatical variables is more difficult than for phonological variables since the equivalence for the former may be determined by the subjective interpretation that speakers make of discourse and social contexts.

Proposition 6.17.3

Grammatical variation is difficult to examine (on the basis of natural speech) because opportunities for using a particular construction or a particular meaning may be relatively infrequent, and because it is more difficult to obtain tokens of different variants.

Proposition 6.18

Grammatical variation includes not only changes that are stable over a long period of time, but also refers to change in the meaning of some constructions that happens within a particular discourse.

Scholium 6-C

David Sankoff distinguished, in his famous study "Sociolinguistics and syntactic variation" (1988), three divergent linguistic research paradigms. The introspective-generative paradigm proposes a theory of language representation in the speaker's mind based on data provided by the linguist's intuitions. The experimental-evaluative paradigm is based on correction criteria and specially focused on teaching the language to those who do not command the varieties of greater social prestige (Martinet 1975) The descriptive-interpretive paradigm is concerned with language variation in its social context and with the use and evolution of language in its speech community. To these paradigms, could be added an interactive-perceptive paradigm, concerned with describing the language system on the basis of its discursive usage originating in communicative interaction. Cognitive sociolinguistics falls within the latter paradigm. Beyond the social functions that were the focus of sociolinguistics of the 1960s and 1970s, it concerns itself with linguistic processes themselves.

With respect to the grammatical, traditional sociolinguistics has gravitated toward the examination of homosemic variation with respect to social classes. That is, it has been concerned with variation that is built from the demonstration of communicative equivalence between two or more variants, which themselves correlate with social, contextual and stylistic factors as well as with linguistic factors (Moreno-Fernández 2009: 28–32, 81–82). From an ethnographic perspective, Muriel Saville-Troike (1982) has explained that, while ethnic markers tend to be expressed on the level of phonology, vocabulary and style, social class and education are (with some notable exceptions) typically indicated on the level of grammar. In addition to the trend of examining the grammatical from the perspective of the social, sociolinguistics has also been interested in variation in internal linguistic processes. Several theories of syntactic variation propose that grammatical structures must be analyzed within discourse because this is where both the instability and versatility of linguistic forms and functions emerge. Typically, rather than develop a so-called "community grammar," elaboration of these theories begins by observing individual behavior. Consequently, sociolinguistic methodology has obtained its samples of usage from recordings of conversations, natural interactions, between members of the same speech community.

In contrast to a dynamic, discourse-based perspective of grammar, generative grammar attempts to provide approximate schematic models of how the human mind would function as it generates and processes structured sequences from lexical elements (Bosque and Gutiérrez-Rexach 2009: 58). The approach gives priority to the individual as such, not as a member of a society, since the functioning of the human mind occurs in the individual. Minimalist syntax (Chomsky 1995) seeks to uncover how natural language facts meet the minimum requirements for a system of sounds and meanings. Within such models, the concept of variation has been of little utility, since the only thing it apparently introduces to the theory are difficulties for the operation of the syntax itself and for its learnability (Henry 2002). However, reality shows that a child acquires her grammar from utterances produced by different speakers whose grammars are probably not identical. Thus, the acquisition mechanism *must* incorporate variation and be sensitive to usage frequencies. Such a mechanism allows the child to acquire not only the language but also to function as a member of the speech community.

The generative approach does not deny the role that social factors play in linguistic variation, nor does it ignore language's multiple geolectal manifestations. What happens is that generativists see social factors as external to the grammatical system itself and, thus, unhelpful in its endeavor to understand the grammatical system (Bosque and Gutiérrez-Rexach 2009: 43). This is where cognitive sociogrammar differs. It takes the position that an account of the social, of the so-called "external," contributes to a better understanding of the language system in its internal dimension. It seems clear that there exist grammatical differences between speakers and that these in turn can also be correlated with extralinguistic factors. It is also the case that the concepts of "acceptability" and "clarity" depend on speakers' perceptions and on the contextualized habits to which they are accustomed. In addition, although the "grammaticality" of a construction usually indicates compliance with the principles governing the grammatical system, it can also indicate compliance with other cognitive systems whose operation depends originally on inter-individual action. Finally, it is also true that syntactic variables—those of homosemic nature—constitute a fact that must also be explained internally. Yet the explanation can only be obtained by analyzing the constructions that compete in particular contexts; between some constructions, there may be differences of referential or grammatical value that can be neutralized or whose meaning may be modified from inside of discourse.

Analysis of the contexts where meaning changes and neutralizations occur constitutes the foundation of the interpretive component of cognitive sociogrammar. That is, since we do not have access to the speakers' intentions or to the subtlety of their communicative intentions, the alternation of forms within contextualized discourse constitutes the clearest indicator of the roles of alternating constructions and of how neutralizations are produced in speakers. Thus, alternating forms do not originate in the internal relationship between syntactic structures but in the sharing elements at the pragmatic level (Sankoff 1988), as discourse is what provides access to a referential or functional equivalency.

What kind of phenomena or grammatical variables require an analysis of this nature? Pedro Martín-Butragueño established in 1994 a typology distinguishing morphological, categorical, functional and positional variables. *Morphological variables* rarely involve the syntactic and pragmatic levels and are often determined by sociolinguistic, stylistic, historical and geographical factors (as is often the case in English for the past tense or the past participle of several variable verbs: *bet-betted, got-gotten, swung-swang, thrived-throve*; in Spanish, the *-ra/-ría* alternation in the imperfect subjunctive, the *-ste/-stes* alternation in the second person singular of simple past tense inflections, or the functional or referential value of the clitics *le, la, lo*). *Categorial variables* affect, in some cases, elements of morphology and, in almost all, the syntax, whose variation sometimes involves the semantic and pragmatic levels. Such variables are rarely determined by sociolinguistic, stylistic, historical and geographical factors. They may be determined by these factors quite irregularly (in Spanish, the use of preposition sequences: *voy por agua/voy a por agua* 'I will bring water;' US English can omit a preposition in *I'll see you (on) Friday* or *He works (by) day(s) and studies (at) nights(s)*). *Functional variables* mainly affect syntax and do not usually correlate with other semantic factors. On the other hand, they are often determined by historical, geographical, sociolinguistic and stylistic factors, though this is not always the case (the presence/absence of personal subject pronouns in Spanish; the variation between *have* and *have got* in English: *He has a cold/He has got a cold*). *Positional variables* usually involve pragmatic factors of various kinds but are not of a morphological or semantic nature (subject-verb word order, verb-complement word order, adjective-noun word order, etc.). The variants of positional variables are commonly associated with different stylistic usages and, with a few exceptions, do not correlate with historical, geographical or sociolinguistic constraints factors. Generally, the variants of all of these types of variables not only show alternating usage but such usage reveals, quite frequently, gradience typical of linguistic variation (Bybee 2010).

Finally, we must insist on the fact that grammatical constructions obey socially accepted and shared linguistic conventions. All grammars, therefore, are sociolinguistic in essence; they are established when categories and constructions become tied to with language use in interactions and when structures become established on the basis of social convention and their acceptability by the speakers. Similarly, grammatical complexity and dynamics can be affected by the speakers' social characteristics, especially by their educational level and social background. It has been shown, for example, that working class speakers tend to favor syntactic and morphological reduction. This fact was highlighted in Basil Bernstein's (1964, 1965) studies on *deficit*, which we have already alluded to. Bernstein studied the socialization process with attention to the role of language in that process and its relationship to psycholinguistic principles, social class, educational attainment and the context of interaction. Deficit theory distinguishes two codes: a restricted code and an elaborated code. In his initial observations, Bernstein associated the restricted code with working class children and the elaborated code with middle class children. He subsequently offered a broader interpretation, associating the codes with interaction styles, processes of psychosocial cognition and different ways of interpreting the social structure. In so doing, he highlighted the more predictable nature of a restricted code and the less predictable of an elaborated one. For Bernstein (1965), all speakers, regardless of social class, have access to a restricted code, but only some groups have access to an elaborated code. In the latter, the restricted code is reserved for certain situations, usually involving family communication.

Debate: Linguistic Grammar or Sociolinguistic Grammar?

The debate over the form and meaning of grammar has occupied linguists for over a century. Discussions have been formulated at various levels, affecting both the conceptualization of entities and grammatical processes as well as their various possibilities of relationship and formalization. Claude Hagège's (1985) *theory of the three points of view* proposes a study of language with consideration to its discursive manifestations, that integrates three complementary perspectives.

1. Language system: Morphosyntactic point of view (subject—predicate)
2. Outside World: Semantic Referential point of view (participant—process)
3. Interlocutors: Enunciative—hierarchical point of view (theme—rheme)

The first has to do with the language systems; the second with the relationship of the system to the outside world, according to the meaning that linguistic expressions convey; and the third, considers the system in relation to interlocutors, according to their representation strategy and the established hierarchy between those who enunciate and what is enunciated. In Hagège's approach, all research conducted from a single point of view, isolated from the other two, is artificial and ignores the real and indissoluble links between all three perspectives. Thus, a grammar pursued exclusively from the first point of view would be both artificial and futile given the close relationships between morphosyntactic forms, the meanings attached to their referents and the pragmatic aspects connecting interlocutors and discourse.

In turn, the theory of sociolinguistic variation aims to develop a grammar in which usage variability correlates with the linguistic and extralinguistic factors. In this grammar, the existing correlations are quantitatively assessed and expressed by formal procedures that include statistical information. Such treatment of linguistic variation and, more specifically, of grammatical variation has led to a theoretical opposition between this model and other approaches. One of these opposing models is that of traditional normative grammar, which cannot be reconciled with a usage-based grammar due to its unscientific character and because it follows a prescriptive rather than a descriptive–explicative ideology. Another opposing model is that of generative grammar, whose fundamental conceptualization dismisses the contribution of the "external," of social factors, on internal processes. Conflicting models can even be identified within a non-formalist sociolinguistics, which is less concerned with both the internal workings of grammar and its linguistic formalization (Henry 2002).

Cognitive sociolinguistics visualizes grammar as a set of representations established by linguistic usage and communicative interaction. From this perspective, a grammar cannot disregard usage or the interactions that take place within a speech community. As a result, any theory that approaches grammar from an exclusively linguistic perspective and overlooks the contribution of the speaker to the configuration of a grammar cannot, from a cognitivist perspective, be entertained. Cognitivism always opts for grammatical concepts based of speakers' usage in concrete social environments.

From a social perspective, one cannot ignore the existence of a general distinction between two ways of doing grammar: that based on how language is used (descriptive grammar) and that based on how grammar should be used (prescriptive grammar). Out of these two, the latter is certainly the most socially visible as it formulates judgments about grammatical usage considered either "good" or "bad" and legitimizes negative social consequences for those who do not conform to appropriate models, as well as for those who are accused of ignorance or carelessness. Such ways of understanding grammar, however, do not concern us, especially at this moment, since our focus is on the internal sociolinguistic dynamics of the grammar itself and not so much on its social appraisal. Grammar's social perception is based on three major traditional fallacies: that of logic, that of precision and that of authority (Ghomeshi 2010). These fallacies are of interest to the study of linguistic attitudes rather than to theories concerned with the internal configuration of grammar, however tied to social factors grammar may be.

Conclusion

The foundations of cognitive grammar are well rooted in the proposals of specialists such as Langacker and Lakoff. In turn, cognitive sociolinguistics approaches the study of grammar from the general perspectives of a cognitivist, but it emphasizes the influence that social, situational and contextual factors have on grammatical form. Besides knowing the language, speakers learn sequences and structures, use them in context, contribute to creating categories, perceive analogies and similarities and are aware of the frequency of use of the various units. Furthermore, they are able to establish grammatical equivalencies during interaction and to modify signifiers according to the presence or absence of certain linguistic or extra linguistic elements.

The sociolinguistic study of grammar has, for decades, faced doubt and suspicion because of having exclusively embraced variationist methods to implement analysis. The difficulties in analyzing sociogrammatical variation are well known: low number of occurrence of variants in everyday speech, difficulty in demonstrating their semantic values, relative incidence of social variables. Yet, these challenges have discouraged very few sociolinguists. Those who capitulated to the difficulties simply abandoned variationist sociolinguistics to augment the ranks of discourse analysts, who, incidentally, acknowledge not only the weight of social contexts, but also the importance of how language is perceived by speakers. The case of Beatriz Lavandera (1984) constitutes a good example of a well-known researcher who left variationist sociolinguistics for discourse analysis.

Cognitive sociolinguistics reclaims a social space within grammar, a space that, in its nature, transcends mere variation. Social interaction, communicative dynamics and the speaker's perception are crucial for understanding the origin of grammar, its configuration and its dynamics as well as how grammar, in intimate connection with the phonological and lexical–semantic, changes.

References

Bernstein, Basil, 1964. "Elaborated and restricted codes: their social origins and some consequences." In *The Ethnography of Communication, American Anthropologist,* Eds., J. J. Gumperz and D. Hymes, 66: 99–116.

Bernstein, Basil, 1965. "A sociolinguistic approach to social learning." In *Penguin Survey of the Social Sciences,* Ed., J. Gould, 144–168. Harmondsworth: Penguin.

Bosque, Ignacio and Javier Gutiérrez-Rexach, 2009. *Fundamentos de sintaxis formal.* Madrid: Akal.

Bresnan, Joan and Marilyn Ford, 2010 "Predicting syntax: processing dative constructions in American and Australian varieties of English." *Language,* 86–1: 186–213.

Bybee, Joan, 2001. *Phonology and Language Use.* Cambridge: Cambridge University Press.

Bybee, Joan, 2010. *Language, Use and Cognition*. Cambridge: Cambridge University Press.
Bybee, Joan and Paul Hopper (Eds.), 2001. *Frequency and the Emergence of Linguistics Structure*. Amsterdam: John Benjamins.
Chomsky, Noam, 1995. *The Minimalist Program*. Cambridge, MA: MIT Press.
Claes, Jeroen. 2014. "Sociolingüística comparada y gramática de construcciones. Un acercamiento a la pluralización de haber presentacional en las capitals antillanas." *Revista Española de Lingüística Aplicada*, 27(2) 338–364.
Clark, John, Colin Yallop and Janet Fletcher, 2007. *An Introduction to Phonetics and Phonology*. 3rd ed. Oxford: Blackwell.
Company, Concepción, 2003. "La gramaticalización en la historia del español." *Medievalia*, 35: 3–61.
Croft, William, 2007. "Construction grammar." In *The Oxford Handbook of Cognitive Linguistics*, Eds., D. Geeraerts and H. Cuickens, 463–508. Oxford: Oxford University Press.
Croft, William and D. Alan Cruse, 2004. *Cognitive Linguistics*. Cambridge: Cambridge University Press.
Cuenca, Maria Josep and Joseph Hilferty, 1999. *Introducción a la lingüística cognitiva*. Barcelona, Ariel.
Ellis, Nick, 2002. "Frequency effects in language processing: A review with implications for theories of implicit and explicit language acquisition." *Studies in Second Language Acquisition*, 24: 143–188.
Fillmore, Charles J., 1988. "The mechanisms of 'Construction Grammar'." *Proceedings of the Annual Meeting of the Berkeley Linguistics Society*, 14: 35–55.
Fillmore, Charles J., 1995. *Construction Grammar. Lecture Notes*. Stanford, CA: CSLI Publication.
Ghomeshi, Jila, 2010. *Grammar Matters. The Social Significance of How We Use Language*. Winnipeg: Arbeiter Ring.
Givon, Talmy, 1979. *On Understanding Grammar*. New York: Academic Press.
Givon, Talmy, 1984. *Syntax: A Functional-Typological Introduction*, 1. Amsterdam: John Benjamins.
Givon, Talmy, 1986. "Prototypes: between Plato and Wittgenstein." In *Noun, Classes and Categorization*, Ed., C. Craig, 77–102. Amsterdam: John Benjamins.
Goldberg, Adele E., 1995. *Constructions: A Construction Grammar Approach to Argument Structure*. Chicago, IL: University of Chicago Press.
Goldberg, Adele E., 2006. *Constructions at Work: The Nature of Generalization in Language*. Oxford: Oxford University Press.
Gras Manzano, Pedro, 2010. *Gramática de construcciones en interacción. Propuesta de un modelo y aplicación al análisis de estructuras independientes con marcas de subordinación en español*. Barcelona: Universitat de Barcelona.
Hagège, Claude, 1985. *L'homme de paroles. Contribution linguistique aux sciences humaines*. La Fléche: Fayard.
Henry, Alison, 2002. "Variation and syntactic theory." In *The Handbook of Language Variation and Change*, Eds., J.K. Chambers, P. Trudgill and N. Schilling-Estes, 267–282. Oxford: Blackwell.
Hopper, Paul and Elizabeth Traugott, 1993. *Grammaticalization*. Cambridge: Cambridge University Press.
Jackendoff, Ray, 2002. *Foundations of Language. Brain, Meaning, Grammar, Evolution*. Oxford: Oxford University Press.

Kristiansen, Gitte and Dirk Geeraerts (Eds.), 2013. "Contexts of use in Cognitive Sociolinguistics." *Special Issue. The Journal of Pragmatics* 52: 1–104.
Lakoff, George, 1987. *Women, Fire, and Dangerous Things. What Categories Reveals about Mind.* Chicago, IL: The University of Chicago Press.
Langacker, Ronald W., 1987. *Foundations of Cognitive Grammar. Volume I. Theoretical Prerequisites.* Standord, Stanford University Press.
Langacker, Ronald W., 2005. "Construction grammars: cognitive radical, and less so." In *Cognitive Linguistics: Internal Dynamics and Interdisciplinary Interaction*, Eds., F. J. Ruiz de Mendoza and S. Peña Cervel, 101–159. Berlin—New York: Mouton de Gruyter.
Lavandera, Beatriz, 1984. *Variación y significado.* Buenos Aires: Hachette.
Martín Butragueño, Pedro, 1994. "Hacia una tipología de la variación gramatical en sociolingüística del español." *Nueva Revista de Filología Hispánica*, 42: 29–75.
Martinet, Jeanne (dir.), 1975. *De la teoría lingüística a la enseñanza de la lengua.* Madrid: Gredos.
Meillet, André, 1921. *Linguistique historique et linguistique générale.* Paris: Champion.
Moreno-Fernández, Francisco, 2009. *Principios de sociolingüística y sociología del lenguaje.* 4th ed. Barcelona: Ariel.
Pierrehumbert, Janet B., 2003. "Phonetic diversity, statistical learning, and acquisition of phonology." *Language and Speech* 46 (2–3): 115–154.
Quine, Willard Van Orman, 1960. *Word and Object.* Cambridge: MIT Press.
Sankoff, David, 1988. "Sociolinguistics and syntactic variation." In *Linguistics: The Cambridge survey, vol. IV. The sociocultural context*, Ed., F. J. Newmeyer, 140–161. New York: Academic Press.
Saville-Troike, Muriel, 1982. *The Ethnography of Communication. An Introduction.* Oxford: Blackwell.
Szmrecsanyi, Benedikt, Jason Grafmiller, Benedikt Heller and Melanie Röthliberger. 2013. *Probabilistic Variation in a Comparative Perspective. The Grammar of Varieties of English.* Leuven: KU Leuven.
Tagliamonte, Sali, 2002. "Comparative Sociolinguistics." In *The Handbook of Language Variation and Change*, Eds., J.K. Chambers, P. Trudgill, and N. Schilling-Estes, 729–762. Oxford: Blackwell.
The Five Graces Group, 2007. "Language is a Complex Adaptative System." Santa Fe Institute. Obtained from: www.santafe.edu/media/workingpapers/08-12-047.pdf (accessed, 15 December, 2015).
Traugott, Elizabet, 1995. "Subjectification in grammaticalization." In *Subjectivity and Subjectivization*, Eds., S. Wright and D. Stein, 31–54. Cambridge: Cambridge University Press.
Traugott, Elizabeth and Ekkehard König, 1991. "The Semantics-Pragmatics of Grammatizalization Revisited." In *Approaches to Grammaticalization*, Eds., E. Traugott and B. Heine, 189–218. Amsterdam: John Benjamins.
Ungerer, Friedrich and Hans-Jörg Schmid, 1996. *An Introduction to Cognitive Linguistics.* Cambridge: Cambridge University Press.

7

SOCIOPHONOLOGY AND COGNITION

The projection of phonetics and phonology to the geosocial level raises numerous profound questions, including the following: *How are phonological systems of different regions linked into a single suprasystem? How does the connection between systems and suprasystem take place in the speaker's (psychological) realm and in the sociological domain?* With respect to variation, there are facts that have not been sufficiently explained within any given theoretical model. Nevertheless, for structuralism, combinatory variants are considered combinatory only within a given speech community; thus, the same elements do not combine in the same way in all communities sharing a language, that is, in all its geolects. How are, then, these variants organized within a supralinguistic system? Moreover, while optional individual variants are particular by definition, it is possible to find certain regularity in the alternation of variants within a community, a social group or even an individual. How should these regularities be represented in a phonological model?

Traditionally, sociolinguistic research followed an orientation that did not grant the cognitive a central explanatory role. We have, consequently encountered the strange paradox that Labovian sociolinguistics (Labov 1966), which in its very beginning used transformational generativism as a referent—a generativism that left no room for the social or the external and that privileged the psychological—has been unable to articulate the link between the individual and the social, the external and the internal: a link that is essentially cognitive in its nature. We agree, then, with Rocío Caravedo (2003) when she says that variationism has granted priority to the observation of variation in microcontexts linked to a few, not always well-defined, social and situational categories. In so doing, variationist sociolinguistics has ignored or undervalued the study of variation in broader contexts. As a result:

additional research in an analytical direction has become necessary. That is, we need to define the macro contexts, types of societies and value systems of the speakers that are part of them, to understand the changes in the organization of language and reinterpret them in line with the cognitive background of the speakers involved. Of course, all of this would be approached socially rather than individually.

(Caravedo 2003: 547, my translation)

This change of direction, to which we adhere, has already begun to occur and can be perceived in the proposal of integrative models such as the one offered by cognitive sociolinguistics.

A. On the Configuration of the Phonological Level

Proposition 7.1

From a cognitive perspective, phonemes can be interpreted as sets of exemplars associated with a "schema."

Proposition 7.2

From a social perspective, phonemes are prototypical projections of the norms of a language.

Proposition 7.3

The internal structure of a phoneme adopts a radial arrangement in which some of its exemplars (variants) may overlap with those of other phonemes.

Proposition 7.4

The sounds of a language are not perceived the same way by all speakers; some of them even go unnoticed.

Proposition 7.5

Phonemic variants allow the formation of complex entities, through categorization processes.

Proposition 7.6

Phonemic gestures are the smallest units of phonetic description. They are tools that are deployed during speech production and whose consequences can be observed in the movement of the speech articulators.

Proposition 7.7

The sounds of a language are not only associated with a closed set of phonemes; they also affect suprasegmental levels of language.

Proposition 7.8

Phonemic units are closely connected with lexical units and grammatical constructions.

Proposition 7.8.1

Morphological units require the involvement of phonemic, lexical and grammatical units.

Proposition 7.8.2

Suprasegmental elements, especially intonation, require the existence of a connection between phonology and syntax and semantics.

Proposition 7.8.3

Phonemic features give rise to different variants of a phoneme when realized in lexical units; this makes it possible to categorize and store them according to their contexts of occurrence.

Scholium 7-A

Cognitive phonology provides valuable information on how phonemic features are perceived, categorized and stored by speakers (Nathan 2007). To start, it proposes, of course, that the units called "phonemes" and their variants are to be interpreted as categories subject to the basic principles and concepts of cognitivism. Particularly, the traditional notion of "phoneme" can be reformulated through the cognitivist concepts of "prototype" and "schema."

A prototype is a perceptual phonemic category: a set of variants perceived as a set because of their similarity. A particular prototype category is built from a series of specific, concrete manifestations that are taken to be "central" representatives or "best exemplars" of all possible various manifestations. Once created, specific manifestations of a phoneme are no longer relevant and are valued insofar as they approximate the category's central member, or "best exemplar." These prototypes, i.e., categories, then represent norms about what the sounds of a language are and what they should be. With subsequent exposure to sounds as used in words, listeners sort the features perceived to be acoustically relevant for the identification of phonemic categories (Pierrehumbert 2003), prioritizing the information that helps identify the category to which it may belong and diluting other concrete acoustical information that may not be central to category identification. The determination of what is relevant, and the related process of categorizing a concrete sound, is done by comparing it with the exemplars associated with a particular prototype, i.e., category. Each exemplar is, in turn, stored with respect to the social and contextual conditions of its production.

Schemas, like prototypes, are categories built from concrete specimens. On the other hand, while prototypes are perceptual categories, sets of close variants grouped together because of their similarity, schemas are abstract and emerging cognitive categories built with respect only to "exemplars." Because they are abstractions, schemas are compatible with all the exemplars that have been used to create the schema.

The units traditionally known as "phonemes" are units treated by cognitivism either as schemas or as prototypes. There is, however, an advantage of working with "schemas" instead of "phonemes." The abstract nature of a "schema" connects it directly with each exemplar manifestation and to its set with the result that, while the existence of exemplars unconnected to a schema is possible, a schema unconnected to exemplars cannot exist. In other words, every exemplar is fully compatible with its schema; the compatibility of any manifestation with its prototype is relative (Langacker 1987: 371; Taylor 1995: 65–68). When "schema" is applied to the field of phonemics, we must accept a set of theoretical premises, discussed by Langacker (1987):

a. As has been advocated from the perspective of autosegmental phonology, also known as prosodic or dependent phonology, the sounds of a language are not isolated from other levels of linguistic expression, but rather affect suprasegmental levels.
b. The sounds of a language are not perceived the same way by all speakers; some of them even go unnoticed.
c. Phonemic variants can occur both at a level of consciousness and at an unconscious level.
d. The sounds of a language can be considered exemplars that reflect their allophonic variation possibilities.

These theoretical principles account for the cardinal elements of a homosemic phonemic variation, understood as different alternatives for saying the same thing, regardless of whether an alternative is employed in response to linguistic or extralinguistic factors. At the same time, through the concept of "schema" and the not incompatible notion of "prototype," these principles offer an interpretation of the concept of "phoneme" beyond its conceptualization within a structuralist paradigm. In fact, Kristiansen (2001) speaks of the existence of linguistic stereotypes formed by variants or groups of variants that would be perceptually distinctive and functionally exclusive. Pierrehumbert (2003) affirms

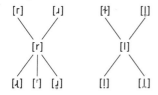

FIGURE 7.1 Radial Arrangement of the Structure Corresponding to the English Phonemes /r/ and /l/

that two forms are identical only if they are identical at discrete level (perceived data) and at parametric level (category). The groups of phonemic variants would be organized in prototypical structures such as the "radial category" that Lakoff proposed in 1987. Once again, the "network" is featured as a fundamental to linguistic organization (Figure 7.1).

Cognitive phonology works with radial categories. In these categories, components are distributed in the form of a centralized network with the possibility that some of their exemplars connect, in turn, with exemplars that are also connected to reticular centers. This results in networks that overlap, creating an overall decentralized network pattern, would seem to facilitate a better understanding of phenomena such as phonetic neutralizations or acoustic equivalences. In this way, then, we leave behind the artificial conceptualization of the phoneme imposed by twentieth century linguistics. According to Quine (1960: 89), although the concept of "phoneme" has enabled linguists to uncover phonetic norms in a language, the technical segmentation that has been imposed by the linguist has resulted in a conceptualization of those norms that is of a different order from how they exist in language. In keeping with this observation, Quine, for his part, described the phoneme in terms of "statistical norms" and downplayed the existence tightly circumscribed, non-overlapping categories.

Finally, we cannot lose sight of the fact that, for cognitive phonology, it is natural to speak of specific, actual sounds, fully specified exemplars, rather than of nonspecific entities. Those sounds result from articulatory gestures, which are acts performed during speech production and considered to be the basic units of description and the level of language from which variations and linguistic change arises (Browman and Goldstein 1992). The analysis of the perception of sounds is the domain of perceptual phonetics (Pickett 1999).

B. On the Sociocognitive Dynamics of Phonology

Proposition 7.9

Phonemic variation occurs at various levels of abstraction: the level of the schema, the prototype level and the physical level.

Proposition 7.9.1

The level of the schema, the most abstract, corresponds to what speakers, as a result of their experience using language in the community, believe is pronounced.

Proposition 7.9.2

The prototype level corresponds to what speakers believe *should* be pronounced; concrete phonemic realizations—their own and those of others—could be characterized according to their degree of (dis)similarity with respect to the prototype.

Proposition 7.9.3

The physical level corresponds to those sounds that are actually pronounced even if they are not perceived by the speaker or evidence unusual characteristics. The physical level also includes cases where a sound is not produced, but speakers perceive its presence.

Proposition 7.10

Listeners perceive features of sounds and identify those features as acoustically relevant or not. They prioritize the information associated with the categorical identity and dilute other information about its concrete acoustical form.

Proposition 7.11

The frequency of phonemic facts is fundamental in establishing phonological categories and their schemas and prototypes.

Proposition 7.12

The perceived similarity of the features in context is crucial in establishing categories, their schemas and prototypes.

Proposition 7.13

The variable use of phonemes in communicative interaction occurs in the relationship between what is said, what is believed to be said, and what is believed should be said.

Scholium 7-B

The gap between the social and the psychological in the models that treat linguistic variation has been problematic enough in recent years so as to have spurred the development of several theoretical proposals attempting to bridge that gap. In models aimed at integrating the essential components of variation—linguistic, social and psychological—cognitive elements have been crucial. Cognition processes are key to understanding and explaining how it is possible to articulate, as part of competence, the linguistic, social and psychological matter. Cognitivism has undeniably permeated, in one way or another, William Labov's variationist proposals beginning with his work in the 1960s where he established the concept of "variable rule." In fact, the inclusion of statistical probabilities within the variationist model presupposed a cognitive element, which has nonetheless remained theoretically underdeveloped. That is, proposing statistical probabilities took as given that linguistic competence, at the psychological level, incorporates a quantitative component, specifically probability, which governs the appearance of some variants or others in a given situational context or with respect to speakers of a particular sociological profile. For Labov (1994), probabilities reveal a biological capacity of the human brain and are part of individual linguistic competence. In other words, the speaker is able to calculate the probabilities involved in using particular linguistic variable and choose the most suitable variant for each socio-communicative circumstance. So the question arises: if Labov's variationism has not hesitated to utilize cognitive concepts in accounting for variation in sociolinguistic competence of speakers, why has it not dedicated more resources toward deepening our understanding of cognitive processes or moved resolutely toward a cognitive sociolinguistics?

Rocío Caravedo noted in 1990 that attending to the gap between Labovian variationist theory and the functional structuralist tradition constitutes a more natural move than attempting to link Labovian variationism with generative principles, which prioritize the internal and the psychological aspects of language to the point of marginalizing the social and external. Caravedo, thus, approaches variability from a functionalist perspective and proposes to account for it, not in terms of the variants of particular phonemes, but in terms of "spaces of variability," whose boundaries could be defined in terms of where a representative meaning functions or ceases to function. Caravedo denounces the concept of "phoneme" as an invariant unit and proposes to replace it with that of "functional zone" with flexible, movable boundaries, according to the communities and groups being studied in each particular case. In this interpretation, linguistic variants shift or alternate within the same zone. Concurrently, zones can relax their boundaries or re-create them according to phonological, morphological and syntactic conditioning factors, or even in response to extralinguistic constraints (time, geography, society, situation). This type of alternation then becomes possible at other linguistic levels thanks to semantic or homosemic equivalency occurring among units that appear in the same contexts and situations.

Caravedo's theoretical formulation distinguishes the following three conceptual levels (1990: 66):

Functional zone: This is a space of phonemic realization on a continuum whose boundaries may coincide with the ability to discriminate meaning in lexical units. For example, the stop and fricative variants of the Spanish phoneme /b/ belong to the same functional zone; as well as the vowels [ɔ] and [ɑ] in English.

Variability space: This is an area of variation that usually coincides with a functional zone but can move between different zones or affect several zones simultaneously under certain linguistic circumstances. For example, in Spanish the possible use of /b, g, d/ in syllable-final position—a relaxed area—(e.g., [ob.ser.'bar], [og.ser.'bar], [od.ser.'bar] *observar* 'to observe') occurs because the three units can appear in the same space of variability. In English the sound [ɾ] can be linked to /t/ or /d/ in a common area of variation, when they occur intervocalically in unstressed syllables.

Variation: This is the differentiated and organized expression of variability in visible and recognizable entities in phonological analysis. When variation does not produce a change in meaning, it is called "non-functional variation." When variation leads to a modification of the original meaning, it constitutes "functional variation."

With respect to quantification as an inherent characteristic of variability, Caravedo does not deny that language proficiency may include a statistical or quantitative component. She draws attention to some significant facts, one of them being that not all variation phenomena occur to the same extent. She also notes that there is not necessarily a predictable relationship between frequency and relevance. That is, not everything that is quantitatively frequent may be relevant for the speaker and not everything that is infrequent is irrelevant. Moreover, it is necessary to emphasize that the criterion of frequency loses explanatory power when in the realm of functional variation (variation in meaning), when different variables and variants intersect (a highly usual linguistic phenomenon) or when variation occurs in asymmetric or conflicting social contexts, with different uses, models and variations in situations of varieties in contact (Blommaert 1999). In these cases a speaker's perception of sociolinguistic facts as well as the cognitive elements associated with perception carry greater weight. Variation, thus, integrates the cognitive dimension and is reinterpreted from a psychological position without neglecting its social and situational components.

Caravedo's theoretical proposal, as it turns out, aligns well with a cognitive phonology that interprets the concept of "phoneme" as a category with a radial structure, a structure that may begin as a centralized network with the possibility of becoming a broader decentralized network. Her proposal is also akin to the interpretation of phonemic variation as a set of exemplars any one of which may become the basis for the emergence of new or altered schemas and prototypes. What Caravedo calls "functional zones" would be somewhat equivalent to the concept of schema, which includes sets of homosemic variants. Cognitive sociolinguistics could distinguish two or more levels of abstraction in its conceptualization of variation as follows.

1. The level of the *schema*, the most abstract, would correspond to what speakers *believe is pronounced*. As a concept, "schema" could be identified with the traditional concept of "phoneme" as well as with all the aforementioned differences in its configuration and evolution. The storage of those exemplars constituting the schemas would be associated with the storage of words, whose organization is realized on the semantic base and on the phonemic foundation itself. Its organization would also incorporate quantitative information relative to usage frequencies although not a probabilistic apparatus in its own right.
2. The *prototype* would constitute a second level. This level would correspond to what speakers *believe should be pronounced*. At this level, concrete phonemic realizations—their own and those of others—are characterized according to their degree of similarity as compared with the prototype, and are stored as either more central or more peripheral within a category. Socially, prototypes may reflect convention and operate as the norm. What speakers believe should be pronounced includes sounds with characteristics different from those perceived. The characteristics of perceived sounds, however, are what is stored in the speaker's brain. It is associated with corresponding schemas but incorporates information about linguistic usage in context.
3. *The sounds that are actually pronounced* would constitute a third level of specificity although the sounds specified at this level may include characteristics that are either unusual or that the speaker does not perceive. This level also includes cases of the absence of sounds that are not perceived as such.

To illustrate the structuring of these theoretical concepts, we will use phenomena related to the realization of syllable-final /s/ in Spanish (e.g., *caras* 'faces,' *olas* 'waves,' *manos* 'hands'). We represent schemas within parentheses preceded by the letter "E." For instance, E(s) represents a "voiceless alveo-dental sibilant schema." The prototype is indicated within parentheses and preceded by the letters "PT." For example, PT(s) represents a "voiceless alveo-dental sibilant prototype." We represent sounds within square brackets, which, in turn, are presented within parentheses. For instance, ([s]) represents a "voiceless alveo-dental sibilant sound." The use of parentheses in this case as well as in all previous cases allows for the inclusion of information pertaining to contextual elements that may be part of the speaker's perception. Thus, (-[s]) represents a voiceless alveo-dental sibilant sound in syllable final position. In this way, the cognitive interpretation of the variation corresponding to syllable final /s/, would make us think of a schema E(-s), which would correspond to the abstraction of the phoneme /s/, fixed in the speakers' minds through its frequency of use and other means, especially writing. In many Hispanic communities, particularly in the most conservative ones, this schema is (proto)typically associated with a sibilant pronunciation, as indicated in the notation: PT(-s). Its various phonetic manifestations are associated with the same schema. Although they could share either more or fewer features with the PT, they are clearly connected to the speaker's perception (e.g., sibilance (-[s]), aspiration (-[h]), assimilated consonant sound, modification of an adjacent sound). In all these cases, the speaker has the perception of referring to the same schema E(-s). Moreover, on numerous occasions the speaker believes that he is articulating a central or prototypical sound PT(-s) although the actual pronunciation may very different and not even specifically perceived by the speaker.[1]

At this second level, what the speaker believes should be pronounced may even be an abstract element PT(-X). This would indicate that the speaker knows that he pronounces something even if he may not know or have to know exactly what it is.

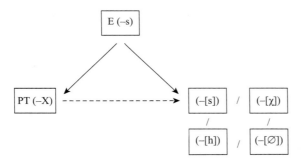

FIGURE 7.2 Schema of -s in Spanish in Communities of Conservative Implosive Consonantism

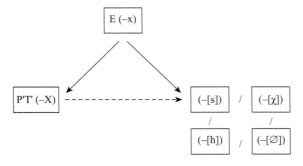

FIGURE 7.3 Schema of -s in Spanish, in Innovative Implosive Consonant Communities (I)

Sociophonology and Cognition **137**

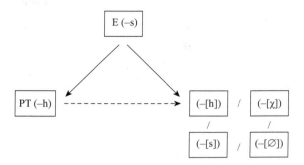

FIGURE 7.4 Schema of -s in Canary Islands Spanish

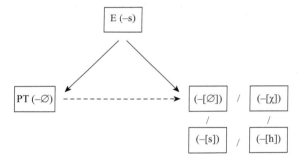

FIGURE 7.5 Schema of -s in Spanish, in Innovative Implosive Consonant Communities (II)

In the most innovative Spanish communities, such as the Canary Islands, the schema could be the same, but with the aspirated variant as the prototype. There may be a collective consciousness that the PT is not a sibilant but aspirated. The rest of the complex category would be organized similarly to the previous case.

We could also find cases in which the PT was the absence of sound, which would happen in communities where final −s lenition is commonplace (e.g., the Caribbean and the Southern Cone). So much so that we could find the conviction that the speaker would be capable of interpreting as a phonetic zero actual phonemic realizations, including the sibilant.

Anyway, in all the possibilities discussed, various phonetic variants could be associated with certain sociolinguistic and stylistic values. Based on this, it would be possible to compose the inventory of schemas and prototypes for speech communities throughout the Hispanic world in a descriptive formalization exercise to be conducted in due course. In such exercise, we should avoid, by all means necessary, the practice that frequently occurs in phonology of interpreting phonemic variants as derivations of a supposed standard language. Let us recall that the concept of "standard language" originated in the sociology of language rather than in linguistics proper, for the purpose of teaching and disseminating (Moreno-Fernández 2010).

C. On Sociophonetic Variation

Proposition 7.14

Phonetic variation is homosemic by nature and it is articulated through a set of different forms or alternative ways to say the same thing.

Proposition 7.15

Phonetic variants utilized in concrete linguistic, social and situational contexts constitute a group of exemplars associated with those contexts.

Proposition 7.16

Phonetic variation is established on the basis of communicative equivalence between certain variants, which can correlate with social and stylistic factors as well as with linguistic factors.

Proposition 7.17

Phonetic variation is easy to quantify because any variant will usually have multiple opportunities for being manifested within virtually any defined context for variation.

Proposition 7.18

Phonetic variation and change can be determined by the speakers' social characteristics, especially by their educational attainment and their social background.

Scholium 7-C

In the chapter devoted to semantic issues, we discussed the fact that part of a unit's meaning depends on context and is negotiated by speakers in interaction. Just as semantic boundaries between lexical units and constructions are blurry, then, so are phonological units' phonemic boundaries. This is so much the case that it becomes preferable to speak of schemas and functional zones rather than of specific phonemes. However, if we understand variation as the alternation between different ways to say the same thing, variation processes at the phonemic level have been traditionally treated from a dual linguistic perspective: that of structuralism, especially Eugenio Coseriu's, and that of William Labov's variationism. For European structuralism, linguistic variation is located fundamentally at the most superficial levels of language—that is, the norm and speech—although the most abstract level, the system, is also sufficiently variable and unstable so as to admit the possibility of language change (Coseriu 1973). Variants found at the level of the norm are called *combinatory variants* or *alo-* (*allophones, allomorphs*) units. At the phonological level, allophones are produced in the process of realizing a phoneme, when the whole speech community produces, for a given phonological environment, a particular concrete sound and not any other. These variants are in complementary distribution, as is the case of [p] and [pʰ] in English or [b] and [β] in Spanish. Therefore, both variants never appear simultaneously in the same phonological context. According to the structuralists, the variants that occur at the level of the norm are abstract in nature and are linked to the realm of *langue*; that is, they constitute realizations accepted by a sociocultural norm.

Along with the norm's variants, we find the speech variants—concrete and individual in nature—that are called *facultative variants*. In this case, they are free variants, which can appear in the same context and that mutually alternate without necessarily causing meaning differences. This is the case of [s], [h] and [Ø], as variants of the phoneme /s/ in syllable-final position in Spanish. Facultative variants can be individual when the alternation occurs in a speaker's pronunciation. They can be general, when a variant has widespread use, as with the predorsal sibilant variant of /s/ in Andalusia, the Canary Islands and the Americas. The interpretation of free variation was resolved by the structuralists with the notion of "polymorphism" (Allières 1954; Alvar 1965–1966; Lope Blanch 1979).

These concepts are very well known. They have been part of the training of many generations of language scholars especially in Europe. However, when variation has to be accounted for, structuralism does not seem to provide all the required answers. Geolinguistic and sociolinguistic reality make evident some of structuralist phonology's difficulties and raises formidable questions. When Henriette Walter (1975) presents an empirical study of phonological diversity in a speech community—that of Paris—, she points out the heterogeneity observed in her reference group due to age, geographical origin or language level. She also proposes to approach variation starting with the analysis of idiolects, whose comparison would allow the discovery of common elements. This idiolectal phase of the analysis leads to the description of the phonological diversity of her informants from the "École Pratique des Hautes Études" and to the proposal of more than half a dozen phonological systems. We emphasize here that these systems are indeed "phonological." That is, the observed individual variants rise to the rank of abstract elements related to an individual. These elements only become common or communal when comparing the systems of several speakers. In other cases, however, the explanation of the variants is restricted to the phonetic level, without recognizing in them a certain level of abstraction. López Morales (1984) interprets in this way, for example, cases of open and closed vocalism in eastern Andalusian speech. Resolving "phonological" diversity among different communities was largely achieved with Uriel Weinreich's (1954) concept of "diasystem" or "suprasystem." However, the same concepts seem less easily applied when trying to explicate the connection between what occurs at the level of the individual speaker and the apparent "unity in social diversity" observable at the community level.

Generativist proposals have not solved several of the underlying issues raised here. American variationists have always been conditioned by their transformational generative environment. Against the proposal of the *optional rule*, a theoretically flimsy concept, sociolinguistics proposed an alternative aimed at enriching the generative model: *the variable rule* (Labov 1969). This rule provided a very suitable theoretical framework to account for variation: in its formulation, the segment /X/ variably manifests itself through [X] or [Z] and this occurs with fluctuating probability in different contexts and conditions. The information corresponding to its likelihood of application is added to the linguistic formulation. Thus, the variable rule would explain the extent to which, and under which linguistic and social conditions a given phenomenon holds. Facing proposals such as that of the "ideal speaker-listener" and "homogeneous community" sociolinguistics proposes the experience of certain real and representative uses. A dialectical opposition with generativism appears from the moment that variationism turns these proposals into axioms (Moreno-Fernández 1988: 128–130). The variationist sociolinguistics' emblematic analysis is, thus, known by the name of *variable rule analysis*. Indeed, variationism has devoted part of its energy to perfecting a statistical test capable of measuring how far a number of linguistic (contextual and functional) and extralinguistic (social and situational) factors determine the appearance of each of the variants of a variable linguistic phenomenon (Sankoff, Tagliamonte and Smith 2005).

Closely linked to these theoretical concerns is how to position sociolinguistic variation, or variability in general, within the totality of language system. Variationist sociolinguistics starts from the idea that the variable rule is linked to linguistic competence. However, in the explanations of this hypothesis that have been formulated, distinct shades of intensity can be observed. For Labov, variable rules are *production rules*, most of which can also be characterized as rules of actuation, although they clearly constitute an aspect of competence. To Cedergren and Sankoff (1974), actuation is a statistical reflection of competence and variable rules include a probabilistic component of the linguistic and the social, respectively. We could say that some scholars have more radically advocated for a concept of "variable rule" as the exclusive property of competence, while others have associated it with less abstract levels of language. These perspectives are more equipped than structuralist perspectives to explain variation in the individual and in relation to his speech community. It is not easy, however, to escape difficulties stemming from these concepts of sociolinguistic competence. Where does the psychological end and where does the social begin in individual competence? How is the quantitative embedded within competence? How can we connect individuals' and communities' phonological diversity with the homogeneity that is necessary for the existence of a group or community?

The foundation for a cognitive study of phonetic variation has been gradually developing since the 1960s. It was established in Langacker's (1987) seminal work and has developed robustly as part of "usage-based linguistics" (Bybee 2010). In our opinion, "usage-based phonology" offers an appropriate foundation to explain sociophonetic variation within the context of a cognitive sociolinguistics. That is why it is important to understand its theoretical foundations. Linguistic habits contribute to shaping the form and content of phonological systems. The frequency with which words or strings of words are used and the frequency with which segmental and suprasegmental patterns recur in language affect both the mental representation and the phonetic form of words. When we speak of language usage, we refer not merely to language processing but to all social and interactive uses to which the language is exposed. The frequency with which we use certain words, phrases or sequences eventually has an effect on their phonological structure. All of this brings us to an interesting debate.

Debate: Variation as a Structural Fact and as a Cognitive Fact

Let us return to the issues raised at the beginning of this chapter: What is the mechanism that links the phonological systems of different geographical regions in a single supra-system? How does the connection between systems and suprasystem take place in the speaker's mind and in the domain of the community? A traditional viewpoint in linguistics has led to proposing the existence of a suprasystem that articulates partial subsystems as well as the entire repertoire of geographically distributed functional variables. However, this idealized or "modeled" interpretation of linguistic reality is not supported by communicative reality. Combinatory variants are combinatory within specific speech communities; the same variants may not function the same way in all speech communities sharing a language or in all geolects. So, how are all these variants articulated within the overall system? For their part, the facultative variants that structuralists call "general," precisely for being general in a community, would not be sporadic variants or variants in complementary distribution but constant elements, susceptible, therefore, to being components of a phonological system, though they may not be shared phonemes. This occurs, for example, with pronunciation /aː/, as in *castle*, *path* or *laugh*, in Received Pronunciation and with /æ/ in General American English. In Spanish it occurs with predorsal [s] of many regions (Western Andalucía, Canarias, the Americas), compared with apical [s] in other areas (northern Spain). Individual facultative variants are particular by definition.

However, within a community, a group or even an individual, you may find certain regularity in the alternation of variants. How should we evaluate these regularity patterns in the phonological model? A clear lack of relationship between the psychological and the sociological and between both of these aspects with the linguistic is evident in the structuralist proposal. At the same time, linguistics has not been able to completely solve the equation that connects the phonetic and phonological levels in the realm of variation due to the fact that it has been hidden under the imprecise cover of polymorphism. Articulating this relationship is made more challenging because the concepts of "phonology" and "variation" are usually located at distinct linguistic levels.

From a sociocognitive perspective, phonological reality, including its variation, is constructed in an emergent way as part of communicative interaction, being conditioned by context. In fact, sound symbolism and social iconization are also at work in variation (Eckert 2012: 96). This is an interaction that produces concrete results, the experiencing of which accumulates in the knowledge possessed by speakers, social groupings and communities. The speaker's perception is, consequently, a partial and contextualized perception that is limited to the scope of the phonetic realizations of his community or group. Contact between varieties is what makes possible the extension of the perceptual experience of individual speakers. It is the linguist's job to abstract such experiences and present them as an integrated system that also possesses a core unity.

Conclusion

Cognitive sociolinguistics proposes that the units called "phonemes" and their variants be reinterpreted according to the fundamental principles of cognitivism. Cognitive phonology is concerned with how phonological features are perceived, categorized and stored by speakers, who prioritize information related to category identity over specific acoustic information. Both the frequency of phonetic facts and similarity in the features of different sounds perceived by the speakers are crucial in the establishment of the categories.

Concurrently, usage-based phonology provides the necessary foundation to reinterpret sociophonetic variation. The concepts of "schema" and "prototype" are part of that foundation. Langacker enunciated a set of premises that condition additional theoretical and methodological facts related to a sociocognitive phonology. These premises include the following: the sounds of a language are not perceived the same way by all speakers; phonological variants may occur both at the levels of consciousness and unconsciousness; and phonological variants allow the formation of complex entities through categorization processes. These theoretical principles articulate phonological variation, understood as the alternation between different forms or alternatives for saying the same thing, including variations linked to extralinguistic factors.

Note

1 We represent with (-[X]) the pronunciation of any other consonant phone that could appear in what Caravedo calls the same "space of variability." Since the speaker may not recognize the sound being produced, we utilize a capital X.

References

Alliéres, Jacques, 1954. "Un exemple de polymorphisme phonétique: le polymorphisme de l's implosif en gascon garonnais." *Via Domitia*, I: 70–103.
Alvar, Manuel, 1965–1966. "Polimorfismo y otros aspectos fonéticos en el habla de Santo Tomás de Ajusco." *Anuario de Letras* VI: 353–377.
Blommaert, Jan (Ed.), 1999. *Language Ideological Debates*. Berlin—New York: Mouton De Gruyter.
Browman, Catherine P. and Louis M. Goldstein, 1992. "Articulatory Phonology: an overview." *Phonetica*, 49: 155–180.
Bybee, Joan, 2010. *Language, Use and Cognition*. Cambridge: Cambridge University Press.
Caravedo, Rocío, 1990. *Sociolingüística del español de Lima*. Lima: Pontificia Universidad Católica del Perú.
Caravedo, Rocío, 2003. "Problemas conceptuales y metodológicos de la lingüística de la variación." In *Lengua, variación y contexto. Estudios dedicados a Humberto López Morales*, Eds., F. Moreno-Fernández, F. Gimeno Menéndez, J.A. Samper, M.L. Gutiérrez Araus, M. Vaquero and C. Hernández, 541–557. Madrid: Arco/Libros.
Cedergren, Henrietta and David Sankoff, 1974. "Variables rules: performance as a statistical reflection of competence." *Language*, 50: 333–355.
Coseriu, Eugenio, 1973. "Forma y sustancia en los sonidos del lenguaje." In *Teoría del lenguaje y lingüística general*. 3rd ed. 115–234. Madrid: Gredos.
Eckert, Penelope, 2012. "Three waves of variation study: the emergence of meaning in the study of sociolinguistic variation." *Annual Review of Anthropology*, 41: 87–100.
Kristiansen, Gitte, 2001. "Social and linguistic stereotyping: A cognitive approach to accents." *Estudios Ingleses de la Universidad Complutense*. 9: 129–145.
Labov, William, 1966. *The Social Stratification of English in New York City*. Washington, DC: Center for Applied Linguistics.
Labov, William, 1969. "Contraction, deletion, and inherent variability of the English copula." *Language*, 45, 715–762.
Labov, William, 1994. *Principles of Linguistic Change. Vol. I. Internal Factors*. Oxford: Blackwell.
Lakoff, George, 1987. *Women, Fire, and Dangerous Things. What Categories Reveals about Mind*. Chicago, IL: The University of Chicago Press.
Langacker, Ronald W., 1987. *Foundations of Cognitive Grammar. Volume I. Theoretical Prerequisites*. Stanford, CA: Stanford University Press.
Lope Blanch, Juan M., 1979. "En torno al polimorfismo." In *Investigaciones sobre dialectología mexicana*, 7–16. México: UNAM.
López Morales, Humberto, 1984. "Desdoblamiento fonológico de las vocales en el andaluz oriental: reexamen de la cuestión." *Revista Española de Lingüística*, 14: 85–97.
Moreno-Fernández, Francisco, 1988. *Sociolingüística en EE.UU. Guía bibliográfica crítica*. Málaga: Ágora.

Moreno-Fernández, Francisco, 2010. *Las variedades de la lengua española y su enseñanza*. Madrid: Arco/Libros.
Nathan, Geoff, 2007. "Phonology." In D. Geeraerts and C. Hubert, *The Oxford Handbook of Cognitive Linguistics*, 611–632. Oxford—New York: Oxford University Press.
Pickett, J. M., 1999. *The Acoustics of Speech Communication: Fundamentals, Speech Perception, Theory and Technology*. Boston, MA: Allyn and Bacon.
Pierrehumbert, Janet B., 2003. "Phonetic diversity, statistical learning, and acquisition of phonology." *Language and Speech*, 46 (2–3): 115–154.
Quine, Willard Van Orman, 1960. *Word and Object*. Cambridge: MIT Press.
Sankoff, David, Sallie Tagliamonte and E. Smith, 2005. *Goldvarb X. a multivariate analysis application*. University of Toronto—University of Ottawa. http://individual.utoronto.ca/tagliamonte/Goldvarb/GV_index.htm (accessed 15 December, 2015).
Taylor, John R., 1995. *Linguistic Categorization. Prototypes in Linguistic Theory*. 2nd ed. Oxford: Oxford University Press.
Walter, Henriette, 1975. "Diversidad fonológica y comunidad lingüística." In *De la teoría lingüística a la enseñanza de la lengua*, dir. J. Martinet, 190–206. Madrid: Gredos.
Weinreich, Uriel, 1954. "Is a structural dialectology possible?" *Word*, X: 388–400.

8
METHODOLOGY FOR A COGNITIVE SOCIOLINGUISTICS

The precepts that guide sociolinguistic research do not deviate much from those dictated by René Descartes in his seminal work *A Discourse on Method*.

> The first was never to accept anything for true which I did not clearly know to be such; [. . .]. The second, to divide each of the difficulties under examination into as many parts as possible, and as might be necessary for its adequate solution. The third, to conduct my thoughts in such order that, by commencing with objects the simplest and easiest to know, I might ascend by little and little, and, as it were, step by step, to the knowledge of the more complex; [. . .]. And the last, in every case to make enumerations so complete, and reviews so general, that I might be assured that nothing was omitted.
>
> (Descartes 1637)

Santiago Ramón y Cajal, in *Los tónicos de la voluntad*, interpreted the Cartesian proposals as meritorious, more because they were formulated clearly and rigorously, after having benefitted from them in his philosophical and geometric meditations than because they had been tested by their author. Good research formulations are to be accompanied by adequate experimentation.

The methodology of a cognitive sociolinguistics does not provide substantially different foundations regarding the collection of spoken language samples and their analysis from those which have sustained sociolinguistics since the 1960s. Arguably, it continues to be a "science of surveys," as William Labov (1972) said of urban sociolinguistics. However, cognitivism has also left its mark on it, affecting methodological decisions which grant primacy to language usage, communicative interaction, and the perception of linguistic production. Methodologically speaking, it is not possible to practice a usage-based linguistics without studying actual usage, as instantiated, for instance, in spontaneous language production or even as a result of elicitation in experimental settings (Kristiansen and Geeraerts 2013). Good research requires the establishment of an appropriate relationship between a theoretical model and a methodology as well as between the methodological principles and analytical and procedural decisions. Thus, sociocognitive research has to reinterpret traditional norms for sociolinguistic investigation from the viewpoint of speakers' cognition.

Cognitive sociolinguistics presents its methodology not as unique or definitive but as an alternative. Naturally, this approach, as would any approach, has limits, as rightly pointed out by Feyerabend (1978). Yet, it is significant that a discipline decidedly built around observable reality, such as sociolinguistics, admits that not all of its components and processes are absolutely observable; indeed, explanatory power may even depend on facets of "reality" that cannot be attested or which may not have happened at all. Cognitive sociolinguistics, however, proposes that what is perceived is as significant and real as what is observed. Let us not forget, in the words of artist Georgia O'Keefe, that sometimes nothing is less real than realism.

A. On the Methodological Basis of Cognitive Sociolinguistics

Proposition 8.1

Sociolinguistic research must develop within a comprehensive, integrative and cognitively realistic conceptual framework.

Proposition 8.1.1

Cognitive sociolinguistics should not adhere to any particular set of methodological proposals; it should evaluate existing methodological alternatives and implement the most suitable ones.

Proposition 8.1.2

In cognitive sociolinguistics, any reductionist approach fails completely when it faces a complex reality.

Proposition 8.2

Cognitive sociolinguistics must systematically address the way reality is perceived by speakers as well as the subjective models created by them.

Proposition 8.3

Cognitive sociolinguistics, in analyzing language based on usage, must work through systematic observation.

Proposition 8.3.1

Sociolinguistic observations should, to the extent it is possible, be triangulated with observations obtained through different methodologies, perspectives, frameworks or disciplines.

Proposition 8.3.2

Since the perception of environment and surroundings is arbitrary, its observation is difficult.

Proposition 8.3.3

The uncertainty principle influences sociolinguistic observation; the very act of making a measurement modifies the data being measured in some way, introducing erroneous elements into those measurements.

Proposition 8.4

Sociolinguistic facts need to be explicitly or implicitly accounted for in terms of how they are produced and why they occur.

Proposition 8.5

Sociolinguistic research should distinguish the physical, conceptual or mnemonic nature of the data that is analyzed.

Proposition 8.6

Experimental studies have to present valid data for the proper understanding of linguistic cognition.

Proposition 8.7

The more synchronic the data is, the more balanced the linguistic system appears to be, although it is difficult to empirically demonstrate that a linguistic systems is balanced.

Scholium 8-A

Sociolinguistic methodology offers two features that, together, give it a distinct personality within the field of linguistics as a whole. One of them is attention to the social dimension of language and its epistemological implications. It is interested in the use of language in society, assessing the interactions of actual speakers considered to be subjects, groups or communities. Its other feature is that it works with empirical data, giving inductive approximations scientific validity.

We are facing a way of conceiving research that is applicable to virtually all forms of doing sociolinguistics, including the cognitivist. If cognitive linguistics is practiced from a perspective based on usage, it must necessarily take into account social diversity. In such a case, it is essential to work from the basis of observation. This is achieved, for example, by building spoken and written language corpora. Geeraerts proposed in 2005 a schematic characterization of four basic approaches to language and its observation, according to where the approach fell along two axes, the social and the empirical:

a. − Social − Empiricalb. − Social + Empirical

c. + Social − Empiricald. + Social + Empirical

Examples of Case a above would include the basic foundational Chomskyan perspective, which, in principle, operates on an ideal speaker (i.e., not subject to empiricism) and on speech communities conceived as homogeneous (i.e., non-social). An example of Case b above corresponds to a trend that has been progressively embedded within generativism, however. This trend involves the examination of linguistic corpora for theory-building, leading to a theory enriched by observation. Case c above, meanwhile, characterizes theories that employ a social (not psychological) conception of language and which, nonetheless, do not practice empiricism, but rely on the linguist's intuitions for understanding how language works. This resource is, thus, very similar to the pure introspection practiced by theoretical linguistics for decades (Itkonen 2003). Finally, an example of Case d above would be the perspective and methodology of cognitive sociolinguistics, which is based on empiricism and espouses a social conception of language.

It seems clear that cognitive sociolinguistics must be elaborated on the basis of empirical data. Such data must be assessed both qualitatively, to explain why things are *what* they are, and quantitatively, to explain why things are *as* they are. Further, we cannot forget the role that this discipline reserves for the perception of reality, which makes the concept of "data" more complex than typically conceived. Cognitive research—especially psychology and sociology of knowledge—distinguishes among three types of data: sensory data, conceptual data and mnemonic data. Sensory data are physical, and therefore recordable and measurable, realities. Conceptual data are representations of the former, entities interpreted and processed by researchers, defined by subjective criteria although there might be a real basis on which to construct a concept. Finally, mnemonic data are sets of abstracted properties fixed in our memory or symbolic entities that identify a fact in a simplified way thus facilitating its memorization (Landi 1995). Each one of these conceptualizations of "data" is applicable to sociolinguistic analysis. Let us consider the study of the /d/ in intervocalic position in Spanish, as in *lado* 'side,' or the study of [ð] in intervocalic contexts in English, as in *mother*. Recorded examples (sensory data) are not typically the data that sociolinguists work from. Rather, they often prefer to reduce the sensory data to a handful of categories (fully realized, weakened and absent) that become the objects of a theoretical account (conceptual data). The data can also be considered mere phonic manifestations of norms or rules that operate in speakers, according to which it is appropriate, for example, to use in Spanish /d/ with endings in *–ado* or to use [ŋ] in verbal *–ing* in English (mnemonic data). These distinctions, thus, may benefit cognitive sociolinguistics by serving as a basis for a systematic addressing of how reality is manifested, the way it is perceived and the subjective models created by the speakers. This typology of data, indeed, also corresponds to some extent with the distinction between the *etic* (reality) and the *emic* (interpretation of the subject) established in 1954 by Kenneth Pike for linguistics and subsequently applied in the social sciences.

For Barbara Johnstone (2000), research consists basically in attempting to find answers to a set of questions. It requires systematic observation, on the basis of which literature searches are conducted and data is collected. But because direct observation is not always entirely reliable, observations should be performed from different perspectives and using various methodologies. And given its meta-theoretical nature, cognitive sociolinguistics, does not compel researchers to work with one particular set of methodological practices. Rather it embraces the use of alternatives that are comprehensively evaluated and integrated into a cognitively realistic conceptual framework. And, because sociolinguistic reality—both the manifest and the perceived—is characterized by its great complexity and responds to the behavior of systems composed of multiple interacting elements, any reductionist approach fails completely (Solé 2009: 19). At the same time, as specialists in human ecology have confirmed (Hawley 1986), since the identification of the context (environment) is subject to arbitrariness, observation can be difficult. According to Vidal de la Blache (1922), the environment can be both a permissive and a limiting condition. Moreover, it makes it difficult to prove whether a system is in total balance or imbalance.

The arbitrariness of observation is precisely one of the workhorses of the study of linguistic reality and many conflicts have been raised in that regard at all levels of research practice. One of them is the "observer's paradox," whereby a simple observation may affect the form and content of language (Labov 1972), placing researchers in the realm of permanent doubt over the reliability of their observations. The observer's paradox is a manifestation, focused on the study of language, of what Werner Heisenberg formulated in 1927 as the "uncertainty principle," according to which, by the very fact of performing a measurement, the researcher somehow modifies the data being measured, introducing an error that is impossible to reduce to zero, no matter how perfect his instruments might be. In the field of physics, measuring the position and velocity of an electron requires striking it with a photon of light, which in turn modifies its position and velocity (Heisenberg 1961). The uncertainty principle proposes the existence of fundamental limits on the accuracy of measurements and, further, that if a real system is described, say in terms of classical physics, it can only ever approximate the reality. In other words, the validity of the uncertainty relation leaves us in a situation where our most accurate procedures for observing reality could only ever be characterized as "measurement by approximation," and our means for ranking the appropriateness of competing procedures would be according to the quality of the approximation obtained.

B. On the Principles of Cognitive Sociolinguistic Analysis

Proposition 8.8

Cognitive sociolinguistic analysis does not consider quantitative and qualitative procedures incompatible. Instead, it utilizes them jointly for a better understanding of both perception and the social use of language.

Proposition 8.9

Cognitive sociolinguistic analysis should be guided by factuality; the theory must be consistent with the data.

Proposition 8.10

Cognitive sociolinguistic analysis should be guided by economy. It should also seek simplicity in description.

Proposition 8.11

Cognitive sociolinguistic analysis should be guided by explicitness, which means accepting that formalization is not an end in itself but a means for understanding, and that the application of formal methods must be reasoned, judicious and appropriate.

Proposition 8.12

Cognitive sociolinguistic analysis should be guided by generality, which supposes seeking general rules as well as universal principles, and treating those rules as relative.

Proposition 8.13

Cognitive sociolinguistic analysis should be guided by predictability; the most preferable analysis is one that minimizes deviation from natural tendencies unless there is evidence to the contrary.

Scholium 8-B

In 1987, Ronald W. Langacker confessed that he was not an expert in scientific methodology, but that did not prevent him from devoting many interesting pages to methodological issues, particularly in the form of a compendium on a well-established epistemology in the philosophy of science (Kuhn 1962; Popper 1972; Feyerabend 1978). The methodological principles on which Langacker settled his cognitive grammar were those of *factuality*, *economy*, *explicitness*, *generality* and *predictivity* (Langacker 1987: 31 ff.). We will devote due attention to these principles in the following paragraphs.

Factuality

The principle of factuality states that theory must be consistent with the data. This implies that it is preferable to have more data rather than less and that the description of data should be as careful and detailed as possible. From this perspective, outlier data cannot be disregarded, as it has an impact on the social perception of linguistic features (Labov, Baranowski and Dinkin 2010: 189). Cognitivism gives great importance, on the one hand, to the discrete elements of language and, on the other, to the symbolic capacity of linguistic units that represent the conventions of a speech community. Because of this, it approaches with skepticism any acceptability or grammaticality judgment that is detached from social context. This fundamental principle adheres to approaches similar to those proposed by Authier and Meunier or by Dittmar in the 1970s.

Economy

The principle of economy compels us to seek simplicity in linguistic description. This principle is by no means unique to cognitivism. It constitutes part of the basic decalogue of Popperian philosophy and is expressly formulated from the perspective of generativism through the allegory of Occam's razor, capable of shaving the "entanglements" of Plato's beard. We can, however, appreciate some clear differences between cognitivism and generativists in this regard; generativists seek general rules or principles and reject lists of facts and figures, which are natural and very convenient materials for cognitivists. At the end of the day, economy is achieved by the cognitivist when theory is constructed with respect to well-defined data sets, whether they reflect simple realities or complex, dynamic facts.

Explicitness

The principle of explicitness seeks precision in linguistic description and explanation. To that end, we need to develop an adequate level of formalization, always recognizing that there is no necessary correlation between empirical adequacy and degree of formalization and, further, that formalization is not an end in itself but a means to understanding sociolinguistic reality. As would be required in any scientific investigation, the application of formal methods must be reasoned, judicious and appropriate.

Generality

The principle of generality concerns itself with seeking general rules and universal principles, always treating them as relative rather than as absolute. Language is a curious mixture of regularity and irregularity, from which it is difficult to extract universals, especially when it is analyzed and interpreted with respect to specific sociocultural realities. Unless there is evidence to the contrary, a preferred analysis minimizes deviation from general and natural trends. As for the rules, cognitivism does not opt for rule formulation as a methodological preference, but neither does it radically oppose their formulation.

Predictivity

The principle of predictivity asks that a theoretical model be capable of anticipating behaviors and events that have not yet occurred and positing the existence of, as yet, unattested elements. However, caution must be exercised when assessing predictability in research. Because linguistic systems provide several alternatives for communicating a meaning, and because those alternatives are associated with varying degrees of acceptability (i.e., conventionality), a given prediction, while permissible, may not necessarily occur. In this way, the conceptualization of reality cannot be homogeneous but rather variable, which itself reflects a different degree of conventionality, that is, conditions under which language is used, varies and changes.

Restrictiveness

Langacker considers one more principle: *restrictiveness*. The principle of restrictiveness establishes that language works with a set of permissible elements and structures and through relationships established by their corresponding schemas. Nonetheless, language does not work with absolutely discrete or absolutely oppositional elements, as there is no firm line between the linguistically possible and the impossible.

C. On the Techniques of Cognitive Sociolinguistics

Proposition 8.16

The collection of tokens from communicative interaction is the basic procedure for the sociocognitive study of language.

Proposition 8.16.1

The collecting of tokens does not necessarily generate objective data or data that is well-defined in and of itself.

Proposition 8.16.2

The collecting of language tokens itself gives rise to perceptions that affect all elements of interaction: the speaker, the interlocutor, each interlocutor's referential scope, the perceived context and the communicative situation as a whole.

Proposition 8.16.3

The way that perceptions are deployed during data collection can be correlated with psychosocial, social and situational factors.

Proposition 8.17

The interview is the basic technique employed for collecting spoken language data.

Proposition 8.17.1

The data collected during a sociolinguistic interview are stored and sorted as part of linguistic corpora.

Proposition 8.17.2

Synchronic spoken language corpora are the most frequently used in sociolinguistics. However, diachronic written language corpora are also used.

Proposition 8.17.3

The internal dynamic of a sociolinguistic interview is capable of revealing speakers' subjective perceptions.

Proposition 8.18

Questionnaires allow access to knowledge of speakers' subjective perceptions and worldviews.

Proposition 8.19

Stored spoken language tokens should be annotated to include information on how the communicative interaction unfolded, attempting to avoid including the subjective judgments of the researchers manipulating the data.

Proposition 8.20

The application of sociolinguistic research techniques must comply with the principles of quantification, accountability and representativeness.

Scholium 8-C

Cognitive sociolinguistics shares many criteria with other approaches that have similar roots. Pedro Martín-Butragueño (2011: 11), for instance, speaks of a *realistic linguistics*, where, in order to be so considered, an investigation would have to comply with three characteristics:

1. use of data from natural contexts rather than laboratory data obtained by means of introspection;
2. focus of observations on speakers and their interactions rather than on language as an abstract object out of context; and
3. making the object of research the speech community rather than the competence of idealized speakers.

Research in cognitive sociolinguistics especially appreciates the potential that qualitative methodology offers and fully exploits the possibilities of the proper coordination of qualitative and quantitative analyses (Maynts, Holm and Hübner 2005). In 1998, Isadore Newman and Carolyn Benz constructed an interactive continuum showing the relationship between qualitative and quantitative research methods, which perfectly depicts the investigative techniques most valued by a cognitive sociolinguistics. It begins with a quantitative-type activity, the assessing of a theoretical model, which is supported in the documentation of the assessment using available literature. From there, we can formulate hypotheses to be tested.

Eventually, analysis of the data leads to conclusions that, when evaluated qualitatively, again offer the possibility of formulating hypotheses serving as a basis for a theoretical model. The last link in the cycle could effectively become the first link in a new cycle. This overlap effectively closes the cycle, bringing together the qualitative and the quantitative.

For Phil Scholfield (1994: 32), the collection of data for quantification can be approached in four different ways. First, by *observation* (of both oral and written materials), which constitutes a natural and non-reactive method. Second, through *questionnaires* which, in turn, can be of two types: closed (e.g., *surveys*, a reactive approach that includes opinions) and open (also a reactive approach, but one that involves discursive production on the part of the subject or informant). Questionnaires, whatever type they may be, are able to uncover speakers' worldview and subjective perceptions (Bartmiński 2010: 35) in relation to discourse, the type of language, his interlocutors or the communicative situation. This technique often resorts to using speakers as judges and can be applied in multiple ways, both directly and indirectly. Among them, it is worth highlighting, because of their potential for cognitive sociolinguistics, opinion polls, stimulus recording and the "matched-guise" technique (Moreno-Fernández 2010).

There remains a fourth method of singular relevance to sociolinguistics: *the interview*. The interview is a reactive method, which seeks the elicitation of materials through an interaction that attempts to approximate naturally occurring communicative interactions. Data are extracted from interviews and organized into large collections called corpora, which often include the transcripts of oral materials. Naturally, the construction of such transcripts often implies the intervention of a new agent-speaker who, of course, also carries individual attitudes, perceptions and representations, which must also be taken into account when it comes to data extraction and analysis. In any case, for cognitive sociolinguistics, corpus studies, both synchronic and diachronic, as well as experimental studies provide a type of data that is essential for understanding the cognitive representation of language. Likewise, data gathered into a corpus allow the construction of probabilistic models that reveal the predictive capability of speakers; that is to say, their knowledge about the probability of occurrence of a particular grammatical option (Bresnan and Ford 2010). In effect, then, sources of data for a usage-based linguistics, such as that practiced from the perspective of cognitivism, are more varied and inclusive than those used in generative or structural linguistics.

Debate: The Speaker's Place in Sociolinguistic Methodology

One of the most interesting issues raised in sociolinguistic methodology since the 1970s is the role of the speaker, although it had been a topic of discussion among sociologists for some time. The issue is linked to other pressing issues, such as (a) the opposition between qualitative and quantitative research techniques;

(b) the convenience of a functionalist stratificational sociology vis-à-vis an ethnomethodological sociology; and (c) the conceptualization of language as a variable sociolinguistic competence or as a polylectal complex.

The debate, we propose, could be formulated as follows: Should sociolinguistic methodology create a theoretical space for what might be classified as behaviors pertaining to the individual; or should it subsume the role of the speaker within more abstract categories such as class, group or network? Cognitive sociolinguistics, being sociolinguistics, builds its analysis based on social categories consisting of groups and networks. Nevertheless, attention to the perceptions of individual speakers and their cognitive processes requires specific consideration and treatment because of their status as protagonists in communicative interaction processes and as agents of linguistic production and perception.

Part of the methodological attention paid to the individual will inevitably involve analyzing the linguistic behavior of the leaders of groups and communities, especially when those groups are particularly complex or evidence tendencies for linguistic change. Working with leaders requires the application of specific observation and interview techniques focusing, in regards to content, on the very role that the focal speaker plays and his relationship to the rest of the group. The creation of a methodological space for focus on leaders does not, however, preclude the study of other types of speakers. The treatment of these individuals would not end with an analysis of their speech as individual per se, but would likely be analyzed, quantitatively and qualitatively, in conjunction with the speech samples of other individuals occupying parallel roles in the community. Far from simply subsuming these individuals to a group identity or losing their behavior in a mass of collective samples, however, their individual behavior can be preserved through the use of several and various statistical techniques (Moreno-Fernández 1989; 1994).

Conclusion

Cognitive sociolinguistics proposes that research develops within an integrative, cognitively realistic, and non-reductionist metatheoretical framework. Processes of observation derived from a social conceptualization of language and from preferential attention to language usage are decisive for its development. However, the observation itself, even cloaked in the aura of realism and objectivity, is subject to subjective perceptions and must wrestle with arbitrariness, a situation that also reminds us of the importance of taking into account the "uncertainty principle."

The cognitive study of language requires quantitative analyses and experimental procedures, with the goal of providing valid data and results for a clear understanding of the cognitive representation of language. Cognitive sociolinguistics develops its analysis incorporating the methodological principles proposed by Langacker in 1987. These principles are those of *factuality, economy, explicitness, generality* and *predictivity*.

As far as the application of research techniques is concerned, sociolinguistics responds to the principles of *quantification, accountability* and *representativeness*, with the interview, corpus building and the administration of survey questionnaires being among its best methodological tools.

References

Authier, Jacqueline and André Meunier, 1972. "Norme, grammaticalité et niveaux de langue." *Langue Française*, 16: 49–63.
Bartmiński, Jerzy, 2010. *Aspects of Cognitive Ethnolinguistics*. London: Equinox.
Bresnan, Joan and Marilyn Ford, 2010. "Predicting syntax: processing dative constructions in American and Australian varieties of English." *Language* 86–1: 186–213.
Descartes, René, [1637] 2005. *A Discourse on Method*. The Gutenberg Project E-text.
Dittmar, Norbert, 1973. *Soziolinguistik. Exemplarische und kritishce Darstellung ihrer Theorie und Anwendung. Mit kommentierter Bibliographie*. Frankfurt, Athenaum Fischer Taschenbuch. Trans. Eng. *A Critical Survey of Sociolinguistics: Theory and Application*. New York: St. Martin's Press, 1977.
Feyerabend, Paul, 1978. *Against Method*. London: Verso.
Geeraerts, Dirk, 2005. "Lectal variation and empirical data in Cognitive Linguistics." In *Cognitive linguistics. Internal Dynamics and Interdisciplinary Interaction*, Eds., F.J. Ruiz de Mendoza and M.S. Peña, 225–244. Berlin—New York: Mouton de Gruyter.
Hawley, Amos H., 1986. *Human Ecology. A Theoretical Essay*. Madrid: Tecnos.
Heisenberg, Werner, 1961. *Physik und Philosophie*. Ullstein: Frankfurt-Berlín.
Itkonen, Esa, 2003. *What is Language. A Study in the Philosophy of Linguistics*. Turku: Åbo Akademis trickery.
Johnstone, Barbara, 2000. *Qualitative Methods in Sociolinguistics*. Oxford: Oxford University Press.
Kristiansen, Gitte and Dirk Geeraerts (Eds.), 2013. "Contexts of use in Cognitive Sociolinguistics." *Special Issue. The Journal of Pragmatics* 52: 1–104.
Kuhn, Thomas, 1962. *The Structure of Scientific Revolutions*. Chicago, IL: The University of Chicago Press.
Labov, William, Maciej Baranowski and Aaron Dinkin, 2010. "The effect of outliers on the perception of sound change." *Language Variation and Change*, 22: 179–190.
Labov, William, 1972. *Sociolinguistic Patterns*. Philadelphia, PA: University of Pennsylvania Press.
Landi, Paolo, 1995. *Percezione e inferenza*. Joppolo: Clinamen.
Langacker, Ronald W., 1987. *Foundations of Cognitive Grammar. Volume I. Theoretical Prerequisites*. Stanford: Stanford University Press.
Martín Butragueño, Pedro (Ed.), 2011. *Realismo en el análisis de corpus orales*. México: El Colegio de México.
Maynts, Renate, Kurt Holm and Peter Hübner, [1969] 2005. *Introducción a los métodos de la sociología empírica*. Madrid: Alianza.
Moreno-Fernández, Francisco, 1989. "Análisis sociolingüístico de actos de habla coloquiales. I." *Español actual*, 51: 5–52.
Moreno-Fernández, Francisco, 1994. "Sociolingüística, estadística e informática." *Lingüística*, 6: 95–154.
Moreno-Fernández, Francisco, 2010. "Elementos para una fonología cognitiva de la variación." In *De moneda nunca usada. Estudios filológicos dedicados a José María Enguita,*

Eds., R.M. Castañer Martín and V. Lagüéns Gracia, 471–490. Zaragoza: Institución Fernando el Católico.

Newman, Isadore and Carolyn R. Benz, 1998. *Qualitative-Quantitative Research Methodology. Exploring the Interactive Continuum*. Carbondale-Edwardsville: Southern Illinois University.

Pike, Kenneth, [1954] 1967. *Language in Relation to a Unified Theory of Structure of Human Behavior*. 2nd ed. The Hague: Mouton.

Popper, Karl, 1972. *Objective Knowledge: An Evolutionary Approach*, Oxford: Clarendon.

Ramón y Cajal, Santiago, 1899. *Reglas y consejos sobre investigación científica (los tónicos de la voluntad)*. Alcalá la Real: Formación Alcalá, 2009.

Scholfield, Phil, 1994. *Quantifying Language. A Researcher's and Teacher's Guide to Gathering Language Data and Reducing it to Figures*. Clevedon: Multilingual Matters.

Solé, Ricard, 2009. *Redes complejas. Del genoma a Internet*. Barcelona: Tusquets.

Vidal de la Blache, Paul, 1922. *Principes de géographie humaine*. Paris: Armand Colin.

9

THE SOCIOLINGUISTIC INTERVIEW

The cognitive sociolinguistics research program requires attention to a key variationist research technique: the interview. In 1972, William Labov delineated for sociolinguistics the goal of providing the study of language with a new research methodology, which included the sociolinguistic interview as an essential tool. Consequently, the interview has been the subject of many of the most important publications treating methodological issues (cf. Frattini and Quesada 1994; Ander-Egg 1995; Arfuch 1995). A volume devoted to cognitive sociolinguistics shall not deviate from that tradition.

The sociolinguistic interview has been utilized as the main resource for obtaining analyzable materials within a quantitative variationist perspective. For that reason, several of its dimensions have received ample theoretical attention. These dimensions include its stylistic value, its representativeness in connection with the vernacular, its thematic content and its discursive dynamics (duration, context, situation and interlocutor characteristics). Yet, despite the fact that the interview also has definitive cognitive dimensions, these have only been treated partially or else as tangential to some other dimension of more primary focus. For example, stylistic assessments of the interview have been made on the basis of the attention that speakers/interviewees give to their own discourse. In this approach, the *monitor theory*, the role of cognition is clearly present in notions like "attention." But this theory, as well as several others, fails to give coherent, consistent attention to the cognitive. What is needed then, is a perspective that does not exclude the contribution of other perspectives, but, in shifting focus, provides a comprehensive cognitive interpretation of the sociolinguistic interview.

A. On the Foundations of the Interview

Proposition 9.1

The sociolinguistic interview constitutes a communicative interaction in which various factors are involved, including the participant structure and the organization and content of discourse, along with cultural, social and contextual factors.

Proposition 9.2

The semi-guided interview is the most appropriate means to obtain samples of spoken language in the quantity and quality required for quantitative analysis.

Proposition 9.3

The semi-structured interview constitutes the most suitable means for the systematic recording of the linguistic object called the *vernacular*, in which minimal attention is paid to speech itself.

Proposition 9.3.1

The semi-guided interview should be designed and constructed with attention to the effect of the observer's paradox.

Proposition 9.3.2

The search for naturalness in the interview has been oriented toward two methodological alternatives: influencing the content of the interview and modifying its dynamics.

Proposition 9.4

Each semi-directed interview presents different characteristics throughout its development.

Proposition 9.5

The participant structure of an interview can change during the interview's progression from that of a semi-guided interview (i.e. interviewer-interviewee) into, for example, a participant observation (i.e. participant as observer).

Scholium 9-A

For classic variationist sociolinguistics, *the principle of the interview* is one of the methodological axioms formulated by William Labov, who stated: "Face-to-face interviews are the only means of obtaining the volume and quality of recorded speech that is needed for quantitative analysis. In other words, quantitative analysis demands data obtained through the most obvious kind of systematic observation" (Labov 1981:29). With respect to its characterization on the pragmatic and discourse level, the sociolinguistic interview, characterized as "semi-formal" and "semi-guided," would have the following features indicated by Marta Albelda (2004: 112).

- Primary features: transactional purpose, semiformal tone; planned and designed with interlocutors' prior agreement.
- Situational or colloquializing features: relationship of varying social equality between interlocutors; relationship of functional inequality; experiential relationship: mutual unfamiliarity between interlocutors; unfamiliar, infrequent context of interaction; unspecialized subject.

Albelda's comparison of colloquial conversation to a semiformal interview has highlighted several ways in which these two types of interaction differ with respect to their situational and discursive parameters (Table 9.1). Semiformal interviews, in particular, tend toward a predetermined pattern for turn taking, which she discusses as a characteristic that causes a reduction in conversational dynamism.

According to Labov, the interview is not only the most effective means of obtaining quantifiable materials, but it is also effective for observing the linguistic object known as the "vernacular," which, as he explains in another of his methodological axioms (1981: 29), provides the most systematic data for analysis:

TABLE 9.1 Comparison Between Colloquial Conversation and Semiformal Interview According to Situational and Discursive Parameters

Comparative Parameters	Coloquial Conversation	Semi-formal Interview
1. Relationship between speakers	PROXIMITY	NO PROXIMITY
2. Interactional frame	FAMILIAR	TRANSACTIONAL
3. Social/functional relationships	SOCIAL AND FUNCTIONAL EQUALITY	+/− SOCIAL EQUALITY/ FUNCTIONAL INEQUALITY
4. Themes	NON-ESPECIALIZED	NON-ESPECIALIZED
5. Turn taking	NON-PREDETERMINED	PREDETERMINED
6. Mood	INFORMAL	FORMAL
7. Planning	ABSENCE	+/− PRESENCE
8. Finality	INTERPERSONAL	TRANSACTIONAL
9. Dynamism/dialogic tension	YES	NO OR A LITTLE

Source: adapted from Albelda (2004: 113)

> The vernacular, in which discourse itself is given minimal attention, provides the most systematic data for linguistic analysis. The vernacular is defined as the way of speaking acquired during pre-adolescence. Its highly regular character has been observed empirically. [. . .] Every speaker has a vernacular form at least in one language, which can be a prestige dialect [. . .] or a non-standard variety. In some cases, we can obtain systematic data from more formal speech styles, but we will not be sure of that until the data has been contrasted with the vernacular.

The vernacular, therefore, is an element of primary interest to sociolinguistics, which guides its research program towards obtaining representative samples of this "way of speaking." Note the centrality that Labov gives to speech in his axiom. This is important since speech is a cognitive process of great significance. Moreover, the vernacular has been characterized in two ways: (a) as an unmonitored variety and (b), as the variety acquired in pre-adolescence (Labov 1972: 208); these two varieties need not coincide among speakers. But the sociolinguistic literature also offers other definitions of the vernacular. Penelope Eckert (2000: 17) defines it as the language of local communities. Trudgill (2003) refers to the *vernacular* as the local language variety of a given speech community, and defines it as the variety least sensitive to the influence of other varieties and to the notion of correctness.

However, as valid as these characterizations may be, we should not fall into the trap of considering a given speaker's vernacular as their most natural or habitual way of speaking since a person can change their language throughout their lifetime and in accord with a given situational context. Moreover, there are many problems that arise concerning the obtaining of so-called natural speech in the process of recording sociolinguistic interviews. The problem emerges because most sociolinguistic interviews consist of conversations that are semi-guided by a researcher with a voice recorder in plain sight. At the same time, Milroy and Gordon (2003: 50) state that speaking in an entirely natural way throughout an interview is unsustainable. Their position is directly linked to the well-known "observer's paradox," in which the act of observing itself alters the behavior of that which is observed. This results in somewhat of a conundrum for the sociolinguist whose goal is to observe the speech that speakers produce when they do not feel observed. Nevertheless, it is not possible to collect speech samples without resorting to systematic observation.

Sociolinguistic methodology has made every effort to prevent or minimize the consequences of the observer's paradox. Many proposals have been made ranging from the quick and anonymous survey to the secret recording, accepted with few objections in many cultures, including the Hispanic World, but rejected, due to ethical issues in the English-speaking world and its vast scientific influence domain. "Participant observation" constitutes a widely accepted strategy to minimize or reduce the observer's paradox. In fact, it has been shown that sometimes a semi-guided interview can become a bona fide participant observation (Niedzielski and Preston 2003: 34), as happened to Lesley Milroy: "The intention was to allow the interviewer to simulate a conversation and, after a period of time, proceed to a symmetrical interactive relationship, so that the interview style came to resemble participant observation" (Milroy 1987: 69).

Faced with the simple strategy of creating one- to two-hour-long communicative interactions with the goal of obtaining large samples of spoken language, Labov suggests a counter-strategy: the attitude of the "apprentice" with the interviewer taking a position of lower authority than his interlocutor. However, according to Briggs (1986), this strategy does not work with some subjects. The learner's attitude favors the cooperative principle of communicative interaction. At the same time, we cannot forget that, in Western society, an interview creates a clearly defined communicative situation with the frequent appearance of a formal speech style. The interview, as a communicative event, does not favor discourse spontaneity. It is a dyadic interaction between strangers with participatory roles that give more weight to the interviewer and turn-taking rights unevenly distributed. One of the goals of the researcher is to reduce the formality of the situation, to help the interviewee relax and produce a greater amount of speech. This is not always easy since interviewees may become confused or even annoyed if the format of the interview does not meet their expectations.

Generally, our quest for the interviewee's implied emotional involvement, with the outcome of obtaining the greatest possible quantity of natural speech, has been pursued using two methodological strategies (Milroy and Gordon 2003: 65): (a) influencing the content of the interview; (b) altering the interpersonal dynamics between interview participants. The former is typically achieved by introducing specific topics, such as life-threatening situations, descriptions of terrible events, recounting ghost stories or explanations of childhood games. A technique for achieving the latter is to modify the number and function of participants by, for example, employing interviewers that belong to the same social network or group as the interviewees; such a strategy makes cognitive factors centrally relevant.

With respect to interview topics, it is essential to know what directly influences the internal structure of an interview. A strategy oriented toward sequential discussion of different topics is given the name of "networks of modules" or "conversational modules" (Labov 1981). It consists of bringing up, as naturally as possible and without pressuring the interviewee, issues that provoke the production of different types of discourse and, along with it, different elements of language that related to various social domains such as childhood, neighborhood, workplace, friendships and anecdotes. For these networks of thematic modules, the researcher's questions are of paramount importance.

In addition, the content and internal configuration of the interview have direct implications for complex issues such as the obtaining and cataloging of various speaking styles. In fact, in Labov's inventory of speech styles, he connects the "interview" with "careful," "spontaneous," "casual" and "reading" styles. The

164 The Sociolinguistic Interview

classification of speech styles, as described by Allan Bell (2001) is somewhat different, and makes explicit some of the cognitive mechanisms involved in the creation of a speaker's speech style. For Bell, a style is classified, first, with respect to "audience design." That is, speakers identify the social profiles of the groups they address. Next, with respect to "recipient design," they then construct a prototypical

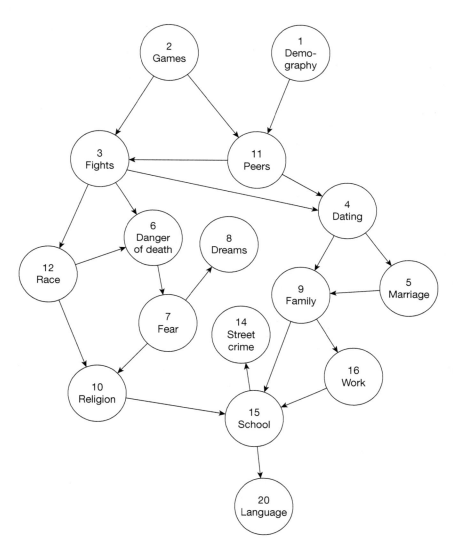

FIGURE 9.1 Network of Thematic Modules Configuration for Adolescents and Young Adults, Based on Labov (1981)

Source: Milroy and Gordon (2003: 59)

speaker characteristic of the group they have in mind. Their own speech style then models the speech style they have associated with the profiles of the individuals they believe make up their audience ("design initiative"), regardless of whether such constructed recipients are in fact present in the audience. In addition, for our present purposes, it is important to note that fragments of several styles of discourse can appear within a given interview. That is, because style is created or selected in response to a situation—sometimes created by the introduction of a particular topic or meaning—, and different situations can occur throughout an "interview situation," one interview is likely to present a variety of styles.

In short, the semi-guided sociolinguistic interview is a discourse activity that involves diverse factors, including the participants' willingness, the discourse structure and content as well as the speakers' underlying assumptions (Preston 1994; Schiffrin 1994), to which we must add the influence of ethnographic factors together with contextual and cultural constraints. All of the interview components just discussed are reflected, in one way or another, in spoken language corpora. These corpora, therefore, provide us with very valuable information for analysis, from a cognitive perspective, both of spoken discourse as well as, specifically, of the sociolinguistic interview itself.

B. On the Cognitivist Interpretation of the Sociolinguistic Interview

Proposition 9.6

The sociolinguistic interview can be characterized according to the configuration of participants and other components that are physically present, to the specific objectives with which it is developed and to the way in which the interlocutors perceive all of the above elements.

Proposition 9.7

The sociolinguistic interview requires, between interviewer and interviewee, adherence to the maxims of quantity, quality, relation and manner.

Proposition 9.8

The sociolinguistic interview usually responds to a cultural script that is set according to interaction patterns accepted in the western world.

Scholium 9-B

The cognitive study of the interview is closely related to the development of cognitive theories of discourse. Among its predecessors, we have Dell Hymes's theories (1972) and Gary B. Palmer's cultural linguistics (1996), which have addressed discourse scenarios as well as perceived contexts. In fact, the concept of "scenario" has proven crucial in the study of discourse. Deborah Tannen and Cynthia Wallat (1993) have discussed interactive frames, defining them as cognitive and cultural models of discourse events, as well as knowledge schemas that reflect the expectations the participants in an interaction have about people, objects, events and situations in the world. Schiffrin, meanwhile, speaks of "situational models" and explains them as information states that include what a speaker and a listener know in their interaction, resulting in broader representations of the social context. Although, in theory, discourse scenarios would be located within situational models, in practice it can be problematic to differentiate between them. A situational model possesses a relatively stable context, not constructed or negotiated by the participants in a communicative situation. According to Gary Palmer (1996), discourse scenario are cognitive models of verbal interaction made up of sequences of pragmatic speech act schemas.

Thus, we have a series of concepts, all closely related, even tautological, which constitute a foundation providing coherence to the study of interactions since interlocutors have to share elements such as their worldviews, discursive scenarios and situational models. However, the possibilities of interpretation of the sociolinguistic interview from a cognitive perspective are many and diverse. One of them is based on the maxims that define Paul Grice's (1989) *cooperative principle*. From this perspective, a pragmatic interpretation of the sociolinguistic interview's development would include arguments, such as those presented below, with regard to his four classic premises (Moreno-Fernández 2009: 146):

- *Maxim of Quantity. Make your contribution as informative as necessary.* The application of this maxim to the sociolinguistic interview raises several difficulties. From the perspective of the interviewee, the main difficulty lies in deciding to what extent their contribution is being informative given that the final decision does not depend on them. The interview dynamics gives the interviewer an authority role, with criteria, therefore, to judge the amount of information provided as either fair, excessive or insufficient. From the interviewers' perspective, the difficulty lies in regulating their own discourse in order to seek a balance between brevity in their conversational turns, encouraging a sense of confidence in the interviewee and maintaining the necessary conversational tension for adequate interview development. At the same time, the "quantity" of discourse required might be conditioned by the desire to address a network of thematic modules planned in advance.
- *Maxim of Quality. Say only what you believe to be true and what you can adequately prove.* The limit of this maxim for the interviewer simply lies in that the interviewee could discover falsity or baseless arguments, particularly in relation to the purpose of the interview. Thus, while one might think

that a researcher may not be concerned with adherence, his own or that of the interviewee, to the Maxim of Quality, as a "real" speaker and conversationalist, he needs to ensure that he does indeed comply with it. With respect to the interviewee, his speech may be conditioned in at least one of two ways in light of the fact that he is being observed and recorded by a stranger. He could try to make his discourse "absolutely" truthful given or, to safeguard his image and that of his group, he could choose deception. The monitor effect, in this way, is noticeably at work for the interviewee and can cause cognitive conflicts or dissonance, which on many occasions is solved with fallacious speech.

- *Maxim of Relation. Be relevant.* Compliance with this maxim in the sociolinguistic interview is strongly conditioned by the topics discussed and by how these are proposed as conversational material. If there are previously established thematic modules or if the modules are sequenced, or arranged a part of a grid or network, a more strict adherence to relevance is required.
- *Maxim of Manner. Make your contribution easy to understand; avoid ambiguity, overextension, and obscurity of expression.* In the case of the Maxim of Manner, both interlocutors' conversational dynamics could follow colloquial conversation patterns. There would be, however, a conflict of interest with respect to the degree of brevity required in the conversational turns. The interviewee tends to try to adhere to one characteristic of this maxim in particular, that of "be brief," while the interviewer, in pursuit of a greater amount of analyzable data, tries to ensure that the interviewee is not.

The sociolinguistic interview can also be analyzed with respect to Anna Wierzbicka's (1994) concept of "cultural script." Cultural scripts help to configure communicative strategies that reflect cultural differences, related also with different ways of thinking. A script is a tacit system of cultural rules that organizes and articulates communicative interactions. In the case of the sociolinguistic interview, it is also possible to develop a cultural script according to the concept of "interview" that prevails in the Western World. That interview script's internal configuration would be different for both interviewer and interviewee.

Interviewer's Sociolinguistic Interview Script

a. It is good if I adopt a friendly and intimate attitude in the conversation.
b. It is good if I seem spontaneous in the conversation.
c. It is good if I speak as little as possible.
d. It is good if the interlocutor takes very long turns.
e. It is good to talk about all the modules I prepared.
f. It is good that the recorder works and goes unnoticed.
g. It is good if I do not blank out.

Interviewee's Sociolinguistic Interview Script

a. It is good if I can find out what the interviewer wants/feels/thinks about me.
b. It is good if I do not tell the interviewer everything that comes to my head.
c. It is good if I do not make any compromising statements.
d. It is good if I do not say much in the interview because whoever hears it may think something bad about me.
e. It is good if I use language well because my speech will be recorded.
f. It is good if I safeguard my social group's standing and reputation.
g. It is good if I participate in a research project.

These cultural scripts correspond both to the enactment of Grice's maxims (described above) as well as to knowledge schemas and the discursive stage of the sociolinguistic interview.

C. On the Perception of the Sociolinguistic Interview

Proposition 9.9

The sociolinguistic interview is configured differently from a conventional conversation with respect to both the discourse produced as well as how participants perceive the elements involved in the interaction.

Proposition 9.10

The sociolinguistic interview offers different formats that can be sequenced according to perspective schemas, incorporating a metadiscourse component that turns speakers into observers.

Proposition 9.11

In the sociolinguistic interview, the conceptualization of a discourse event as a whole is maximally subjective on the interlocutor's part.

Proposition 9.12

In the sociolinguistic interview, the recorder is a part of the interaction and has a significant influence on the monitor; because of this, interlocutors evaluate the discourse of the interview as having consequences that extend beyond the interview interaction itself.

Proposition 9.13

The interviewee's sphere of perception is constructed as a whole unit that includes both the speaker-interviewer and the recorder.

Proposition 9.14

The interviewer's sphere of perception is principally related to the interlocutors of the conversation, with focused attention on the interviewee himself.

Proposition 9.15

The researcher-transcriber's sphere of perception constructs the interview as a whole interactional unit, including all participants and discourse produced.

Proposition 9.16

In the sociolinguistic interview, the topic of language is to be avoided, minimized or contextualized.

Scholium 9-C

A cognitive interpretation of the sociolinguistic interview utilizes as a starting point the concept of "discourse scenario" as understood by Palmer (1996): that is, as a cognitive model of interaction formed by sequences of speech act schemas. These schemas are analytical categories that would account for different dimensions of the ensuing interactions. Among them would be those called *prospect schemas*, which derive from the way participants in the interaction perceive one another. Thus, the speaker is not only a discursive agent, but also an experiencer and observer of his environment and, in particular, an observer of his interlocutor. Langacker established in 1990 that the conceptualization of interaction can be objective, if done from outside the perceptual field of interaction (outside observer), or subjective, if done from within the interaction itself (interlocutors in action).

Given the fact that they include a metadiscursive component that makes speakers observers, sociolinguistic interviews can be structured in a variety of ways, in particular with respect to perspective schemas. In general, the conceptualization of the interview as a discursive event is maximally subjective with respect to each interlocutor. Nonetheless, we can differentiate between the conceptualizations held by the interviewer and those held by the interviewee. For example, the interviewer focuses his observations on the interlocutor. The interviewee probably conceptualizes interaction more comprehensively and is perhaps more sensitive to each of the elements—verbal and nonverbal—which make up the interaction.

170 The Sociolinguistic Interview

To understand how perspective schemas work within the various conditions of the sociolinguistic interview, we begin with a representation of how they work an ordinary or neutral colloquial conversation (Figure 9.2).

"H1" indicates speaker one/the interviewer; "H2" stands for speaker two/the interviewee; and "O" means scene observer. The rectangle contains the discursive event as a whole; that is, the full extent of the observer's perceptual field (Langacker). The shaded area encloses the part of the discursive event conceptualized by the speaker. In short, this graphic of an ordinary conversation includes two speakers who reciprocally observe, perceive and conceptualize the other interlocutor and his own environment. Both act as observers of the other interlocutor and both have similar environments (the shaded area). In this type of exchange, there is no need to posit substantial apriori differences with respect to either the way participants are perceived, the illocutionary force of their actions, how they will sequence their interventions or the perspective that will govern their respective conceptualizations of their environment and each other.

The sociolinguistic interview, however, despite having characteristics in common with conventional conversation, is configured differently in terms of interaction conceptualization and discourse itself. One element that makes the conventional sociolinguistic interview unique is the incorporation of an element that is absent from neutral conversations: the recorder/camera. The recorder/camera is a prop of the interview, and therefore also part of the interaction. Due to its presence, interlocutors evaluate the discourse of the interview as having consequences that extend beyond the interview interaction itself; this perception in turn has a significant influence on the monitor. Along with the recorder, other instruments (notes, questionnaires) may be utilized, which may also affect the discourse of the interview. But to fully understand the interview, we must distinguish between the perspective of the interviewer and that of the interviewee, resulting in an asymmetry that cannot be presupposed, for example, in ordinary conversation.

From the interviewer's point of view (Figure 9.3), the central zone of perception is the interviewee's space (the shaded circle), to which the interviewer gives his direct attention (as indicated by a solid-line arrow). And he gives focal attention to the interviewee himself (indicated by the thick-lined circle).

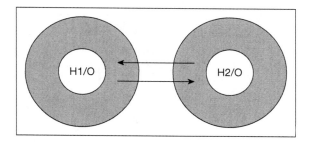

FIGURE 9.2 Subjective perception of colloquial conversation situation

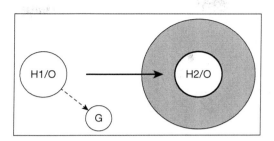

FIGURE 9.3 Subjective Perception of the Sociolinguistic Interview from the Interviewer's Perspective

At the same time, there is a secondary attention, or a weak perceptual relationship (indicated by the dashed-line arrow), to some technical support element (indicated by "G"), usually a voice recorder, a camera, a notebook or a questionnaire, whose operation tends to be monitored throughout the interview (in case it malfunctions or stops, for instance).

In the direct attention that the interviewer pays the interviewee, the interviewer often employs sets of strategies intended to shape the direction of the interview, with the aim of, ultimately, influencing the discourse produced. One set of strategies has to do with eliciting a certain type of reaction from the interviewee. Most generally, interviewers aim to reduce an interviewee's self-monitoring by creating a sense of relaxation for the interviewee, who might otherwise be very tense due to the context of interaction (i.e., the interview). Techniques include conversation starters or "icebreakers" in order to facilitate the initiation of conversation, usually the most tense part of an interview. Another technique includes regulating physical proximity of the interlocutors, the use of linguistic elements to create a feeling of solidarity between the speakers and thereby obtain more "spontaneous"-type speech and use of the researcher's native language, which conditions both the interview style, its discursive content and the topics discussed. One topic that is typically avoided or minimized in order to avoid an intensification of the monitor effect is that of the language variety being used in the interview. This also applies to the topic of language in general, unless it has been contextualized within the natural development of the interview. Nonetheless, the topic of language is sometimes introduced in interviews, sometimes on purpose, sometimes inadvertently, sometimes due to one of the interlocutors' emotional involvement in an issue and sometimes because informants know that their interviewers study language or linguistics (Niedzielski and Preston 2003: 34). Even Preston (1994) has proposed a list of interview topics in which language is discussed (the participants, the interaction and the code), generally for the purpose of studying linguistic beliefs or attitudes. Finally, sharing a pleasant experience or something else in common with the interviewee usually contributes to creating a relaxed conversational atmosphere. Thus, when the interviewers tell stories about

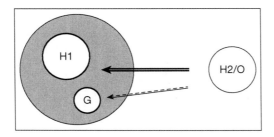

FIGURE 9.4 Subjective Perception of the Sociolinguistic Interview from the Interviewee's Perspective

themselves, they should avoid including too much detail or emotion, which can lead an interviewee to believe that he has nothing to add or to conclude that the interviewer is perhaps unapproachable, an authority who possesses a great deal of symbolic capital. From the interviewee's point of view, his perception zones during the interview are similar to those of the interviewer, but are for the most part inverted, creating a mirror effect, which is, however, not complete (Figure 9.4). The field of perception (the shaded area) of the interviewee (H2) includes both the speaker-interviewer (H1) and the interview tools used by the interviewer (G). Both receive—or are susceptible to receiving—the interviewee's preferential attention (as indicated by the dark-lined circles). The interviewee will pay more attention to one or the other according to several factors: the phase of the interview, G's physical appearance, H1's attention to G, among other things. Proper development of the interview should diminish or even eliminate attention paid to G. Nevertheless, this is difficult to achieve due to the quantity and unpredictability of the factors involved, including the interviewer's ability to create (and the interviewee's receptivity to) a cooperative and friendly atmosphere.

We have indicated that the need to minimize the observer's paradox has encouraged the development of methodological strategies aimed at changing the context and atmosphere of the interaction during a sociolinguistic interview. To this end, another strategy includes increasing the number of participants in the interview, which can be done in various ways. One is to include several interviewers. In this case, all interviewers and element "G" fall within the interviewee's sphere of attention (Figure 9.5).

While each element within the interviewee's perception area (the shaded circle) is a foci in its own right (dark-lined circles), none receives more concentrated attention than another, even if among the interviewers (H1a and H1n), one is considered the main interviewer. Either way, attention to each foci within the sphere of perception must become discontinuous (dashed-line arrows). In such a situation, the interviewer's maneuvers to manage element "G" (note taking, handling the recorder) can be done more naturally given the more dispersed attention of the interviewee.

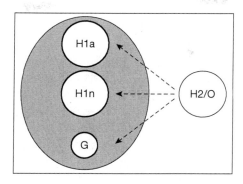

FIGURE 9.5 Subjective Perception of an Interview with Multiple Observers from the Interviewee's Perspective

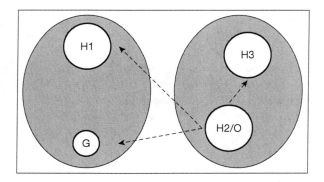

FIGURE 9.6 Subjective Perception of an Interview with Multiple Subjects from the Main Interviewee's Perspective

Another strategy to modify the structure and content of a discourse consists of gathering several interviewees, usually members of the same network or sociolinguistic reference group (Nordberg 1980). Supposedly, interviewees exert social control over one another such that it would be unacceptable for one of them to use speech patterns other than those of their group or network. The field of perception of each of the interviewees, in that each is himself a main interviewee, differs from his perceptive structure presented under other conditions (Figure 9.6).

First of all, we will note that the interviewee (H2) will have not one, but two well-differentiated perception areas within the same interaction. The first, as before, includes the observer's area (H1) and includes element "G." The second encompasses the area of the other interviewees (H3) who are members of the same social group. As can be seen from the figure, the interviewee's main attention is directed, as in the case of a two-participant interview, to the interviewer (H1) and secondarily to element G, but attention to each focal element is weakened since it is also being directed toward other participants (H3) who, although not primary foci, are still perceived by the interviewee. This interview structure encourages the emergence of linguistic and conversational differences between speech directed toward H1 and speech directed toward H3. The former, in principle, would be subject to more monitoring than the latter.

The various participant structures of the sociolinguistic interview have also been tweaked for a variety of sociolinguistic investigations. One adaptation is having a small child accompany the interviewer to the interview, since children, often associated with non-threatening conditions, facilitate the creation of a relaxing atmosphere. However, this arrangement is also discouraged because children tend to absorb attention and monopolize conversation topics. Another technique, of considerable interest, records two or more informants conversing without the presence of the researcher. In this case, any monitor effect caused by the element G would be offset by the intensified interaction with and attention to a member of the same group, who might even play the role of interviewer. This technique was used with good results by Stuart-Smith (1999) in Glasgow (UK) and Cestero Mancera (2000, 2007) in Alcalá de Henares (Spain), to name a few. A minor variation of this, the interview conducted by an insider, a member of the interviewee's social group or network, was practiced by Labov, Cohen, Robins and Lewis in 1968, among others. This technique brings the communicative exchange even closer to one that mirrors a colloquial conversation, with the modification that it includes a recorder (an element G) (Maurer 1999: 116).

A cognitive approach to the sociolinguistic interview is also capable of revealing underlying organizational schemas that would lead to undesirable interview outcomes. One of these is the situation where the interviewer who, despite focusing on the interviewee, might not be able to escape self-perception, that is perceiving himself as an element of the interaction. In this circumstance, one of the following scenarios is likely to come about:

a. The interviewer becomes so involved in the interaction that he loses control over other aspects of the conversational dynamic, such as self-control during his speaking turns, monitoring the recorder or otherwise keeping in mind that the interview's primary focus is the interviewee and his discourse. While such a scenario may not have an unequivocal negative impact on the interaction, it is not unlikely that it has undesirable side-effects, most particularly a decline in the quantity and quality of discourse contributions made by the interviewee.
b. The interviewer becomes so self-aware that he becomes the main focus of his observation. These cases are rare with seasoned researchers but relatively frequent among inexperienced interviewers who might be concerned by a desire to fulfill a modular script to the letter, who may fear that their interviewing techniques will be questioned by external observers or who may

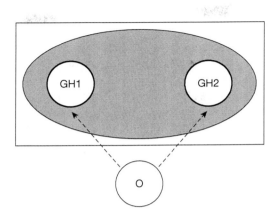

FIGURE 9.7 Objective Perception of a Speech Event from the Transcriber's Perspective

simply be self-complacent. In such situations, the monitor effect may be so strong that it blocks the interviewer from focusing on anything besides his own discourse, including even that of the informant.

The schemas discussed so far reflect subjective conceptualizations of the sociolinguistic interview from the point of view of some participant or other and from within the perceptual field of the interaction itself. There is yet another general perspective schema related to the sociolinguistic interview to consider: that of the observer who is entirely outside the speech event. In such a case, the conceptualization of discourse by the observer is maximally objective, conceived of as alien. A clear example of this objective conceptualization is that which occurs when a researcher transcribes or transliterates sociolinguistic interviews recorded at a different place or time (Hidalgo and Valesco 2005). This perspective schema is represented in Figure 9.7.

As can be seen, a transcriber (O) perceives the sociolinguistic interview from outside the interaction (i.e., outside the inner rectangular box) and he perceives it as a whole, including all participants in it and all statements produced. In a way, the element G is also present since noise and recording quality affect the way in which the interview is objectively perceived. The transcription work—long and hard—is usually done with headphones and in the solitude of the researcher's work space.

Debate: Is the Semi-Guided Interview Adequate?

An examination of the sociolinguistic interview from a cognitive perspective has encouraged reanalysis of its structure, its development and, especially, the quality of the materials obtained. And that is precisely where doubts and debates about the interview arise: Are the materials and data obtained by means of semi-guided interviews the best suited for sociolinguistic analysis?

Given the schemas underlying the customary structure of sociolinguistic interviews, we might wonder which is most suitable for obtaining quality samples of spoken language. To answer this question, we can analyze the outcome that the various schemas we have examined would create with respect to a set of criterion factors that we deem as desirable for obtaining quality data. For example, to obtain quality data, we want interactions that are, on the one hand, "spontaneous," or which approximate natural speech. On the other hand, we also want interviews of a certain "length," that is, that include a sufficient amount of speech. Using these two criteria, we can establish a basic interview typology, as depicted in Table 9.2.

The most spontaneous interactions (+ Spontaneity) are those that occur in normal, everyday conversation. Hence covert or secret recordings (i.e., the "Clandestine interview") provide both spontaneous speech as well as a good amount (+ Length) of speech for quantitative and qualitative analysis. The downside is that they do not usually provide optimal data, either for technical reasons (quality of recordings in natural contexts tends to be poor) or for ethical or legal reasons (invasion of privacy by secret recording). Another good source of more spontaneous speech is the multiple informant interview. However, in these interviews, the amount of speech per speaker and the length of their speaking turns tend to be reduced because conversational dynamics encourage an overall greater quantity of speaking turns over the course of the interview. While each type of interview has advantages and disadvantages, it seems advisable to opt for the multiple-observer interview. Despite its limits with respect to spontaneity, and the fact that it has been characterized as [– Length], it still has a good likelihood of producing natural speech (since, with multiple interviewers, it isless likely that the interviewee's attention will be on his speech) and nonetheless produces sufficient data for analysis. The other recommended technique, the most frequently used, is the two-person semi-guided sociolinguistic interview. When conducted by an external investigator, it is generally very effective for producing sufficient quantities of data. When conducted by a group insider, it succeeds in producing not only sufficient quantities of data, but data of a more spontaneous character since it generally approximates everyday conversation to a greater extent.

TABLE 9.2 Conversational Interaction Typology According to Length and Spontaneity

	+ *Length*	– *Length*
+ Spontaneity	Normal conversation Clandestine interview	Multiple informant interview
– Spontaneity	Sociolinguistic interview	Multiple observer interview

Conclusion

From a methodological point of view, the interview is one of the best-known techniques of sociolinguistic research. In this chapter, the great majority of its characteristics have been discussed in detail. The discussion focused, as to be expected, on aspects that contribute to the cognitive framing of the interview itself and, thus, that influence the ensuing discourse. Nonetheless, it will be necessary in the long run to present an exhaustive explanatory and interpretative model of the sociolinguistic interview entirely from a cognitive perspective. Cognitive features hitherto sporadically or partially treated must be included for a complete and coherent presentation.

Cognitivism has shown interest in discourse, but has only rarely been interested in its purely sociolinguistic implications or in quantitative studies of spoken discourse. Those perspectives that have taken interest have proven particularly useful and have contributed toward deeper appreciation of conversational dynamics. In particular, initiatives within cultural linguistics (e.g., Palmer 1996) have served to treat the sociolinguistic interview as a discursive scenario and been able to reveal the importance, not only of the various components of the interview, but of perspective schemas for understanding the shape of interview discourse. Moreover, these insights can be integrated with the conceptual foundations of other theoretical proposals, such as Grice's maxims (1989) or Wierzbicka's cultural scripts (1994, 2006).

What other useful insights might sociolinguistics obtain from a cognitive treatment of the sociolinguistic interview? It is likely we will acquire more detailed knowledge of the perceptual mechanisms that come into play as part of conversational interaction. These mechanisms would shed light on dimensions of the sociolinguistic interview that are not sufficiently well known and could potentially correlate with other social and linguistic factors. This, ultimately, would contribute toward a better understanding of the sociolinguistic interview itself.

References

Albelda, Marta, 2004. "Cortesía en diferentes situaciones comunicativas. La conversación coloquial y la entrevista sociológica semiformal." In *Pragmática sociocultural: estudios sobre el discurso de cortesía en español*, Eds., D. Bravo and A. Briz, 109–136. Barcelona: Ariel.

Ander-Egg, Ezequiel, 1995. *Técnicas de investigacion social*. 24th ed. Buenos Aires: Lumen.

Arfuch, Leonor, 1995. *La entrevista, una invención dialógica*. Barcelona: Paidós.

Bell, Allan, 2001. "Back in style: reworking audience design." In *Style and Sociolinguistic Variation*, Eds., P. Eckert and J.R. Rickford. Cambridge: Cambridge University Press, pp. 139–169.

Briggs, Charles L., 1986. *Learning How to Ask: a Sociolinguistic Appraisal of the Role of the Interview in Social Science Research*. Cambridge: Cambridge University Press.

Cestero Mancera, Ana María, 2000. *El intercambio de turnos de habla en la conversación. Análisis sociolingüístico*. Alcalá de Henares: Universidad de Alcalá.

Cestero Mancera, Ana María, 2007. "Cooperación en la conversación: estrategias estructurales características de las mujeres." *Linred*. Obtained from: www.linred.com/articulos_pdf/LR_articulo_24042007.pdf (accessed 15 December, 2015).

Eckert, Penelope, 2000. *Linguistic Variation as a Social Practice*. Oxford: Blackwell.

Frattini, Eric and Montse Quesada, 1994. *La entrevista. El arte y la ciencia*. Madrid: EDUDEMA.

Grice, H. Paul, 1989. *Studies in the Way of Words*. Cambridge: Harvard University Press.

Hidalgo Navarro, Antonio and Grupo Valesco, 2005. "La transcripción de un corpus de lengua hablada." In *Actas del II Coloquio Internacional del programa EDICE*, Ed., J. Murillo Medrano, 275–318. Universidad de Costa Rica-Universidad de Estocolmo. Obtained from: www.edice.org/2coloquio/2coloquioEDICE.pdf (accessed 15 December, 2015).

Hymes, Dell, 1972. "Models of the interaction of language and social life." In *Directions in Sociolinguistics. The Ethnography of Communication*, Eds., J. J. Gumperz and D. Hymes, 35–71. New York: Holt, Rinehart & Winston.

Labov, William, 1972. *Sociolinguistic Patterns*. Philadelphia, PA: University of Pennsylvania Press.

Labov, William, 1981. *Field Methods of the Project on Linguistic Change and Variation. Sociolinguistic Working Paper No. 81*. Austin, TX: Southwest Educational Development.

Labov, William, Paul Cohen, Clarence Robins and John Lewis, 1968. *A Study of the Non-Standard English of Negro and Puerto Rican Speakers in New York City*. Philadelphia, PA: U.S. Regional survey.

Maurer, Bruno, 1999. "Jeu de rôles et recueil de données socio (¿) linguistiques." In Louis-Jean Calvet and Pierre Dumont (dirs.). *L'enquête sociolinguistique*, 115–123. Paris: L'Harmattan.

Milroy, Lesley, 1987. *Observing and Analysing Natural Language*. Oxford: Blackwell.

Milroy, Lesley and Mathew Gordon, 2003. *Sociolinguistics. Method and Interpretation*. Oxford: Blackwell.

Moreno-Fernández, Francisco, 2009. *Principios de sociolingüística y sociología del lenguaje*. 4th ed. Barcelona: Ariel.

Niedzielski, Nancy and Dennis Preston, 2003. *Folk Linguistics*. Berlin—New York: Mouton de Gruyter.

Nordberg, Bengt, 1980. *Sociolinguistic Fieldwork Experiences of the Unit for Advanced Studies in Modern Swedish*. Uppsala: FUMS.

Palmer, Gary, 1996. *Toward a Cultural Linguistics*. Austin, TX: Texas University.

Preston, Dennis, 1994. "Content-oriented discourse analysis and folk linguistics." *Language Sciences*, 16, 2: 285–331.

Schiffrin, Deborah, 1994. *Approaches to Discourse*. Oxford: Blackwell.

Stuart-Smith, Jane, 1999. "Glasgow: Accent and voice quality." In *Urban Voices*, Eds., P. Foulkes and G. Docherty, 203–222. London: Arnold.

Tannen, Deborah and Cynthia Wallat, 1993. "Interactive frames and Knowledge Schemas in Interaction: Examples from a Medical Examination/Interview." In *Framing in Discourse*, Ed., D. Tannen, 57–76. New York: Oxford University Press.

Trudgill, Peter, 2003. *A Glossary of Sociolinguistics*. Edinburgh: Edinburgh University Press.

Wierzbicka, Anna, 1994. "Cultural scripts: A new approach to the study of cross-cultural communication." In *Language Contact and Language Conflict*, Ed., M. Pütz, 69–87. Amsterdam: John Benjamins.

Wierzbicka, Anna, 2006. *English: Meaning and Culture*. Oxford: Oxford University Press.

10
THE PERCEPTUAL DYNAMICS OF THE SOCIOLINGUISTIC INTERVIEW

One aspect of the sociolinguistic enterprise that can be fruitfully analyzed using a cognitive framework is the semi-guided interview, conceived as a discourse scenario composed of perspective schemas. Perspective schemas are dynamic models that highlight the nature, area, strength and direction of the attention of a particular interview participant. These perspective schemas include perception areas and foci receiving priority attention. Perception areas and priority attention foci may vary according to the participant structure of the interview and the presence of other interactive elements. Although we have already learned much about the perceptual dynamics of the interview using these perspective schemas, it is possible to know still more by moving beyond the overview provided in the previous chapter and toward details of its perceptual micro-dynamics. It is to this level of internal dynamism that we now turn our attention.

A. On the Basics of Perceptual Dynamics

Proposition 10.1

Interlocutors are recipients of the communicative situation, its development and its results.

Proposition 10.2

Interlocutors project into discourse their perception of a communicative situation, its development and its results.

Proposition 10.3

The projection of perceptions by the interlocutors can be of a linguistic or a non-linguistic nature.

Proposition 10.4

The linguistic projections of perceptions affect all components of the interaction: both interlocutors, each interlocutor's referential and conceptual realm and the whole communicative situation.

Proposition 10.5

The particular way in which linguistic perceptions materialize may be correlated with psychosocial (presentation of *self*, interpersonal relationships), social (age, educational level, gender) or situational (context, audience) factors.

Proposition 10.6

The way in which the linguistic projection of perceptions materializes may be correlated with stylistic discourse varieties.

Scholium 10-A

To analyze the dynamics of the sociolinguistic interview, we begin with several general premises that necessarily frame and determine the form it eventually takes. We begin, as mentioned in the previous chapter, with the principle that interview informants perceive the communicative exchange in its totality as well as each of its components. Other theoretical premises that underlie the interview are listed above in propositions 10.1–10.6. Among these, of paramount importance, is the premise that speakers' perceptions are materialized as linguistic projections in the discourse of the interview.

In particular, speakers' perceptions, their "reality," are manifested in discourse as a heterogeneous entity and as existing on various levels. At the *object level*, speakers construe reality by referring to perceived facts as if they had objective independent existence. On this level, two speakers can either agree on what the perceived facts are or may behave so as to shed doubt on the "reality" of an interlocutor's perceived facts. At the *experience level* of discourse, reality is revealed in descriptions of how it is lived differently by different individuals. Finally, at the *narrative level*, speakers configure their information in different ways to achieve specific effects in their interlocutors (Pollner 1987).

The way in which perceptual dynamics are manifested in interaction and the different levels on which reality is construed, among other factors, have led to what is known, outside of sociolinguistics, as the "cognitive interview." Such interviews attempt to obtain statements from interviewees by facilitating their recall process and by encouraging manifestation of their attitudes, all while ensuring the accuracy and reliability of their narratives. Perhaps unsurprisingly, its origins and development have been closely linked with police interrogations as well as with interviews developed for other professions (medical, legal, laboral) (Ibáñez 1979; Callejo 2001; Arao 2005; Willis 2005).

As can be seen, although interview dynamics respond to factors on the pragmatic level—in fact, linguistic projection is achieved, in large part, by elements that discourse analysis calls *meta-communicative* (Schegloff and Sacks 1973; Stubbs 1983)—we are in the presence of a different understanding of pragmatics, discourse analysis and conversation analysis. This perspective allows us to formulate research questions such as the following:

- What are the most significant factors in the perception of the elements of an interview?
- Where are speakers located with respect to the factors of perception?
- How do perceptual factors correlate with the speakers' social profile?
- How do perceptual dynamics of an interview function from a linguistic and sociolinguistic perspective?

These questions have received preliminary answers from the quantitative analysis of nine sociolinguistic interviews conducted in Alcalá de Henares, a Spanish-speaking city in the center of the Iberian Peninsula, only 30 km from Madrid, as part of the Proyecto para el Estudio Sociolingüístico del Español de España y América (PRESEEA) (cf. Moreno-Fernández 1996; Moreno-Fernández and Moreno Martín de Nicolás 2011).

B. On the Indicators of Perception in Communicative Interaction

Proposition 10.7

Perceptions about the *discourse* of the interview are evidenced in the discourse itself by means of the following indicators: *interview organizers*, *discourse evaluators* and *communicative intention fixators*.

Proposition 10.8

The perception of self as a speaker is evident in discourse by means of the following indicators: deontic modality markers, self-regulators, markers of doubt, discursive modality markers and referential distance markers.

Proposition 10.9

The perception of the *you* as interlocutor is evident by means of the following indicators: focalizers of otherness, politeness signals, agreement requests, focalizers of understanding and hetero-regulators.

Proposition 10.10

The perception of referential and contextual environment is evident in discourse by means of the following indicators: referential appeals, situational descriptors and marked interrogations.

Scholium 10-B

Perceptions about the dynamics of the interview are linguistically projected, which means that the spoken discourse itself contains concrete elements that reflect those perceptions and that, consequently, it is possible to categorize and analyze those projections. A general framework within which to analyze these perceptions is as follows:

a. perception of *discourse* delivered during the interaction;
b. perception of *self* as a speaker;
c. perception of *you* as an interlocutor; and
d. perception of referential and contextual realm.

These four types of perceptions correspond largely with the components included in perspective schemas. On the other hand, referential components, although possibly outside the scope of the interaction, are relevant and "present" in so far as they are (explicitly) mentioned in the discourse itself.

For each of these principal areas of perception (*discourse, self, you, context*), linguistic markers or indicators that reveal or reflect each category can be identified. In other words, and more specifically, we are now in a position to outline a typology in which, for each type of perception, a core set of related linguistic indicators can be enumerated. This typology, based on the results of the Alcalá de Henares investigation, is presented below, together with illustrative examples. As will be seen, not all of the linguistic indicators directly reveal a perception in itself, but all, one way or another, *do* presuppose a previous exercise of perception by the speaker.

A. Perception of the Emergent Discourse of the Communicative Interaction

Interview organizer A metadiscursive conversational element that helps to build interaction: let's talk for a moment; let's think of this example; let's talk about . . .; let's end.

Discourse evaluator An element used to evaluate, assess or comment on any aspect of the delivered discourse: what you've said is an outrage; if you'll excuse the repetition.

Communicative intention fixator A deictic element that signals or reflects the speaker's communicative intention: that's what I was getting at; that's what I'm talking about; listen to what you're saying . . .

B. Perception of the "Self" as a Speaker

Deontic modality marker An element that reflects attitudes related to the expression of will or the affective: well; I accept that . . .; it's good that . . .; I understand that . . .; wow!; it's true.
Self-regulator An element that regulates the speech of one speaker: I will explain; I'll tell you one thing; I don't want to keep talking.
Doubt marker An element that expresses doubt, either rhetorical or actual: what would I tell you?; how would I tell you?; what could we call it?; I don't know what to call it; don't ask me.
Discursive modality marker An element that expresses a speech mode adopted by the speaker: I say; I remember; I affirm; in my point of view; I don't understand you; does that make sense?
Referential distance marker An element that establishes a distance between the speaker's discourse and discourse presented as alien or foreign: regarding that thing called . . .; as they say; if we were to say that . . .; as they say in; as the ____ say.

C. Perception of the "You" as an Interlocutor

Otherness focalizer An element of discourse development that appeals to the interlocutor or fixes attention on him/her: man; woman; look; listen; you see; let me tell you; imagine (that) . . .
Politeness signal An element that expresses courtesy, generally ritualized: I beg your pardon; excuse me; I'm sorry.
Agreement request An element used to request or confirm the agreement of the interlocutor: you'll agree with me that . . .; right?; you would say the same.
Understanding focalizer An element used to verify the interlocutor's understanding or request their agreement: do you understand?; do you know what I mean?; you know?; do you know what I'm saying?; does that make sense?; right?
Hetero-regulator An element that sequences or intends to sequence the interlocutor's discourse: tell me; explain that; describe . . .; would you mind telling me?

D. Perception of the Referential and Contextual Realm

Referential appeal An element that makes reference to objects, concepts or ideas outside the interaction: you may have heard of . . .; you may have noticed that . . .; I'm talking about . . .

Situational descriptor An element that appeals to or describes an aspect of the interaction circumstances: it's hot; this is a tough situation.

Marked interrogation A statement that contains an interpretive orientation indicator (Escandell, 1999: 3985) and often affects referential or contextual elements (linguistic or non-linguistic) of the interaction. Here we would include rhetorical, attributive, repetitive or anticipatory questions: *¿y por qué me tengo que ir a la cama para que la niña se duerma?* 'and why do I have to go to bed for her [the little girl] to fall asleep?' (PRESEEA-ALCALÁ-ES. 42. M11.); *¿que fuera con esas intenciones?* 'what in heaven was he thinking?;' *¿que no fuera esa persona?* 'what if it wasn't that person?' *¿que fuera otra que venía a robarme?* 'what if it was someone else coming to rob me?' *no lo sé las intenciones no lo sé* 'I don't know what their intentions are, I just don't know' (PRESEEA-ALCALÁ-ES. 42. M11).

With respect to marked interrogation statements, doubt has been raised with respect to their inclusion as perception indicators and, also too, where in this taxonomy they would belong. They have been included here as indicators because explicitly using such interrogative statements is possible only if the speaker holds a special perception of communicative interaction and is aware of this perception. As for which category they are best included in, the fact that they take the form of an interrogative might seem to suggest an appeal to a *you*. Yet, despite their interrogative form, these statements are not intended to elicit an action on the part of the listener. That is, they are not intended to carry a perlocutionary force. On the other hand, an assessment of their semantic content would seem to suggest that these indicators have to do with the speaker's own communicative intentions (i.e., *self*). However, they do not seem to be formulated in order to express or define the *self* but to express an attitude of the *self* towards a message or state of affairs. That is, in context, these statements seem to be appealing to situations beyond both the *you* or the *self*; they are about a prevailing state of affairs in which the *you* or the *self* (or both) find themselves. Notwithstanding, it should be noted that these types of statements tend to occur extremely infrequently in discourse.

This treatment of perception indicators does not pretend to be exhaustive. The same goes for the examples provided, among which, it will have been noted, there is some overlap between categories. This is, of course, to be expected since one and the same utterance may carry different illocutionary forces in different contexts. Neither, on the other hand, must this classification be taken as a contradiction or invalidation of other analytical proposals such as Haverkate's (1994) theory of politeness or the discourse analysis meta-communication (Stubbs 1983), into which, we believe, several of its components could be easily accommodated. For example, expressions such as *I think* or *I believe that . . .* are among those that Antonio Briz (2003) calls "strictly pragmatic attenuators" and other expressions—such as the deontic modality markers—are included in well-known catalogs (Martín Zorraquino and Portolés 1999). Be this as it may, from within a cognitive linguistics, these elements still serve as perception indicators.

C. On the Perceptual Dynamics of the Sociolinguistic Interview

Proposition 10.11

The perceptual dynamics of the interview oscillates between two poles: that of the speaker—in relation to the context, the interlocutor and the discourse itself—and that of the interlocutor—as a mechanism that contributes to the organization of discourse.

Proposition 10.11.1

The perceptual dynamics of the sociolinguistic interview move between the mechanisms that facilitate a correct interpretation of what is said, those that position the speaker with respect to the interlocutor and those aimed at the organization of discourse.

Proposition 10.11.2

In the sociolinguistic interview, interviewees make discursive movements guided primarily by the need to allow an appropriate interpretation of their messages and, secondarily, by a desire to position themselves within the conversational dynamics.

Proposition 10.11.3

An interviewer begins a sociolinguistic interview by employing discourse organizing criteria, which ultimately help shape the dynamics of the interaction. Subsequently, the interviewer gives increasing importance to the appropriate interpretation of his own speech over other potential objects of attention.

Scholium 10-C

To understand the perceptual imperatives that are most at work during the sociolinguistic interview, we can submit our data to statistical analysis. After quantifying the extent to which each speaker uses each type of perceptual indicator (our dependent variables), a "principal component" analysis is carried out. This analysis creates a linear sequence of certain variables to reveal which ones are most correlated with each other and which ones account for the greatest amount of variance in the data. Once the variables, in our case the indicator types, have been put into their correlated "groupings," the researcher is responsible for discovering what qualitative arguments support these alignments and correlations.

Statistical analysis of our Alcalá de Henares sociolinguistic interviews identified two main groupings of perception indicators. The first included communicative intention fixators (e.g., *that's what I was getting at; listen to what you're saying . . .*) and politeness signals (e.g., *I beg your pardon; excuse me*), reflecting the link between the two types of markers, together with understanding focalizers (e.g., *you know?; does that make sense?; right?*) and Otherness focalizers (e.g., *man; look; imagine*). In other words, the perceptual dynamics of the interview seemed to gravitate toward two primary areas: (i) the speaker's own position in relation to the context, his interlocutor and the discourse itself and (ii) the interlocutor, as a means to help the speaker organize his own discourse. The second grouping of perception indicators included modality markers (discursive [e.g., *I affirm; in my point of view*] and deontic [e.g., *well; it's good that . . .*]) and hetero-regulators (e.g., *tell me; explain that*) together with discourse evaluators (e.g., *what you've said is an outrage*). It makes sense that the indicators of perception of the *self* would be located together with those that introduce the expression of opinions, feelings or thoughts. It also makes sense to appeal, on the opposing level, to the *you* (e.g., *tell me; explain to me*).

More generally stated, our analysis reflects a perceptual dynamics that shifts between linguistic mechanisms that promote a correct interpretation of what is said (most often offered by the interviewee), those that position the speaker with respect to the interlocutor and the discourse and those markers oriented toward discourse organization (typically offered by the interviewer). Said differently, interviewees make discursive moves that are guided, first, by a desire to have their messages adequately interpreted and, second, by a desire to position themselves within the dynamics of the conversation. Interviewers, for their part, commence interviews by making discursive moves primarily aimed at organizing the discourse itself; this organizing, in turn, shapes the dynamics of the interview in the long run. At a later stage in the interview, interviewers tend, like interviewees, to make discursive moves that are principally aimed at leading their listeners to an appropriate interpretation of their utterances. A schematic representation of these findings is located in Figure 10.1.

In conclusion, we have seen how some of the components that make up an interaction (e.g., the interlocutors) are ranked in importance in a speaker's discourse. More precisely, what we have discussed is how those components are *perceived* and the relative importance that speakers give to those perceptions, as reflected in the use of various discourse devises. Particularly, we have seen that, for speakers, two things are of paramount importance: (i) the *you*, in so far that the *you* has arrived at a satisfactory interpretation of the speaker's meaning and (ii) the *self*, in the sense of relating—appreciable in the perception of references. Because semi-guided interviews were used to explore these questions, analysis of the discourse devises employed also revealed that speakers were additionally giving

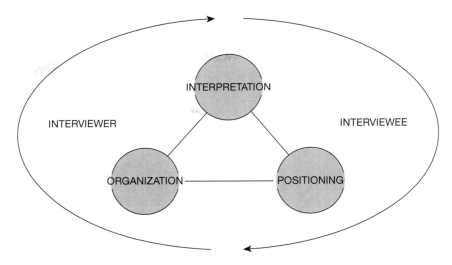

FIGURE 10.1 Representation of the Sociolinguistic Interview's Internal Dynamics Guided by Three Criteria: Performance, Positioning and Organization

ample perceptual attention to discourse organization and to regulation of the interviewer's interventions.

Debate: Do Social Factors Affect the Interview Dynamics?

Researchers with some experience conducting sociolinguistic interviews have had opportunity to observe differences in how to organize their discourse for speakers with different social and individual profiles. Such observations suggest that perhaps the interactive dynamics of an interview respond to more than discursive or communicative factors. They may also respond to factors such as the interviewee's age or educational level. Or perhaps it is better to ask: Is the way that one perceives the development of the interview, is his perception of the *you* and the *self*, different depending on his social profile and the social profile of his interlocutors? It may in fact be so.

Research has shown that older individuals seem to be more aware and involved in the form and organization of discourse. Furthermore, evidence suggests that the youngest consultants disfavor perception indicators corresponding to the *you* compared with what is customary in older individuals.

With respect to education, it appears that more educated speakers not only use perception indicators corresponding to the *you* less frequently than less educated individuals, but they show more frequent use of indicators of the perception of the *self*. In addition, less educated speakers favor the use of referential and contextual perception indicators. It so happens that women, more so than men, also favor the use of indicators of *reference* and *context*.

In sum, then, it seems that the dynamics of a sociolinguistic interview is not homogeneous with respect to how utterances in particular, and the communicative situation in general, are perceived by speakers. Instead, it is conditioned, at least partially, by the social profile of the individual speaker.

Conclusion

The semi-guided sociolinguistic interview can be used to reveal the speakers' perception regarding the discursive scenario and the elements that constitute the general framework of the interaction. Their perception can be seen, for example, in the use of perception indicators (words, expressions), which themselves in part comprise the discourse of the interview. These indicators can be classified into four main groups according to the principal object of perception: the *discourse*, the *self*, the *you* and *the referential and contextual realm*.

Quantitative analysis of perception indicators yields abundant data that augment our understanding of the sociolinguistic interview's perceptual dynamics. Thus, in the interview we have observed a greater frequency of use of the indicators referring to the *self* and to the *you*, and a lower probability of occurrence of perception indicators referring to *discourse* and the *contextual realm*. By correlating the four kinds of indicators with the factors like sex, age, education and a participant's role in the interview, we have also observed that the use of a class of indicator, and by extension the participant's particular perceptual interests, can vary according to the social profile of the participant. It was seen, for example, that the use of *discourse* indicators is influenced by the age and role of the speaker in the interview. Older individuals made more reference to the discourse. In addition, *context* indicators varied with the educational level of the speaker, with these being preferred by younger individuals (rather than older). The indicators most influenced by speaker characteristics, however, were those related to the perception of the *you* and the *self*. Both age and educational level conditioned the use of *self*-indicators and *you*-indicators. For example, younger individuals disfavored mention of the *you* (compared with older people). Likewise, more educated individuals also disfavored *you* indicators (as compared with the less educated), but furthermore opted for greater use of *self* indicators. Additionally, holistic assessment revealed that interviewers tend to use certain indicators very frequently, particularly those relating to (in descending order) the *discourse*, the *context*, the *you* and the *self*.

With respect to the perceptual dynamic of the interview overall, we found that it revolves around three main parameters: the interpretation of the discourse delivered by the *self*, the organization of discourse, including appeals to the interlocutor, and the relative positioning of the actors in the interaction, especially that of the *you*. In slightly broader terms, the dynamics of the interview shifts between two different conversational strategies: the interviewer's and the interviewee's where the elements of the interaction acquire greater or lesser relevance depending on the perspective and the role of the participants.

Within the realm of sociolinguistic research methodology, a cognitivist approach to those perceptions that shape semi-guided interviews provides resources that augment our knowledge of its components. In conjunction with quantitative data, we are then able to compare different interviews to determine whether the extent to which each fulfills expectations of what such interactions should be. Finding, for example, that an interviewee employs a perceptual strategy weighted toward the *self* and the *you*, giving comparatively less attention to the context and/or the construction of the *discourse* itself, we could conclude with greater certainty that the interview successfully realized the researcher's goal of creating a "natural" conversational exchange. In other words, the cognitive perspective, paired with quantification and statistical analysis makes possible a systematic evaluation of the appropriateness of the data obtained in a given sociolinguistic interview. Further conceivable would be the establishment of prototypical perceptual parameters expected for sociolinguistic interviews employed for various purposes. These evaluative methods could be quite useful for analyzing the interviews that comprise large spoken language corpora.

References

Arao, Lilian A., 2005. "Modos de organización del discurso en una entrevista de carácter testimonial." In *En torno al discurso*, Ed., A. Harvey, 221–228. Santiago de Chile: Ediciones Universidad Católica de Chile.

Briz, Antonio, 2003. "La estrategia atenuadora en la conversación cotidiana española." In *Actas del Primer Coloquio del programa Edice. La perspectiva no etnocentrista de la cortesía: identidad sociocultural de las comunidades hispanohablantes*, Ed., D. Bravo, 17–46. Estocolmo: Universidad de Estocolmo.

Callejo, Javier, 2001. *El grupo de discusión: introducción a una práctica de investigación*. Barcelona: Ariel.

Escandell Vidal, M. Victoria, 1999. "Los enunciados interrogativos. Aspectos semánticos y pragmáticos." In *Gramática descriptiva del la lengua española. Vol. 3 Entre la oración y el discurso*, dirs. I. Bosque and V. Demonte, 3929–3991. Madrid: Espasa Calpe.

Haverkate, Henk, 1994. *La cortesía verbal*. Madrid: Gredos.

Ibáñez, Jesús, 1979. *Más allá de la sociología*. Madrid: Siglo XXI.

Martín Zorraquino, María Antonia and José Portolés, 1999. "Los marcadores del discurso." In *Gramática descriptiva del la lengua española. Vol. 3 Entre la oración y el discurso*, dirs. I. Bosque and V. Demonte, 4051–4213. Madrid: Espasa Calpe.

Moreno-Fernández, Francisco, 1996. "Metodología del "Proyecto para el estudio sociolingüístico del Español de España y de América" (PRESEEA)." *Lingüística*, 8: 257–287.

Moreno-Fernández, Francisco and Irene Moreno Martín de Nicolás, 2011. "Dinámica perceptiva de la entrevista sociolingüística." In *Realismo en el análisis de corpus orales. Primer coloquio y de cambio y variación lingüística*, Ed., P. Martín Butragueño, 4557–490. México: El Colegio de México.

Pollner, Melvin, 1987. *Mundane Reason. Reality in Everyday and Sociological Discourse*. Cambridge: Cambridge University Press.
Schegloff, Emanuel and Harvey Sacks, 1973. "Opening up closings." *Semiotica*, 8: 289–327.
Stubbs, Michael, 1983. *Discourse Analysis. The Sociolinguistic Analysis of Natural Language*. Chicago, IL: The University of Chicago Press.
Willis, Gordon B., 2005. *Cognitive Interviewing. A Tool for Improving Questionnaires Design*. Thousand Oaks, CA: Sage.

11
THE PERCEPTION OF LINGUISTIC VARIATION

Subjective perception plays an essential role in the origin, development, change and disappearance of linguistic varieties. In fact, every variety owes its form, to some extent, to how it is perceived by its own speakers and speakers of other language varieties. One of the most interesting aspects that the analysis of the perception of varieties reveals is the multiplicity of realities into which they fall. On one hand, the multiplicity of varieties of any language is usually rich and complex since the geographical intersects with the cultural and the social with the situational, to make language use a hodge-podge. To that, we must add that all varieties are constantly changing realities; what is perceived today does not have to coincide with what is perceived tomorrow. For its part, perception—more particularly perception of linguistic varieties—is not straightforward or uniformly applied. Perception can be directed toward individuals or groups, partially or holistically applied and incorporate individual or group information, beliefs, prejudices and biases that potentially impact linguistic activity and extra-linguistic behaviors.

In the study of linguistic attitudes and beliefs and, in general, in the study of perceptions toward language varieties, it is instructive to distinguish between statements advanced by linguists and those held by non-linguists. Interestingly, linguistics pays little attention to the perceptions of non-linguists although these clearly predominate in society and, therefore, have a greater influence on language usage and how the great majority of people evaluate particular languages. Non-linguists' perceptions are quite often widely popular and shared by teachers and language students; and these popular beliefs tend to be so strong that, in an exercise worthy of analysis, one's behavior can be held hostage by them even when theoretical knowledge contradicts these beliefs. Thus, perceptions linked to beliefs and attitudes strongly impact social behavior and institutions. These institutions in turn contribute to giving internal shape to speech communities. Among such institutions, the mass media as well as the school, as an institution that disseminates linguistic ideologies, are worth mentioning.

A. On Linguistic Attitudes Toward Language Varieties

Proposition 11.1

Linguistic cognition may be affected by both what people say and by conscious and unconscious reactions that people have toward language.

Proposition 11.2

Speakers' perceptions and awareness directly and indirectly impact their attitudes and linguistic behaviors.

Proposition 11.3

Pragmatic evaluations, attitudes and accommodations presuppose perceptual activity, but perceptual activity may not automatically result in pragmatic evaluations, attitude or accommodations.

Proposition 11.4

Linguistic attitudes are manifestations of social attitudes. They specifically target a language and its varieties as well as to how varieties are used in society.

Proposition 11.4.1

According to the *hypothesis of inherent value*, two varieties may be compared with the result that one of them is considered to be better or more attractive than the other.

Proposition 11.4.2

According to the *imposed norm hypothesis*, a variety can be considered better or more attractive than another if it is spoken by a more prestigious group.

Proposition 11.5

Linguistic attitudes are determined by speakers' formation and prejudices, by speech characteristics, and by the interlocutors' intentions.

Proposition 11.6

Languages and their varieties are closely related to their user's notion of identity and this relationship is manifested in individual linguistic attitudes.

Scholium 11-A

Linguistic attitude is a manifestation of the individual's social attitude that makes specific reference to both the language and its use in society. For Teun van Dijk (1999), attitudes are part of the cognitive domain of a speaker and can be characterized as an organized set of general evaluative beliefs, usually shared by other members of a social group. Attitudes generally form as a result of social interaction, often act as a defining component of social identity and, simultaneously, may serve as explanatory factors for linguistic change.

Linguist attitudes generally include at least three dimensions: a *competence dimension*, an *evaluative dime nsion* and an *instrumental* or usage dimension. The *competence dimension* refers to the cognitive content of an attitude and draws on the knowledge we have of the community's language, which, as this knowledge increases, tends to bring about favorable attitudes. The *evaluative dimension* refers to the affective component of an attitude, the value conferred upon the object of the attitude, in this case, the language or variety. This valoration is shaped by the belief systems that get manifested in social interaction. Finally, the *instrumental* dimension refers to the conative component of attitude (Sanz 2008). Linguistic attitudes are an integral part and consequence of linguistic awareness, a decisive factor in speakers' behavior in relation to the most prestigious linguistic forms, as well as in the recognition of sociolects and those styles closest to the ideals of culture and education within a community (Milroy and Milroy 1985; Fernández Marrero 1999: 175; Kristiansen 2001).

In the field of cognitive sociolinguistics, the concept of "prestige" has as much significance as that of "attitude." Speakers tend to follow a prestigious model, often considered "correct," but not the same as a "normative model." The prestige of a model may lie in its peculiarities or features that are particular to a community. Prestige traits may be those with a (perceived) long history of use in the community. In such cases, "prestige" traits may further be associated with attitudes of conservatism. Prestige traits could also be new or foreign to the community, in which case "prestige" is further associated with an innovative attitude. Regardless of its other associations, however, prestige traits tend overwhelmingly to be associated with traits present in the speech of women. As sociolinguistics has demonstrated, this is likely due both to a tendency on the part of women to attend and adhere to what is prestigious, as well as the tendency of others to attend to and take up the features that characterize women's speech, making women, thus, models for speech and in many cases also the leaders of linguistic change (Labov 2001). The notion of *covert prestige*, an equally important sociolinguistic concept that has implications for a cognitive sociolinguistics, is the prestige associated with features of language that are recognized as non-normative or as removed from the "appropriate." It is often associated with linguistic features used by less-educated individuals. Further, among the lower sociocultural strata, it tends to be associated with notions such as "masculinity" (Labov 1966; Trudgill 1972). *Covert prestige* positively values linguistic features that are not associated with (overt) *prestige*; that is, it values features of language that are not extantly extolled by a community as being "correct," "appropriate" or "normative." In fact, the persisting use of features openly considered "incorrect," "inappropriate" or "non-standard" typically occurs because such features are associated with a covert prestige. They are, in effect, markers of group solidarity forged by means of nonconformity to and rejection of authority. The existence of this nonconformist behavior, rather than undermine the "standard," seems instead to affirm that the entire community is in fact oriented with respect to (either toward or away from) the model or "standard" for communication.

The classification of a linguistic feature as "prestigious" comes about through judgments about what is "good" or "bad" in language and about what is stigmatized and what deserves respect. Such judgments can be associated to any types of linguistic unit, from the sounds, to the lexicon, to the grammar. Ghomeshi meaningfully entitled a 2010 publication *Grammar Matters*. He explains that the evaluation of what is politically correct in language usage, the characterization of certain linguistic usage as sexist or non-sexist, is a consequence of the action of a prestige whose analysis is as easy in what is superficial as slippery in what is profound. Language matters because history, tradition, social differences and the insecurities caused by changes also matter (Ghomeshi 2010).

B. On Perceptions Toward Language Varieties

Proposition 11.7

The perception of variation and of linguistic varieties responds to a process of categorization based on discriminatory learning.

Proposition 11.8

Awareness and knowledge of varieties of a language other than our own is acquired through both schooling and increasing contact with speakers of diverse provenance.

Proposition 11.9

The perception of a variety as central or peripheral is related to its cultural, political, and economic prestige as well as to its history; that is, varieties come to be classified as relatively more prestigious or less prestigious.

Proposition 11.10

Linguistic perception can have as its object linguistic varieties as well as speech communities, groups of speakers or individuals.

Proposition 11.10.1

The classification of an individual as a good or a bad speaker of a language is based on his or her proximity or similarity to a prototype.

Proposition 11.10.2

The classification of an individual as a good or a bad speaker is done holistically, without distinguishing relative abilities on different linguistic levels.

Proposition 11.11

Linguistic attitudes are mainly determined by two factors: speakers' perception of what in language is pleasant or not and their perception about what is correct or not.

Scholium 11-B

Differences between language varieties come about as a result of very diverse and complex causes, which do not include climate or altitude, as has occasionally been argued. Anthropologists maintain that *Homo sapiens* does not respond to climatic averages (Morán 1993: 80). Overall, we customarily acquire awareness and knowledge of the varieties of our language(s) as well as their variables and variants through schooling and progressive contact with speakers of different origins. It could be argued that this process of acquiring knowledge of language variation reflects linguistic maturity. At the same time, language attitudes held by speakers and learners of that language rely heavily on the degree of their linguistic maturity.

The above arguments are partially related to a research proposal that has achieved a remarkable level of development: *perceptual dialectology*, closely related to *Folk Linguistics*. Dennis Preston is the most prominent representative of this latter line of research who has, admirably, linked the tradition of attitudinal studies, which began with contributions from European dialectology in the 1960s, to variationist sociolinguistics. According to Preston (2004), parallel to the "linguistic theory" offered up by specialists, there also exists "popular theory" of language. In popular language theory, language is something perfectly real, an extracognitive reality, external to the individual, Platonic, yet authentic. Those speakers who have a direct relationship with that language (academics, politicians, teachers) exhibit a "totally correct" or "exemplary" language usage. Nonetheless, they are allowed certain liberties, like minimal deviation from what is strictly correct. Those speakers who do not have a direct relationship with that real language display a "normal" use of the language. In fact, when people are asked about their way of speaking, the vast majority of people respond that they speak "normally." In general terms, the ways of speaking that depart from that "normal language" usually fall either in the category of "dialect," which is how people customarily interpret the speech from other regions where their own language is spoken, or in the category of "errors," which is how the speech of foreigners is interpreted. The relationship between real language and its exemplary or "normal" use is a natural relationship. Thus, many people find it incomprehensible that those who use a "deviant" variety persist in their "errors" for longer than is acceptable. This attitude is even interpreted as a product of laziness or stubbornness, if not of perversity or degeneration, as Lesley and James Milroy (1985) have shown.

Along with dialects and errors, speech could also depart from "normal language" by falling into a category that we might call "vulgar language." Vulgar language would be, in effect, "normal" language with the incorporation of vulgar elements, that is, elements that are not widely socially accepted since they are considered obscene, indelicate or uneducated. The classification of "vulgar language" as a negative deviation from "normal" is exemplified in the Hispanic World, where it is claimed that those who often use expletives or profanities "speak bad." The

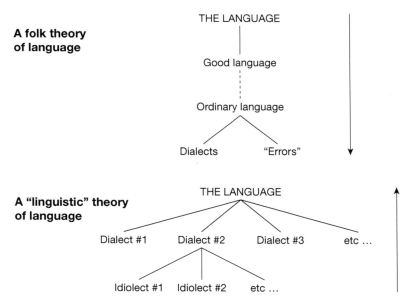

FIGURE 11.1 Folk Linguistic Theory of Language, Based on Preston (2004)

relationships between "language," "exemplar language" and "normal language" (and its deviations) are hierarchically represented in Figure 11.1.

Within the framework of folk linguistics, Preston concludes that there are two factors that determine, if not all, certainly most of the linguistic attitudes speakers hold: (a) the (subjective) perception of languages as more or less pleasant; and (b) correctness in their use. In fact, speakers show a special sensitivity toward "correctness" in language use. Particularly, according to popular belief, language is alien to, outside of, the individual and as such has its own rules to be followed as closely as possible. It is the job of the speaker to attend to the reference model, the "exemplary language," and follow its rules. Nonetheless, speakers remain aware of the internal diversity of language as well as of those elements that are shared across varieties.

C. On the Perception of Prototypes in International Languages

Proposition 11.12

Languages are prototypical mental categories to which dialectal, sociolectal and stylistic varieties are ascribed.

Proposition 11.13

The boundaries between varieties of a language are fuzzy, even with respect to other languages.

Proposition 11.14

Varieties of a language do not have absolutely common properties but a similarity or family resemblance.

Proposition 11.15

Varieties of a language are perceived as either more central or peripheral depending on their relationship to some established "nuclear" language and/or to the language of more prestigious communities.

Proposition 11.15.1

The main prototypes within an "international language" category usually have as their core members varieties directly associated with countries ("Spanish from Spain," "Australian English").

Proposition 11.15.2

A significant proportion of speakers believes that the best variety of a language is associated with a specific territory, which usually features prominently in (hi)story of the development of that the language.

Scholium 11-C

Ángel López García (1998: 13–14) has applied prototype theory to Hispanic dialectology and has reached the conclusion that what is called the "Spanish language" is a prototypical mental category toward which all of its varieties are oriented. Similarly, one could speak of a category called the "English Language." From a perspective akin to that of the prototype theory, three main levels of categorization have been proposed: the basic level, the superordinate and the subordinate (Cuenca and Hilferty 1999: 42 ff.). The basic level constitutes the central and most important level in the general process of categorization of a language variety; the basic level identifies the main exemplars to which other varieties will be compared. The superordinate level loosely groups "basic" varieties according to some similarity or other, but does not establish clear hierarchies between these larger groupings. At the subordinate level, where the greatest cognitive effort is required, varieties included on the basic level are broken into more finely discriminated varieties and grouped according to their attributes. Applying this organization scheme to Spanish languages and geolectal varieties, those varieties considered to represent prototypes, that is, those classified on the basic level, would include "Mexican," "Argentinian," "Chilean," and so forth; for English, this level might include "Southern American," "Bahamian" or "Bangladeshi" English. At the superordinate level, we would find varieties classified into categories such as "Andean Spanish," "Caribbean Spanish" or "Castilian Spanish," and even "American Spanish," on the basis of structural similarity. Such groupings could represent what Montes Giraldo (1995) called "superdialects." Finally, at the subordinate level, we would find varieties classified into categories such as "Havana Spanish," "Montevideo Spanish" and "Madrid Spanish," among many others, or "Bostonian English," "Texan English" or "Estuary English." Within each category, the varieties included would display a substantial, albeit relative, amount of homogeneity among themselves.

For Ángel López García the classification of language varieties is related to cultural, political and economic prestige, which in turns leads to classifying languages as either more prestigious or less prestigious varieties. In addition, historical factors also play a role in how language varieties come to be classified. As we indicated in 2000, the prototype "Castilian," that is the Spanish associated with the northern region of Castilla-Leon in Spain, has had a large impact on how other Spanish varieties throughout the world are perceived and classified. Its influence is also tangible in Spain, where it continues to be touted as the best, most "pure" Spanish. When speakers from other regions of Spain, like Andalusia, Extremadura, Murcia or the Canary Islands, want to speak "proper," they incorporate into their speech features characteristic of northern Castilian. These include more frequent pronunciation of intervocalic *-d* (e.g., in verbal participles such as *acabado* 'finished' and *bebido* 'drunk'); full realization of implosive *-s* in syllable final position and, in some cases, a phonetic distinction between *s* and *z*. Such behaviors, thus, attest to the fact that symbolic features are often used to build categories such as, in this case, "Castilian."

Likewise, in other Spanish-speaking countries, it is also often thought that the best Spanish is that which approximates the Castilian prototype. For example, the Spanish spoken in Camagüey is recognized as the "best" in Cuba, and its features are the most similar to those of Castilian Spanish within that country. Likewise, Colombian Spanish is thought to be more "pure" than that of other regions for similar reasons. In particular, the Spanish of Bogotá has long been regarded as "very well-spoken." *Bogotanos* appear to be genuinely concerned about their language and give much attention to its use and study. It is possible that the conservative nature of some features of this variety—coincidentally those features that are also part of Castilian—has contributed to the prestige *bogotanos* have awarded to their own Spanish as well as to the respect it enjoys in other Hispanic countries. The case of Mexico is also very interesting. Mexico is the country with the largest Spanish-speaking population in the world. One would assume that for Mexicans the best Spanish is that spoken in Mexico, especially that spoken in Mexico City (also conservative in nature). However, many Mexicans adopt, tacitly or expressly, the position that the best Spanish is spoken in Spain. Finally, Argentina presents a very special situation because Argentinians seem to consider their Spanish to be "peripheral" in comparison with some other Spanish prototype they have in mind. The Argentinean variety of Spanish includes elements that, although not exclusive to this Spanish, have become symbols of its territory. These elements include *voseo* (i.e., the use of *vos* for informal singular "you," as in *vos tenés* 'you have') and the palatal fricative sound [ʒ] (Moreno-Fernández 2000).

The hierarchization of language varieties in the English-speaking world mirrors in several ways the situation in the Hispanic world. In both cases, varieties are evaluated with respect to some particular variety that is strongly linked to national or state territories, despite the existence of extensive diversity among the language varieties that exist within each country. In both cases there also exists a historical narrative that gives priority to one of the varieties (that is, the Castilian gets preference in the case of Spanish; the British in the case of English). This occurs even if demographic and economic factors, or the degree to which their cultural manifestations have influenced others, do not actually support the positioning of these varieties as the most privileged within their respective social and linguistic domains.

One example of a classificational approach to Englishes based principally on linguistic considerations but also partially dependent on the idea that prototypical

Englishes are associated with national or state territories was presented by Laurie Bauer in 2002. His system distinguished (a) a group of innovative North American varieties, including Canadian and those of the Midwestern and Southern U.S.; (b) a group of more conservative varieties, such as British, South African, Australian and New Zealand English; and (c) other varieties with very specific or particular traits, such as Southern Hiberno-English or Irish English (Bauer 2002: 20). As occurs in the Hispanic World, the perception that these English varieties are related to specific regions depends on the region of origin of the individual formulating the categorization and on his relative distance from other varieties.

In other ways, however, the evaluation of language varieties in the English-speaking world differs from that of the Spanish-speaking world. Edgar Schneider (2007) has, for example, identified varieties of what he calls "post-colonial English," based on where speakers stand with respect to what he defines as five evolutionary stages: foundation, exonormative stabilization, nativization, endonormative stabilization and differentiation. Naturally, perceptions of "non-linguists" do not necessarily fall in line with linguistic arrangements, although these same perceptions are often the reason why dialectal realities end up the way they do. In a different vein, and since the latter part of the twentieth century, the conglomerate of all varieties of English has often been sorted out with respect to cognitive concepts like "centrality," and particularly with respect to a distinction made between central and peripheral varieties. This type of conceptualization can be seen in the work of several scholars who have organized the varieties of English—the "Englishes" if you will—into a concentric arrangement according to their degrees of "standardization." For example, Manfred Görlach (1990) places a variety he calls international English at the epicenter of his model, around which he places in successively more distant circles regional and national standards, then subregional semistandards, then the Creoles and, finally, the pidgins. Tom McArthur (1998) placed the "world standard English" in the center of his circular model, surrounded by the varieties considered to be standard for each of the world's major English-speaking regions. The concentric circle model that has undoubtedly had the greatest impact on scholarly and popular belief is Braj Kachru's (1988) through David Crystal's (2003) work. Kachru creates three main spaces for English: the inner circle, the outer circle and the expanding circle. The inner circle, for "native language" varieties, contains five Englishes that correspond to "countries" and that are those most often identified *as* varieties of English by non-linguists: Australia, Canada, New Zealand, United Kingdom and the United States of America. In the outer circle, for Englishes spoken as a second language, he places those of Ghana, India, Kenya, Malaysia, Philippines and Singapore, among others. Lastly, the expanding circle is for Englishes spoken as a foreign language and includes varieties of English spoken in Egypt, Indonesia, Israel and Korea. This classification of the varieties of English, clearly, responds not to linguistic, but to social or sociopolitical considerations and the "concentric circle" arrangement appears to correspond more or less with popular or general perception of varieties of English.

The concentric model does have its parallel in a model devised for the Spanish-speaking world, however. A three-circle model was proposed in 1998 by Moreno-Fernández and Otero. However, unlike the world-Englishes model, which classified national varieties of English and did so on the basis of whether English is the first, a second or a foreign language, Moreno-Fernández and Otero's model classified Spanish speakers on the basis of language proficiency (Moreno-Fernández and Otero 2008). The model, depicted in the figure, could nonetheless be applied to any international language.

In Figure 11.2, each circle represents the extent to which the Spanish language is more or less fundamental to the communicative repertoire of a speaker or a group of speakers. The smallest, or nuclear, circle includes those speakers that constitute the Native Skills Cluster (NSC); the medium-sized, or extended, circle corresponds to the Limited Skills Cluster (LSC). The largest, or peripheral, circle corresponds to the Foreign Language Learners Cluster (FLLC), those who acquire Spanish as a foreign language. From this model, the community or group of potential users (GPU) would essentially include the members of the NSC, optionally joined by the members of the LSC and FLLC, as represented in the following equation: GPU = NSC + (LSC + FLLC). In the case of Spanish, the nuclear and extended circles (NSC+LSC) would include speakers from over 40 countries. The peripheral circle, that of the learners, includes international students of Spanish. In the case of English, the nuclear and extended circles (NSC+LSC) include speakers from approximately one hundred countries. The peripheral circle corresponds to almost the entire rest of the world.

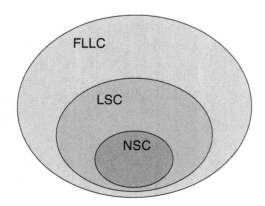

FIGURE 11.2 Levels for a Typology of Speakers of an International Language. NSC: Native Skills Cluster; LSC: Limited Skills Cluster; FLLC: Foreign Language Learners Cluster

Debate: Exemplar Features or Prototypes in Dialectal Perception?

The perception of linguistic variation—and let us not forget that not all variation is consciously perceived—responds to a process of categorization based on discriminatory learning. In turn, categorization is a basic process that involves the sequencing and simplification of reality while maintaining a sufficient degree of adaptation to it (Morales 2007). The way in which this process takes place in the individual, particularly with respect to how the individual perceives and categorizes linguistic varieties, has been explained from various theoretical positions, including *feature theory*, *exemplar theory* and *prototype theory*. A current issue of theoretical debate concerns which of these wields the most explanatory power.

Feature theory posits that the variety of speech that one hears is ascribed to a given geolectal variety given the presence or absence of a particular feature (phonetic, lexical, grammatical, phraseological). The problem with a categorization based on Feature Theory is that not all features are attributable to a single category. In other words, not all linguistic features are unique and exclusive to one linguistic variety. When acting in accord with the belief of exclusivity, we often obtain an incomplete perception of reality, which results in inaccurate categorizations.

Exemplar theory holds that the categorization of objects depends on their association with an exemplar, or a concrete case. Similarity with an exemplar results in classifying the focal object into the same category to which the exemplar belongs. More specifically, the theory posits a principle of generalization whereby we identify as belonging to the same category any case that matches our memory of a first exemplar. Exemplars might take shape out of specific experiences or with respect to speakers thought to be typical or representative of a language variety. One drawback of a theory like this is that all speakers from a given geographical origin may be attributed the characteristics of the remembered exemplar speaker.

Finally, *prototype theory* proposes categorizing linguistic reality according to dialectal prototypes. The categorization process would consist of comparing potential members of a category with the category's prototype in order to verify their degree of association with it (Pearce 1998; Morales and Huici 1999). Prototypes, themselves, may exist at different levels of generality or abstractness. A difficulty with this proposal, then, is the characteristics of a prototype, in being potentially very abstract, may not correspond to any concrete reality and may, for the same reason, also not be easy to identify.

In principle, there may be no extant need to dismiss any of the three theories outlined above. Although all three present some kind of limitation, each also possesses some degree of explanatory power. That is, each makes significant strides toward elucidating the processes associated with the cognitive imperative to categorize and classify, a need that also extends to language (Schütz 1964). Furthermore, the concepts of "feature," "exemplar" and "prototype" are not theoretically mutually exclusive, nor incompatible, when it comes to characterizing the dynamics of dialectal variation. In terms of classifying language varieties, at least, evidence has shown that all three concepts can go some way toward explaining how, and on what basis, geolinguistic and socio-geolinguistic varieties tend to be classified as they are.

Conclusion

Linguistic attitudes are manifestations of psychosocial attitudes. They are embedded in the speakers' cognitive world. They are a set of beliefs shared in common with other members of a respective social group. Linguistic attitudes are manifested toward both our own linguistic varieties and habits as well as toward those of others. However, speakers usually manifest more favorable attitudes toward their own variety, especially if it enjoys a high degree of standardization. It so happens, however, that people do not always perceive their own language variety favorably; they may, in fact, have a negative attitude towards their own language. This is usually the case when the speaker's language variety is not considered prestigious because it does not facilitate upward social or economic mobility or when it restricts access to places or social circles other than our own, as is often the case for minority languages.

The idea that some language varieties are "preferable" to others is deeply rooted. From a cognitive perspective, we can say that there are varieties considered more nuclear and others considered more peripheral with respect to a given prototype. In the Hispanic and Anglo-Saxon worlds, the Castilian and British varieties, respectively, are generally considered nuclear, regardless of their geographical position with respect to other varieties and despite some of their features being quite marked. The perception of centrality (or peripherality, for that matter) is often linked to cultural, political and economic prestige of the speakers of the language, which in turn leads to the classification of their varieties as more or less prestigious. In the Spanish-speaking world, among the prestigious varieties we find the Peninsular, Colombian and Mexican Spanishes. In the English-speaking world, the British, the Midwestern United States and the Australian varieties are among the most prestigious.

Finally, we highlight the great strides that perceptual dialectology studies have taken. This way of doing dialectology is interested in the perceptions of the speakers who are not linguists. These perceptions include both those operating consciously, reflecting a popular linguistics, and those which operate unconsciously, reflecting linguistic attitudes. That is, perceptual dialectology is concerned with the cognitive processes that govern what people say, speakers' unconscious reactions, the conscious beliefs that speakers within a community hold. Understanding these perceptual cognitive processes gives us valuable information about the spatial and social dynamics of language, as well as about the status of processes of language variation and change.

References

Bauer, Laurie, 2002. *An Introduction to International Varieties of English*. Edinburgh: Edinburgh University Press.

Crystal, David, 2003. *English as a Global Language*. 2nd ed. Cambridge: Cambridge University Press.

Cuenca, Maria Josep and Joseph Hilferty, 1999. *Introducción a la lingüística cognitiva*. Barcelona, Ariel.

Fernández Marrero, Juan Jorge, 1999. "Actividad normativa y conciencia lingüística. Técnicas de control de las evaluaciones populares." In *Identidad cultural y lingüística en Colombia, Venezuela y en el Caribe hispánico*, M. Perl and K. Pörtl, 175–185. Tübingen: Max Niemeyer Verlag.

Ghomeshi, Jila, 2010. *Grammar Matters. The Social Significance of How We Use Language*. Winnipeg: Arbeiter Ring.

Görlach, Manfred, 1990. *Studies in the History of the English Language*. Heidelberg: Winter.

Kachru, B., 1988. "The sacred cows of English." *English Today*, 16: 3–8.

Kristiansen, Gitte, 2001. "Social and linguistic stereotyping: A cognitive approach to accents." *Estudios Ingleses de la Universidad Complutense*, 9: 129–145.

Labov, William, 1966. *The Social Stratification of English in New York City*. Washington, DC: Center for Applied Linguistics.

López García, Ángel, 1998. "Los conceptos de lengua y dialecto a la luz de la teoría de prototipos." *La Torre, año III, núm*, 7–8: 7–29.

McArthur, Tom, 1998. *The English Languages*. Cambridge: Cambridge University Press.

Milroy, James and Lesley Milroy, 1985. *Authority in Language: Investigating Language Prescription and Standardisation*. London: Routledge & Kegan Paul.

Montes Giraldo, José Joaquín, 1995. *Dialectología general e hispanoamericana. Orientación teórica, metodológica y bibliográfica*. Santafé de Bogotá: Instituto Caro y Cuervo.

Morales Domínguez, José F., (coord.). 2007. *Psicología social*. 3rd ed. Madrid: McGraw-Hill-Interamericana.

Morales J. Francisco and Carmen Huici, 1999. *Psicología social*. Madrid: McGraw-Hill.

Morán, Emilio, 1993. *La ecología humana de los pueblos de la Amazonia*. México: Fondo de Cultura Económica.

Moreno-Fernández, Francisco, 2000. *Qué español enseñar*. Madrid: Arco/Libros.

Moreno-Fernández, Francisco and Jaime Otero, 1998. "Demografía de la lengua española." *Anuario del Instituto Cervantes. El español en el mundo 1998*, 59–86. Madrid: Arco/Libros.

Moreno-Fernández, Francisco and Jaime Otero, 2008. "The status and future of Spanish among the main international languages: Quantitative Dimensions." *International Multilingual Research Journal*, 2 (1–2): 67–83.

Pearce, John M., 1998. *Aprendizaje y cognición*. Barcelona: Ariel.

Preston, Dennis, 2004. "Language with an attitude." In *The Handbook of Language Variation and Change*, Eds., J.K. Chambers, P. Trudgill and N. Schilling-Estes, 40–66. Oxford: Blackwell.

Sanz, Gema, 2008. *Actitudes lingüísticas de los inmigrantes rumanos en Alcalá de Henares*. Alcalá de Henares: Universidad de Alcalá.

Schneider, Edward W., 2007. *Postcolonial English. Varieties around the World*. Cambridge: Cambridge University Press.

Schütz, Alfred, 1964. *Collected Papers II: Studies in Social Theory*. The Hague: Martinus Nijhoff.

Trudgill, Peter, 1972. "Sex, covert prestige and linguistic change in the urban British English of Norwich." *Language in Society*, 1: 179–195.
Van Dijk, Teun A., 1999. *Ideología. Una aproximació multidisciplinar*. Barcelona: Gedisa.

12
THE PERCEPTION OF LINGUISTIC CONTACT

The integration of studies of "languages in contact" into the field of sociolinguistics has been gradual. The seminal sociolinguistic literature of the 1960s and 1970s (Bright 1966; Lieberson 1967; Giglioli 1972) did not include chapters or monographic studies on languages in contact. Some attention was paid to the situation of certain bilingual communities, but always from a sociological perspective. Scholarly attention to language contact started to become more systematic in the specialty manuals of the mid-1970s. Trudgill (1974) deals with Pidgins and Creoles in a chapter called "Language and Geography." Hudson (1980) includes pidgins and creoles among language varieties, and Wardhaugh (1986) addresses code mixing and language alternation. Currently, all of the most important manuals of this specialty area give due attention to the principal dimensions of linguistic contact, regardless of whether the perspective taken is more introductory (Coulmas 1997; Meyerhoff 2006), more communicative (Coulmas 2005) or more variationist (Chambers, Trudgill and Schilling-Estes 2002; Milroy and Gordon 2003; Bayley, Cameron and Lucas 2013). In addition, there is a large and ever growing literature on bilingualism and language contact (Hickey 2013). Sociolinguistic literature published in Spanish or about the Hispanic world has given special attention to language contact, from the earliest handbooks (López Morales 1989; Silva-Corvalán 1989), to more recent ones (Almeida 1999; Blas Arroyo 2005; Moreno-Fernández 2009a; Serrano 2011; Díaz-Campos 2011, 2014; Silva-Corvalán and Enrique-Arias 2016). The incorporation of a cognitive approach into the field of sociolinguistics provides yet one more reason to consider the study of languages in contact a priority.

Language contact studies came of age with the work of Hugo Schuchardt (1909a, 1909b), a versatile linguist who, being one of the pioneers of sociolinguistics, often dealt with social matters in his treatment of language. Later, starting in the 1960s and especially after the publication in 1953 of Uriel Weinreich's *Languages in Contact*, studies on language contact became more elaborated and complex. In all, it is understandable that the study of languages in contact developed as it did. First of all, language contact requires human contact and this often implicates the influence of social, psychosocial and cognitive factors. Second, theories of language variation and change, typically within the field of sociolinguistics, overlap with theories of language contact, typical within the field of creolist studies, because contact is one of the main sources of change. Moreover, a sociolinguistic interest in bilingual communities leads naturally to the treatment of issues relating to language contact and its various consequences. From this perspective, sociocognitive factors are important in all phases of contact, from initial moments of speaker-to-speaker interaction to the complete formation of bilingual speakers and, subsequently, communities.

A. On Language Contact from a Cognitive Perspective

Proposition 12.1

Language contact situations constitute a uniquely stimulating space for sociolinguistic perception.

Proposition 12.2

Situations of language contact between groups often result from geographical proximity, ethnic contact or social coexistence; they are often a result of population shifts.

Proposition 12.3

Linguistic perception is conditioned by the type of linguistic varieties to which the individual has been exposed, as well as by his worldview and the perceptual system of his community of origin.

Proposition 12.4

A language variety's level of sociolinguistic perception is inversely proportional to the stability of the communicative environment, its level of internal diversity and the amount of linguistic innovations produced.

Proposition 12.5

The size of a speech community directly impacts the chances of survival of its linguistic variety or varieties.

Proposition 12.6

In language contact situations, the greater vitality of a language with respect to another favors its perception by a greater quantity of people and a more positive evaluation of it.

Proposition 12.7

In language contact situations, a language's standardization favors its perception by a greater quantity of people and a more positive evaluation of it.

Proposition 12.8

In language contact situations, a language's longer history over that of another language favors its perception by a greater quantity of people and a more positive evaluation of it.

Proposition 12.9

In language contact situations, the language with greater perceived autonomy receives a more positive evaluation.

Scholium 12-A

A cognitive sociolinguistics treating language contact should devote ample attention to perception processes, the preferential objects of such perceptions and in how languages in contact utilize accommodation strategies. Perception processes affect contact between different worldviews, on one hand, and the mechanism employed to adapt and integrate those worldviews, on the other. From among the most important objects of perception in language contact situations, then, will those varieties considered most legitimate, or those linguistic habits considered as "good" or "adequate," emerge. Let us not forget, as Bourdieu (1977) indicates, that the value of a language—or its varieties—is determined by the status of those who use it in the social market. Linguistic differences among speakers are evaluated with respect to the role that the legitimate language has in the socioeconomic life of the speaker. This factor takes on an enormous amount of importance in multilingual communities, in intercultural settings and in language contact situations (Nishida 1999). In such situations, the dominant ideology, at work in the idea of the *langue légitime*, provokes in speakers a process of language "externalization," a process where the speaker begins to distance himself from the prestige model, with consequences of all kinds, including ethical and aesthetic.

Language contact situations constitute a uniquely stimulating space to examine sociolinguistic perception. We speak of language contact when two (or more) linguistic varieties, either of the same language or of different languages, coexist, albeit always recognizing that the boundaries between varieties may not be obvious or quantifiable. The concept is a broad one; it denotes a diversity of situations including geographic, ethnic or social boundaries, and, more generally, many situations stemming from population movements (Moreno-Fernández 2004).

In situations of language contact, the level of sociolinguistic perception is inversely proportional to the stability of the communicative environment, to the extent of linguistic diversity present within the community and to the strength of social innovations. In a stable sociolinguistic environment within a stable speech community, after the language acquisition process has been completed, and the language has come to serve basic communication needs within the society, functional performance of perception processes, now not strictly required for effective daily communication, decreases. This is the way, for example, that spontaneous and family interactions, which are built through routine mechanisms, occur. That is, family interactions often operate from the automation of routine and do not involve special attention to the interlocutor or to the immediate context. In fact, the reader may have noticed this to be the case when such routines break down, as happens when an individual believes he had heard what routine indicates should be heard, even though something different has in fact been said. Take the following example, where A proceeds to answer a question that has not actually been asked:

A: Good afternoon. <noise = "cough">
B: What a cough!
A: Mostly uneventful.
B: No. I said "what a cough."

For the most ritualized messages, attention to its denotative content is minimized. Consequently, certain differences or nuances in the routine, easily detected by a listener unfamiliar with it, may go unnoticed. There are, however, situations in which the perceptual mechanism is reactivated and its cognitive functioning resumes. In general, these are situations in which communication routines are disrupted and, therefore, require more attention. One such situation is when the speaker is in the midst of a learning process. A common context in which this occurs, then, is in formal schooling as would be provided by the educational system. But this is not the only way. Other ways include professional training activities—with particular attention to those involving communication skills—or through tourism, travel or even the media, where one is likely to discover new realities. In effect, contexts in which communication routines are affected or interrupted, usually because they disrupt social and communicative stability, a speaker's sociolinguistic perception is stimulated.

In language contact situations, clashes or contrasts occur at different levels, such as that of identity or that of language itself. Particularly fascinating is a conflict of worldviews, which may be greater or lesser according to the linguistic and cultural distance between the varieties involved. In order to compare segments of a single community (e.g., in situations of bilingualism)—segments in which different linguistic structures or different patterns of communicative behavior can emerge (Bright 1966: 186)—Whorf's concept of linguistic relativity, used to examine differences among communities (Hopi, Navajo, English-speaking), could usefully serve. Dell Hymes (1966), for example, used the concept of "linguistic relativity" to examine differences regarding the "use" of language. In a complex community, a contrast between components of the language may materialize with speakers perceiving as more important either: (1) the language, (2) the culture, (3) both, (4) neither. Whether the priority component is the language or the culture, attitudes toward linguistic habits may reflect the existence of categories such as "separatism/unification," "loyalty/disloyalty," "overt prestige/covert prestige" and "norm/usage."

As applied to the field of language contact, including teaching and translation, the theory of linguistic relativity could lead to the conclusion that if our mother language always imposes a certain worldview, it is virtually impossible to fully and accurately learn other languages. In this sense, language and worldview theories make it quite difficult to explain at an abstract level how different languages come to coexist in the first place. However, it is possible to avoid these theoretical somersaults. In fact, it is preferable to do so since the existence of many "natural" bilingual speakers (Badia 1969), and the fact that it is possible to successfully achieve interlinguistic communicative exchanges, show that there is no fundamental contradiction in the coexistence of a multitude of human language varieties. One possible way to avoid the impasse would be to relativize the concept of what is transferrable and non-transferrable.

On a different level, the identification of a language with the territory or dominion of a single nation or state has become commonplace. Similarly common is the perception that the best speakers of a language are located in a particular region or territory, especially its most prestigious geographical centers. The individuals of those locations would constitute the core of that geolinguistic reality. Everything that is not clearly identified with that core would fall into the "periphery." Those speakers at the center of a geo-sociolinguistic system rarely experience identity doubts; those located somewhere in the periphery usually do to a greater extent. When we speak of geo-sociolinguistic systems, we refer to situations where a language variety is identified with a well-delimited territory and with well-structured social groups. Examples of this would include the use of the Spanish language in the peninsular territories of Castile, in Spain, or that of the English language on the east coast of the United States.

Despite the fact that the idea that "language = geographic domain" is deeply rooted, the equation is hopelessly incomplete. Just as the use of a language variety can be associated with a territory, it can also be associated with other notions, such as those of "social group" or "ethnicity." In fact, in the same way that ethnolinguists have been concerned with the characterization of human groups of very diverse ethnic origins, traditional urban sociolinguistics has devoted a great deal of effort to the discovery of linguistic features that co-vary with social factors in large speech communities. For instance, language has been shown to be tightly linked to ethnicity in indigenous communities in Africa or Latin America (Zimmermann 2011). At other times, language usages are tightly bound to the practice of a religion, as occurs in Asia, especially with the use of Arabic. In such cases there also often exists a language of more general usage, which articulates the dynamics of these groups within the state where they are located—let us call it a superstructural variety—creating a situation of diglossia. This happens, for example, with English and Arabic in the Philippines; English, Hindi and Arabic in India; French and indigenous languages in Senegal or with Spanish and the languages of certain indigenous groups in Mexico.

If we accept that intimate connections exist between (a) language and territory; (b) language and social group and; (c) language and ethnicity, then we may also come to appreciate that, for each of these connections, both a center and a periphery could be identified. Every area, every group, every ethnicity has an epicenter with boundaries that demarcate its outer limits and, thus, the difference between it and the periphery, where *Other* areas, *Other* social groups and *Other* ethnic groups are found. It is in these peripheral areas where borderline linguistic habits emerge, often intermixing with those of neighboring groups and communities. This phenomena falls under the generic label of "code mixing" and is often accompanied, especially among border speakers, by feelings of low self-esteem, social disintegration fears or even the desire to self-marginalization. In border areas, identity is often constructed as a real problem within the periphery; this "problem" is often felt to be exacerbated by a tangible disregard transmitted from outside the periphery.

Finally, we must remember that the concept of "linguistic variety" includes languages, dialects, sociolects, registers, styles and other types of specific varieties. In 1962, William Stewart classified these varieties according to four attributes: *standardization, autonomy, historicity* and *vitality*. As is known, *standardization* involves the codification and acceptance within a speech community of a set of rules defining correct usage (as would be laid out in an orthography, grammar and dictionary). *Autonomy* is the perception that a linguistic system is unique and independent, although the extent to which this is so may vary. *Historicity* is an attribute given to linguistic systems felt to have resulted from "regular" development over time. Historicity is also usually linked to the existence of a national or ethnic tradition that claims the linguistic system as its own. *Vitality* refers to the extent to which a linguistic system is used by a community of native speakers: the larger the community, the greater the vitality. In fact, the chance that a variety survives in the long run varies directly with the size of the community. Less vitality, and thus lesser likelihood of survival, are associated with those varieties that, from an ecological perspective, Hawley (1986) called "small languages." Applying

TABLE 12.1 Classification of Linguistic Varieties According to Stewart's (1962) Attributes

Attributes	Type	(Examples)
1 2 3 4		
+ + + +	Standard language	(Spanish, English)
+ + + −	Classical language	(Latin, Sanskrit)
+ + − −	Artificial language	(Esperanto, *Volapük*)
− + + +	Vernacular	(Leko-Bolivia, Dahalo-Kenya)
− − + +	Dialect	(Cuban Spanish/Castilian, Norman, Low German)
− − − +	Creole Language	(Apricot, Haitian Creole, Chinook)
− − − −	Pidgin	(Fula pidgin, pidgin Sango)

Note: 1 = standardization, 2 = autonomy, 3= historicity, 4 = vitality.

Source: W. Stewart (1962)

Stewart's attributes in binary fashion, as either "present" or "absent," we could uniquely characterize several types of language varieties (Table 12.1).

Like Stewart, the German researcher Heinz Kloss was also concerned with the social presence of linguistic varieties. In 1967, Kloss introduced to the international literature a number of concepts that have demonstrated substantial durability over time and significant usefulness for our understanding of the social dimension of language, including the consequences of contact in multilingual speech communities. In particular, the concepts have helped us gain greater clarity about how one variety may diversify into many, the relationships these varieties have with one another and how individuals of the societies in which they are used will respond to them. These concepts were those of *Abstand* ("distant") languages, *Ausbau* ("developing") languages and *Dach* ("umbrella") languages (Kloss 1967). These concepts distinguish languages and dialects according to two criteria: the social functions carried out by a linguistic variety and its objective structural properties. *Abstand* languages are linguistically distant with respect to one another; they are not related and never get confused in the communities where they coexist, as in the cases of: Spanish with respect to Basque, Hungarian with respect to German or Guaraní with respect to Portuguese. The *Ausbau* languages are those that, unlike linguistically related varieties or varieties of similar origin, have developed prestige and social status—standardization, education, public use. This is the case for Spanish, for example, as opposed to the local dialects of the Pyrenees, despite the fact that all of them derive from Latin (Bossong 2008). Finally, the *Dach* languages are those whose standardization serves as a point of references for other related varieties. This is the case of *Euskera batua* for all the Basque varieties or that of Modern Arabic with respect to all the Arabic varieties.

By interweaving both Kloss's and Stewart's theoretical concepts, we could say that the languages that are better evaluated and that enjoy greater overt prestige are the *Ausbau* and *Dach* languages: those found in the center of a geo-sociolinguistic system, which enjoy an appreciable amount of autonomy, historicity and standardization and have a exceptional amount of vitality. The linguistic varieties that are on the periphery of a geo-sociolinguistic system manifest these attributes to a lesser degree, if at all, and do not usually enjoy more prestige than that which is covertly attributed to them for certain contexts or among certain speaker groups.

B. On the Consequences of Language Contact

Proposition 12.10

Language contact situations involve the operation of selection processes, which in turn affect all levels of the language varieties involved and their social use.

Proposition 12.11

Language contact situations lead to accommodation processes, which become manifest in the form of convergences and divergences.

Proposition 12.12

Contact situations produce linguistic consequences that are perceived differently by the communities and the speakers involved.

Proposition 12.13

Multilingual situations drive the emergence of sociocultural values, attitudes and beliefs relative to linguistic habits, which involve categories such as loyalty, legitimacy and prestige.

Proposition 12.14

In contact situations, systems perceived as new are conditioned by previously acquired linguistic systems

Proposition 12.15

The learning process and the social use of languages or varieties in a given community determine the linguistic consequences of contact.

Proposition 12.16

As a result of conceptual vagueness and ambiguity arising in language contact situations, speakers will assign new semantic values to words and expressions.

Scholium 12-B

The linguistic consequences of contact include phenomena such as interference, accent and language alternation (Moreno-Fernández 2015). However, in situations of coexistence, these consequences also depend on the type of relationship that becomes established among speakers, such as whether they are considered individually, as groups or as a community. In such situations, sociolinguistic consciousness directly affects language attitudes, since knowledge of the facts of language is essential for making judgments about those facts, and attitudes will influence communicative accommodation. In any case, the effects are detected in both the process(es) of acquisition of the language(s) in contact as well as in the social use of coexisting linguistic varieties. In this regard, it is essential to make a clear distinction between phenomena arising from contact where individuals speak varieties of the same language, varieties of different languages that are from the same language family, or varieties of different language that are from distinct language families. Making this distinction is especially important in situations where a particular variety dominates, that is where one variety is considered the majority or more general language, usually due to extralinguistic reasons.

In his study of the presence of Ecuadorians in Madrid (Spain), Maria Sancho (2014) observed a linguistic accommodation process at the lexical, pragmatic, phonetic and grammatical levels (in that order of intensity from most to least) (Figure 12.1). At the lexical level, adaptation or convergence seems to occur more quickly and more consistently, probably because the use of certain lexical forms may pose the most immediate obstacles to understanding. This often occurs because, even for speakers of varieties of the same language for whom the meaning of certain words may appear to be similar, meanings often do not coincide or because words with shared etymons may have received new semantic values. That is, sometimes, one can have the feeling that there is mutual semantic understanding when there really is not. In fact, even though speakers of varieties in contact may share the same communicative context, they frequently face difficulties transmitting the most basic information. This results in misunderstandings, which are not at all marginal phenomena in linguistic communication and which are direct evidence of vagueness and lexical ambiguity.

As opposed to what happens in the lexicon, differences at the pragmatic (politeness) level go much further in explaining divergence in linguistic usages. This is so because, in general, expressions related to social respect and politeness are immediate reflections of differences in cultural and worldview that bring to

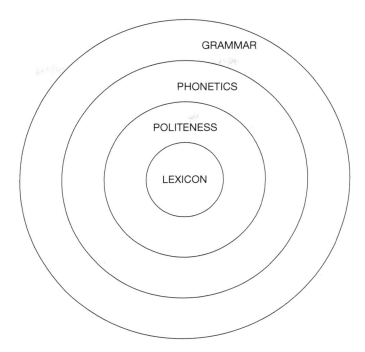

FIGURE 12.1 Intensity of Accommodation on Various Linguistic Levels, from Most (Center Circle) to Least (Outer Circles) in a Situation of Language Contact Resulting from Immigration

Source: Sancho (2014)

the fore concrete reasons why sociolinguistic convergence may be difficult. Accommodation occurs more slowly at the phonetic and grammatical levels.

When varieties of the same language are in contact, there are convergences and divergences. Let us recall that convergence is the process of approximation or mutual influence between two linguistic varieties. This approximation occurs with varying degrees of intensity and can occur at any level of language. Among convergence phenomena would be the transfer of linguistic elements or the alignment of linguistic categories on the phonic, grammatical, lexical or pragmatic level. With regard to the current situation of the languages of Europe, Auer and Hiskens (1996) have highlighted that social and cultural changes quickly affect the nature and social standing of traditional dialects. The minority European languages, for example, are being affected by processes, such as large-scale emigration, that have been leading to convergences both between the dialects of several large immigrant groups and between these immigrant groups and the native local geolects. These convergences can lead to one of two situations with respect to the social standing of the minority variety:

1. Minority variety—Majority prestige variety. In this situation, the minority geolect takes on some of the social prestige of the majority prestige variety, which in turn leads to more convergence and linguistic leveling. On the other hand, the prestigious variety can also be influenced by the new minority geolect.
2. Minority variety—Local variety. In this situation, one geolect exercises greater influence than others, especially in those cases where there is an external prestige variety. This would be the case, for instance, for Ecuadorian immigrant communities in Spain and for communities whose local dominant geolect is other than Castilian (e.g., Andalusia). Similarly, this would be the case for Indian or Philippine inmigrants in London or New York. In these cases, the influence of a local variety on a minority variety may lead to very different outcomes; immigrants may resist local influence from the local host variety(ies) and maintain the ancestral host language. Or, immigrants may accommodate or acquiesce toward the local host variety, among other outcomes. Here, as above, the local variety can also be influenced by the guest geolect.

Speakers of different languages that come to coexist can start off in one of two ways. Incoming speakers (e.g., immigrants) have prior knowledge of the host language (at any level) or they have no knowledge of it (Caravedo 2009; Moreno-Fernández 2009b). If they have prior knowledge of the host language, it may happen that their knowledge is of a different dialect. In this case, differences between the known variety and the host variety can as easily hinder mutual understanding as if incoming speakers had no knowledge. If incoming speakers in fact have no knowledge of the host variety, and the host variety is the dominant or prestigious language, incoming speakers will begin to learn it, evidencing in the process of language acquisition the usual attendant phenomena subsumed by the notions of "transfer" and "interference."

C. On the Perception of Languages in Migratory Environments

Proposition 12.17

In migration contexts, language differences between speakers of different origins are evaluated according to the extent to which the speakers possess legitimacy within the socioeconomic life of the community.

Proposition 12.18

In migration contexts, the linguistic and social consequences of language contact depend on the degree of affinity between the languages and on the complexity of the linguistic situation.

Proposition 12.18.1

Popular perception is acutely attuned to the accent of speakers from other communities and to the fluency of the new speakers' speech.

Proposition 12.18.2

Migratory contexts favor the immigrants' conscious lexical convergence toward the lexicon of the host variety.

Proposition 12.18.3

Migratory contexts favor conscious divergence between politeness strategies between the immigrant population and the host community.

Proposition 12.18.4

Migratory contexts favor the unconscious convergence of the immigrants' phonetics and grammar toward the phonetics and grammar of the host variety.

Scholium 12-C

Migratory environments, as anticipated, are particularly complex contexts for the study of language contact and its sociocognitive implications. In these environments, the degree of affinity of the languages in contact and the complexity of their linguistic coexistence are critical factors (Blommaert 2013). To analyze these issues, it is necessary to establish a scale of linguistic complexity of the host region (as in Table 12.2), whose components could combine with those of a linguistic affinity scale, leading to different types of intersections, whose theoretical value could be assessed in studies of sociolinguistic integration (Chambers 2003). Such studies would start with the hypothesis that integration is less difficult the more similar the languages in contact are and the less complex the host community is.

From a cognitive perspective, it is important to point out that in contexts of migration, contact with the host society activates perception processes. The new system will be perceived through the prism of the previously acquired system, as well as through the speakers' beliefs and attitudes, which can be vastly different

TABLE 12.2 Scale Linguistic Complexity of the Host Community

1. Monolingual community with only one variety – 2. Monolingual community with different varieties – 3. Bilingual community whose second language has little social relevance – 4. Bilingual community with a socially relevant second language

Source: Moreno-Fernández (2009b)

for immigrants as compared with members of the host community. Let us remember that perception is always selective and subjective, and that in the case of immigrants, meta-perception and self-perception also develop. The degree of subjectivity implicit in the perceptions is related to the type of language variety to which the individuals have been exposed, as well as to the perception system transmitted by their elders. By way of example, the use of *usted* 'you [singular]' may be perceived as a sign of formality in some Spanish-speaking contexts and as a sign of closeness in others. Tanja Zimmermann (2011: 382) indicates that both native speaker errors and errors due to contact have either greater or lesser sociolinguistic importance based on the degree to which the attitude they reflect is accepted by members of a community or social group.

In the first migratory phase, the individual begins a very sensitive social perception process in which he associates the way of speaking found in his first contact group with all of the host society. During this phase, contacts with his own networks of origin provide feedback about his beliefs. As Rocío Caravedo (2009, 2010) explains, the first dichotomy immigrants perceive in the host community's sociolinguistic usage is not actually that of "formality/informality," which unproblematically occurs in the acquisition of our native language, but rather that of "majority/minority" and "local/foreign." Nonetheless, they often perceive these "majority/minority" and "local/foreign" dichotomies as distinctions in formality and informality. Hence immigrants practice a particular interpretation of what is formal and what is informal in the host community. Furthermore, since perception is subjective, immigrants, as speakers of a different variety, may not perceive as different elements that objectively are different. When contact results in a speech variety containing some degree of mixing, the variety developed (derived) is usually unstable and perceived with insecurity and distrust by its own users. It seems to often be the case that "hybridization" is associated with negative values and opposes concepts such as "purity," "homogeneity" and "authenticity" (Kabatek 2011).

Finally, varieties that emerge due to mass migrations (resulting in mixes and transfers, among other phenomena) should be analyzed within their own contexts, that is, specific linguistic markets. In these contexts, popular perception is very sensitive to having or not having an "accent," as well as to speech fluency in the new speakers. For minority varieties, occupying a lower social stratus can lead to gradual deterioration and attrition or create radical affective and attitudinal reactions in its speakers (Pavlinić 2001).

Debate: Languages and Mixed Varieties

Given the low status often attributed to peripheral and mixed varieties, features or languages, it may be a question as to whether contact varieties should be considered languages like any other. This, in turn, sheds doubt on whether speakers of such contact varieties could, therefore, be considered full-fledged community members in a given linguistic universe. The issue of whether bilingual mixed language varieties can be considered languages in their own right, it must be acknowledged, is not always debated on purely linguistic grounds. As regards Spanish, the mixed varieties of Spain, America and Asia may come to mind. Despite the several unique peculiarities that develop in these varieties, it is not only possible, but seemingly eminently appropriate, to group them as part of the Hispanic world, since, as has been shown numerous times in the research, these varieties maintain an overwhelming degree of linguistic family resemblance among themselves.

Le Page and Tabouret-Keller proposed in 1985 a "projection model" that defines individual linguistic behavior as a series of actions by which people reveal both their personal identity and their search for a position within a social group. According to this model, speech acts are acts of image projection. That is, speakers project their inner world through language or, in the case of multilingual contexts, through the choice of a language. By means of their linguistic usages, speakers invite their interlocutors to share in their projection of the world and their attitudes towards it. At the same time, speakers are willing to modify their own projections of the world due to the influence of the people with whom they communicate. Le Page and Tabouret-Keller's model includes a general hypothesis that is formulated as follows. Individuals are able to create their own linguistic behavior patterns in order to accommodate to the members of the group or groups they wish to be identified with at each moment. This is how contact and mixed varieties acquire their personality, as adaptations to the linguistic varieties around them. However, compliance with this general hypothesis is determined by four conditions:

a. the existence of a group identifiable as such;
b. that speakers have the ability to modify their own behavior;
c. that access to a group is possible and permits analysis of its behavioral patterns; and
d. the existence of motivation to join a group.

As regards the situation of speakers of Hispanic and Anglo-Saxon contact varieties (pidgins and creoles), we take the fulfillment of the first two conditions as unproblematic. First, with respect to (a), a group is identifiable as a group when it shows particular recognizable features. Second, with respect to (b), speakers of mixed varieties, as most other speakers, have the individual capacity to regulate and modify their behaviors or, at least, their attitudes. Conditions (c) and (d), however, may be more difficult to meet since they are dependent on macrosocial factors that may be out of the control of the individual speaker. The Spanish- and English-speaking worlds would have to be accessible, both on the global scale, and within each one of their respective communities, to the individual members of other groups, especially those considered to be part of the periphery. Not only that, but recognition of linguistic elements shared by both varieties and facilitation of mutual identification among members of the groups must be encouraged. Only in that way, can a sense of community that would result in the enrichment of one's identity be born, develop or strengthen.

In our view, it is important that speakers of mixed varieties feel they are members of a larger linguistic community regardless how particular, special or peripheral their variety may be. At the same time, it is vital that those occupying central areas of the system be aware that the existence of a "center" depends crucially the presence of a "periphery" and that, by disregarding or ignoring the peripheral, they may inadvertently be turning their back on one of the main sources from which innovation, originality and, ultimately, sociolinguistic development of language springs. The evolution of any language is determined as much by its own internal dynamics as by the influence of external agents, most notably the linguistic uses of neighbors and immigrant populations. Under these circumstances the concept of "translanguaging" emerges as a way to explain why language borders are fuzzy (García & Wei 2014). But this concept leads us to another story.

Conclusion

Language contact studies have a strong connection with the ethnography of communication founded by Dell Hymes and John Gumperz (Gumperz and Hymes 1964, 1972). The ethnography of communication provides an easy connection between cognitive sociolinguistics and language contact because, among other reasons, worldview is an issue that falls squarely among the principle concerns of both ethno-linguistics and cognitivism (Bartmiński 2010).

The situations that lead to language contact are varied, but generally come about when members of different groups, that use different languages or language varieties, come to occupy the same geographic space, most commonly as a result of either the occupation of neighboring domains or population displacements from one territory to another. In any case, language contact situations produce similar cognitive and social phenomena that deserve attention. Moreover, many of these situations prompt gradual accommodations, linguistic intersections and language mixtures that, from the perspective of *prototype theory*, often result in varieties considered to be "peripheral." In these varieties, the identification of an individual as a good or bad speaker of a language is based on his or her proximity or similarity with the prototype of the central or core variety.

Language contact situations are particularly stimulating for the speakers involved and singularly affect their cognitive and perceptual resources. The cognitive analysis of language contact contributes to the discovery of perceptions arising from them as well as of the preferred objects of such perceptions. At the same time, language contact situations help to understand the mechanisms of adaptation and integration that operate in environments of linguistic and cultural contact. Outstanding among the emergent objects of perception in contact situations is the sociological distribution of possible types of coexisting language varieties and their degree of legitimacy in the dynamics of the social market.

References

Almeida, Manuel, 1999. *Sociolingüística*. La Laguna: Universidad de La Laguna.
Auer, Peter and Frans Hiskens, 1996. "The convergence and divergence of dialects in a changing Europe." *The Journal of the ESF*, 34: 30–31.
Badia i Margarit, Antoni M., 1969. *La llengua dels barcelonins. Resultats d'una enquesta sociològico-lingüística. Vol. 1: L'enquesta. La llengua i els seus condicionaments*, 1. Barcelona: Edicions 62.
Bartmiński, Jerzy, 2010. *Aspects of Cognitive Ethnolinguistics*. London: Equinox.
Bayley, Robert, Richard Cameron and Ceil Lucas, 2013. *The Oxford Handbook of Sociolinguistics*. Oxford: Oxford University Press.
Blas Arroyo, José Luis, 2005. *Sociolingüística del español. Desarrollos y perspectivas en el estudio de la lengua española en contexto social*. Madrid: Cátedra.
Blommaert, Jan, 2013. *Ethnography, Superdiversity and Linguistic Landscapes: Chronicles of Complexity*. Bristol: Multilingual Matters.
Bossong, Georg, 2008. *Die romanischen Sprachen. Eine vergleichende Einführung*. Hamburg: Buske.
Bourdieu, Pierre, 1977. "The economics of linguistic exchanges." *Social Science Information* 16: 645–668.
Bright, William, 1966. *Sociolinguistics*. The Hague: Mouton.
Caravedo, Rocío, 2009. "La percepción selectiva en situación de migración de un enfoque cognoscitivo." *Lengua y migración/Language & Migration*, 1–2: 21–38.
Caravedo, Rocío, 2010. "La dimensión subjetiva en el contacto lingüístico." *Lengua y migración/Language & Migration*, 2–2: 9–26.
Chambers, Jack K., 2003. "Sociolinguistics of immigration." In *Social Dialectology: In Honour of Peter Trudgill*, Eds., D. Britain and J. Cheshire, 97–113. Amsterdam: John Benjamins.
Chambers, Jack K., Peter Trudgill and Natalie Schilling-Estes (Eds.), 2002. *The Handbook of Language Variation and Change*. Oxford: Blackwell.
Coulmas, Florian, 1997. *The Handbook of Sociolinguistics*. Oxford: Blackwell.
Coulmas, Florian, 2005. *Sociolinguistics. The Study of Speakers' Choices*. Cambridge: Cambridge University Press.
Díaz-Campos, Manuel, 2011. *The Handbook of Hispanic Sociolinguistics*. Oxford: Wiley-Blackwell.
Díaz-Campos, Manuel, 2014. *Introducción a la sociolingüística hispánica*. Oxford: Wiley-Blackwell.
García, Ofelia and Li Wei, 2014. *Translanguaging. Language, Bilingualism and Education*. Houndsmills: Palgrave Macmillan.
Giglioli, Pier Paolo (Ed.), 1972. *Language and Social Context*. Harmondsworth: Penguin.
Gumperz, John J. and Dell Hymes, 1964. The ethnography of communication, *American Anthropologist*, 66—6, parte 2.
Gumperz, John J. and Dell Hymes, 1972. *Directions in Sociolinguistics: The Ethnography of Communication*. New York: Holt, Rinehart & Winston.
Hawley, Amos H., 1986. *Human Ecology. A Theoretical Essay*. Madrid: Tecnos.
Hickey, Raymond., 2013. *The Handbook of Language Contact*. Oxford: Wiley-Blackwell.
Hudson, Richard A., 1980. *Sociolinguistics*. Cambridge: Cambridge University Press.
Hymes, Dell, 1966. "Two types of linguistic relativity (with examples from Amerindian ethnography)." In *Sociolinguistics*, Ed., W. Bright, 114–167. The Hague: Mouton.

Kabatek, Johannes, 2011. "Algunos apuntes acerca de la 'hibridez' y de la 'dignidad' de las lenguas iberorrománicas." In *Variación lingüística y contacto de lenguas en el mundo hispánico. In memoriam Manuel Alvar*, Eds., Y. Congosto Martín and E. Méndez García de Paredes, 271–290. Madrid-Frankfurt: Iberoamericana-Vervuert.

Kloss, Heinz, 1967. *Abstand* languages and *Ausbau* languages. *Anthropological Linguistics* Harvard: Harvard.

Le Page, Robert and Andrée Tabouret-Keller, 1985. *Acts of Identity: Creole-based Approaches to Language and Ethnicity*. Cambridge: Cambridge University Press.

Lieberson, Samuel, 1966. *Explorations in Sociolinguistics*. The Hague: Mouton.

López Morales, Humberto, 1989. *Sociolingüística*. Madrid: Gredos.

Meyerhoff, Miriam, 2006. *Introducing Sociolinguistics*. London: Routledge.

Milroy, Lesley and Mathew Gordon, 2003. *Sociolinguistics. Method and Interpretation*. Oxford: Blackwell.

Moreno-Fernández, Francisco, 2004. "Medias lenguas e identidad." *III Congreso de la Lengua Española*, Rosario. Obtained from: http://congresosdelalengua.es/rosario/ponencias/aspectos/moreno_f.htm (accessed 15 December, 2015).

Moreno-Fernández, Francisco, 2009a. *Principios de sociolingüística y sociología del lenguaje*. 4th ed. Barcelona: Ariel.

Moreno-Fernández, Francisco, 2009b. "Integración sociolingüística en contextos de inmigración: marco epistemológico para su estudio en España." *Lengua y migración/Language & Migration*, 1–1: 121–156.

Moreno-Fernández, Francisco, 2015. "Spanish Language and Migrations." In *The Routledge Handbook of Hispanic Applied Linguistics*, Ed., M. Lacorte, 624–638. New York: Routledge.

Nishida, Hiroko, 1991. "A cognitive approach to intercultural communication based on Schema Theory." *International Journal of Intercultural Relations*, 23–5: 753–777.

Pavlinić, Andrina M., 2001. "Migrants and Migrations." In *Concise Encyclopedia of Sociolinguistics*, Ed., R. Mesthrie, 519–524. Amsterdam: Elsevier.

Sancho Pascual, María, 2014. *Integración sociolingüística de los inmigrantes ecuatorianos en Madrid*. Alcalá de Henares: Universidad de Alcalá.

Schuchardt, Hugo, 1909a. "Die Lingua Franca." *Zeitschrift für Romanische Philologie*, 33: 441–461.

Schuchardt, Hugo, 1909b. *Pidgins and Creole Languages*, Ed., G. Gilbert. London: Cambridge University Press, 1980.

Serrano, María José, 2011. *Sociolingüística*. Barcelona: Serbal.

Silva Corvalán, Carmen, 1989. *Sociolingüística. Teoría y análisis*. Madrid: Alhambra.

Silva-Corvalán, Carmen and Andrés Enrique-Arias, 2016. *Sociolingüística y pragmática del español*, 2nd ed. Washington, D.C.: Georgetown University Press.

Stewart, William, 1962. "Outline of Linguistic Typology for Describing Multilingualism." In *Study of the Role of Second Language in Asia, Africa, and Latin America*, Ed., F.A. Rice, 15–25. Washington D.C.: Center for Applied Linguistics.

Trudgill, Peter, 1974. *Sociolinguistics. An Introduction*, Harmondswoth: Penguin.

Wardhaugh, Ronald, 1986. *An Introduction to Sociolinguistics*. Oxford: Blackwell.

Weinreich, Uriel, 1952. *Languages in Contact*. The Hague: Mouton.

Whorf, Benjamin Lee, 1940. "Science and linguistics." *Technology Review*. 40: 229–231; 247–248. In *Language, Thought and Reality: Selected Writings of Benjamin Lee Whorf*, Ed., J.B. Carrol. New York: Wiley. 1956. Trans. Spa. *Lenguaje, pensamiento y realidad*. Barcelona: Barral. 1971.

Zimmermann, Klaus, 2011. "La construcción ecolingüística del contacto de lenguas (español y lenguas amerindias)." In *Variación lingüística y contacto de lenguas en el mundo hispánico. In memoriam Manuel Alvar*, Eds., Y. Congosto Martín and E. Méndez García de Paredes, 361–390. Madrid-Frankfurt: Iberoamericana-Vervuert.

Zimmermann, Tanja, 2011. *El español hablado por los afrocostarricenses*. Kassel: Kassel University.

EPILOGUE

This monograph has attempted to lay out, through a series of propositions, the epistemological system for a cognitive sociolinguistics. The system is offered as a metatheoretical framework amenable to logical manipulation on the part of its users. The propositions that constitute the basis of the system have been formulated (i) in order to draw attention to the key issues and core elements of cognitive sociolinguistic research and (ii) with the idea that such propositions can be empirically verified if in some cases this has not already been accomplished. The intention of this volume is not, therefore, to provide a simple catalog of sociolinguistic principles or of theoretical postulates of a cognitive nature, but rather it aims to build a verifiable metatheoretical basis for cognitive sociolinguistics. In this endeavor, we have sought order, clarity and rigor. Above all, we have striven for coherence in our conceptualization of language as a complex adaptive system, a conceptualization that we understand as an alternative—although to a certain extent complementary—to formalist and universalist visions.

Far from presenting a highly circumscribed and compartmentalized sociolinguistics, it has been our intention to acknowledge that the cognitive sociolinguistics conceived of here is neither monolithic nor is it always neatly defined. In fact, this monograph commenced by communicating our doubts about whether the project being embarked upon would be better classified as "cognitive sociolinguistics" or as "sociocognitive linguistics." Although the distance between the two may not be very great, each would obviously necessitate different approaches. But because this model is neither autonomous nor hermetic in its arguments, we consider the scholia that have sustained, complemented or illustrated the propositions to be vital. Similarly, we consider the debates near the conclusion of each chapter to be essential. Those debates have attempted to highlight issues that linguistics has treated as controversial or multivocal. In these ways, then, we have been able to draw attention to the fact that cognitive sociolinguistics is an emerging field, where the study of the spoken language in its respective social and cultural contexts will be under constant construction.

One last note to tie up loose ends: the occasion when I was asked whether the main objective of my research was to know language or know the human being was a sociolinguistics seminar in 1988 at Universidad de Málaga. And it was Juan Villena Ponsoda who asked the question following my presentation "The sociolinguistic method." In a way, I have been writing this book ever since.

INDEX

Note: page numbers in italic type refer to figures; those in bold type refer to tables.

Abercrombie, Nicholas 42
Abstand 212
accent 214, 217, 218
acceptability 116, 117, 118, 120–121, 122, 151, 152
accommodation 9, 26, 27
accountability 154, 157
accreditation 62
acquisition 16, 21, 22, 25, 26, 30, 74, 75, 76, 77, 101, 102, 114, 120, 209, 214, 216, 218
act 22, 27, 28
adjectives 116
adolescents *164*
adverbs 98, 116
affective factors 183, 193, 218
affixes 110
Africa 43, 54, 200, 211
age 20, 21, 37, 101, 102, 139, 180, 187, 188
agents, of sociolinguistic reality 22
agreement requests 183
Aijón Ávila, Miguel Ángel 100, 108
Alba, Orlando 99
Albeda, Marta 161, **161**
Alcalá de Henares, Spain 174, 181, 182, 186
Alliéres, Jacques 139
Almeida, Manuel 206
Althusser, Louis 69
Alvar, Manuel 139
America (USA) 200, 219; American English 21, 103–104, 121, 141, 198, 200, 210
analogy 113, 114, 115, 116, 117
Andalusia, Spain 46, 139, 199, 216
Ander-Egg, Ezequiel 159
anthropology 11, 62, 70
Antilla, Arto 78
apriorism 70
Arabic 211, 212
Arao, Lilian A. 181
Arfuch, Leonor 159
Argentina 104, 199
argumentations 17, 62
argumentative dialogue 66
Aristotle 28, 81
Armstrong, Sharon L. 94
Asia 43, 211, 219
Asociación de Academias de la Lengua Española 104
attitudes 8, 19, 26, 37, 50, 68, 124, 155, 171, 180, 183, 191–194, 195, 197, 203, 210, 213, 214, 217, 219
audience 43, 164–165, 180
Auer, Peter 215
Ausbau 212, 213
Australia 104, 200; Australian English 197, 200, 203
Authier, Jacqueline 151

autonomy 115, 117, 208, 211, **212**, 213
available lexicon 95
Ávila, Antonio 102, 103
Azurmendi Ayerbe, María-José 35

Badia, Antoni 210
Bahamian English 198
Bailey, Charles-James N. 28, 81
Baker, Paul 25
Bakhtin, Mikhail 9, 17, 90, 99
   see also Voloshinov, Valentin N.
Bangladeshi English 198
Baranowski, Maciej 151
Barlow, Michael 25
Bartminski, Jerzy 61, 70–71
Bassa 61
Batstone, Rob 76
Baudelaire, Charles 67
Bauer, Laurie 199–200
Belfast, Northern Ireland 4
beliefs 8, 50, 53, 61, 63, 68, 99, 171,
   191–192, 193, 203, 213, 217, 218
Bell, Allen 164–175
Benveniste, Émile 28
Benz, Caroline 154
Berger, Peter 62
Berkowitz, Stephen D. 47
Bernard, Thomas 35
Bernárdez, Enrique 18
Bernstein, Basil 42, 103, 122
Bickerton, Derek 5
Bierwisch, Manfred 94
bilingual 3, 206, 207, **217**, 219
bilingualism 206, 210
biology 85
Blache, Vidal de la 149
Blakemore, Sarah-Jayne 2
Blas Arroyo, José Luis 206
Blommaert, Jan 134, 217
Bolivia **212**
Bortoni-Ricardo, Stella M. 50
Bosque, Ignacio 120
Bossong, Georg 212
Boston, USA 21, 198
Bourdieu, Pierre 18, 52–53, 61, 66, 99,
   208
brain, the 1–2, 15, 92, 133, 135
Bratman, Michael E. 18
Bresnan, Joan 25, 117
Briggs, Charles L. 163
Bright, William 42
British English 199, 200, 203
Briz, Antonio 184

Browman, Catherine P. 131
Brown, Penelope 63
Bruner, Jerome 21, 51
Bybee, Joan 81, 113, 115

Calella, Spain 49, *49*
Callejo, Javier 181
Calsamiglia Blancafort, Helena 66
Calvet, Louis-Jean 37, 43
Camagüey, Cuba 199
Camargo, Laura 63
Cameron, Richard 4
Canada 104, 200
Canary Islands, Spain 137, *137*, 139, 199
Cane Walk, Guyana 43
Caravedo, Rocío 103, 127–128, 133–135,
   143n1, 218
Caribbean 137, 198
Casado, Manuel 70
Casas, Miguel 90, 98
caste 42, 54
Castile, Spain 210
catastrophe theory 85
categories 6, 8, 26, 41, 62, 70, 80, 82,
   86, 95, 112–113, 115, 117, 118, 122,
   124, 127, 129–130, 131, 132, 142, 156,
   169, 184, 197, 198, 199, 210, 213,
   215
categorization 8, 9, 19, 21, 22, 27, 38, 40,
   41, 45, 50, 53, 54, 55, 69, 71, 79, 80,
   82, 87, 92, 94, 110, 112–114, 115,
   128, 129, 130, 142, 194, 198, 200,
   202–203
Cedergren, Henrietta 3–4, 86, 140
Central America 103
central meaning 91
centrality 8, 27, 103, 115, 200, 203
Chambers, Jack K. 206, 217
change, social 34–35, 60
Chicago, USA 97
child language 163
China 52
Chinook **212**
choice 11, 27
Chomsky, Noam 4, 28, 120, 148
chunks 116, 117
city 36, 37
Clark, Herbert H. 19
Clark, John 109
class *see* social class
clauses 110, 115
climate 195
clitic 115, 121

cognition 15; and sociogrammar 109–124; and sociophonology 127–143; and sociosemantics 89–106
cognitive category 8
cognitive ethnolinguistics 61, 70
cognitive grammar 23, 109, 110, 111–112, 124, 151
cognitive interview 180–181
cognitive linguistics 7, 11, 20, 22, 23–24, 26, 27, 61, 74, 109, 111, 148, 185
cognitive maps 26
cognitive psychology 2
cognitive semantics 90, 94
cognitive sociolinguistics 30; fundamental concepts of 26–28; goals of 7–9; methodology for 145–157; objectives of 26; possibility of 9–11; principles of analysis 150–153; research questions 7; techniques of 153–156; theoretical space of 22–26
cognitivism 2, 6, 10, 20, 21, 94, 111, 123, 129, 130, 142, 145, 151–152, 155, 177, 220; cognitivist interpretation of the sociolinguistic interview 165–168
Cohen, Paul 174
colloquial conversation 66, 161, **161**, 167, 170, *170*, *174*
Colombia 103, 104, 199, 203
colonies 3
colors, naming of 61
combinatory variants 127, 139, 141
communication strategy 24
communicative accommodation 11, 24–25
communicative efficiency 76, 104
communicative intention 17, 19, 60, 121, 183, 184
communicative intention fixator 181, 183, 186
communicative interaction 15, 26, 27
communicative meaning 90, 100, 101
communicative use 18
community 28
competence 5–6, 28, 29, 37, 52, 53, 86, 133, 140–141, 154, 156, 193; sociolinguistic 6, 86, 133, 141, 156
complex adaptive system 11, 15, 16, 18–19, 24, 26, 30, 110, 224
complex networks 2–3, 30, 85
compositionality 118
computational model 82
computer science 3, 4
conceptual data 149

conflict 2, 18, 41, 52, 167; conflict theories 34–35
conjunctions 96
consensus 21, 34–35, 41, 63, 72, 101, 103
consensus theories 34–35
conservatism 42, 85, 193
constitutive component 38, *39*
construction 8, 65, 66, 67, 76, 91, 95, 96, 99, 111, 112–113, 114, 115, 116, 117, 118–119, 121, 138; discursive 60, 61–62, 63, 65, 98, 99, 189; grammatical 18, 23, 26, 91, 96, 109–110, 112, 122
construction metaphor 62
constructionism 62, 109–111, 112, 113
context 8, 9, 24, 25, 27, 28, 39–40, 55, 64, 65, 66, 77, 78, 87, 98, 99–100, 109, 110, 113, 117, 132, 135, 138, 139, 141, 142, 153, 154, 159, 166, 180, 182, 185, 186, 188, 189
contextualized meaning 90, 95, 109
conventions 18–19, 30, 111, 112, 113, 115, 116–117, 118, 122, 135, 151, 152, 170
convergence 24, 27, 67, 68, 213, 214, 215–216, 217
conversation 3, 28, 64, 65, 71, 162, 163, 166, 168, 169–171, **176**, 176–177, 185, 186, 189; colloquial 66, 161, **161**, 167, 170, *170*, *174*
conversation analysis 59, 62, 66, 72, 181
conversation citation 63
conversational modules 163
cooperative activity 18
cooperative principle 163, 166
core grammar 112
corpus 27
correctness 69, 162, 197
Coseriu, Eugenio 139
Coulmas, Florian 9, 79–80
Coulthard, Malcolm 67
covert prestige 193–194, 210
Créole **212**
Creoles 45, 200, 206, 219
creolists 5, 9, 207
Croft, William 112
Cruse, D. Alan 112
Crystal, David 200
Cuba 103, 199, **212**
Cuenca, Maria Josep 2, 8, 115, 198
cultural environment 17, 25, 27, 34, 35, 36, 41, 55, 61, 69
cultural script 165, 167–168, 177

culture 28, 38, 39, 41, 47, 59, 61, 70, 71, 72, 98, 103, 162, 193, 210
customs 61
Cuyckens, Hubert 27

Dach 212–213
dahalo **212**
Dahrendorf, Ralf 35
Darwinian paradox 85
data, conceptual 149
David, Kingsley 34
De Vega, Manuel 2
deaf dialogue 66
DeCamp, David 9
deduction 4
deficit theory 103, 122
deictics 84, 183
denotation 98, 99, 106
deontic modality markers 181, 184–185
Descartes, René 145
descriptions 60, 62–63, 112, 131, 150, 151, 152, 180
descriptive grammar 123
determinism 70
Detroit, USA 42
Deutscher, Guy 61
dialect 26, 51, 84, 103, 162, 196, *196*, 198, 200, 202–203, 211, 212, **212**, 215–216
dialogue, argumentative 66
diasystem 140
dictionary 29, 98, 211
diglossia 211
Dinkin, Aaron 151
Dirven, René 10, 101
discourse 9, 10, 16, 21, 27, 90, 91, 95, 96, 98, 99, 102, 103–104, 110, 112, 114, 115, 116, 119, 120–121, 155; and the sociolinguistic interview 159, 160, 161, 163, 165–167, 168, 169, 170, 174, 175, 177, 179, 180, 181, 182–183, 184, 185, 188–189; worldview and society 59–71
discourse analysis 39, 59, 62, 124, 181, 184
discourse evaluators 181, 182, 186
discourse scenarios 16, 166, 169, 179
discourse styles 21
discriminatory learning 194, 202
discursive modality markers 181
disloyalty 210
Dispaux, Gilbert 66
ditransitives 110
Dittmar, Norbert 5, 151

divergence 25, 27, 67, 68, 213, 214, 215, 217
Dominican Republic 99, 103
Dorian, Nancy 5
dualities 28–29
Ducrot, Oswald 105
Dumais, Susan T. 95
Dunbar, Robin 2
Durkheim, Émile 8
dynamic sociology 27
dynamics, of sociolinguistic reality 22

Eccles, John 80
Echevarría, Max 96
Eckert, Penelope 3–4, 12, 25, 31, 56, 100, 107, 142, 143, 162, 177, 178
Eco, Umberto 21
ecolinguistics 24, 25, 28, 39
economy 82, 85, 150; principle of 151–152, 156
ecosystem 28
Ecuadorians 214, 216
education 2, 52, 101, 193, 209; level of 42, 46, 49, 100, 102, 103, 118, 120, 122, 138, 180, 187–188
Egypt 200
elaborated code 122
elderly people 44, 45
Ellis, Nick 15, 84, 117
embodiment 18, 27
emergence 16, 17, 45, 52, 55, 98, 99, 116, 134, 174, 213
emergent grammar hypothesis 115
emergent meanings 92, 105, 106
emerging realities 3, 16, 25
emic 149
energeia 28
Engels, Friedrich 35
English language 77, 78, 84–85, 98, 103–104, 116, 121, *131*, 134, 139, 149, 198, 199–201, 203, 211, **212**; American English 21, 103–104, 121, 141, 198, 200, 210; Australian English 197, 200, 203; Bahamian English 198; Bangladeshi English 198; Bostonian English 198; British English 199, 200, 203; Estuary English 198; international English 197, 200, 201; Irish English 200; New Zealand English 104, 200; post-colonial English 200; South African English 200; Southern Hiberno-English 200; Texan English 198

énoncé/énonciation 28
enunciation 29, 122–123, 142
enunciative-discursive level 75
environment 7–8, 17, 28, 50, 60–61, 80, 81, 87, 98, 99–100, 147, 149, 169, 170, 207, 209, 220; cultural 17, 25, 27, 34, 35, 36, 41, 55, 61, 69; linguistic 76, 77–78; of linguistic usage 35–39; migratory 216–218; natural/physical 8, 41, 55; objective 37, *38*; perceived 37, *38*; situational 35; social 1, 8, 25, 27, 36, 37, 47, 49, 68, 69, 94, 123
ergon 28
errors 63, 84, 150, 196, *196*, 218
Escandell, Victoria 184
Escoriza, Lius 98
Esperanto **212**
Estuary English 198
ethnic groups 211
ethnography 41; of communication 22, 220
ethnolinguistics 61, 70, 220
ethnomethodology 28, 35, 94
etic 149
etymological fallacy 95
Europe 45, 139, 195, 215
Euskera batua 212
evaluation 19, 66, 189, 192, 194, 200, 208
Evans-Pritchard, Edward 8
everyday life 28, 35, 98
exemplar 8, 25, 79, 80, 81, *81*, 112, 113, 128, 129, 130–131, 134, 135, 138, 198, 202, 203
exemplar theory 25, 112, 202
exemplary language 195, 197
experiential cognitive linguistics 23
experiential principle 113
experts dialogue 66
explicitness 150, 151, 152, 156
Extremadura, Spain 199

face-to-face interaction 35, 36, 37, 41, 44, **44**, 45, 66, 161
factuality 63, 150, 151, 156
facultative variants 139, 141–142
family resemblance 27, 94, 197, 219
Feature Theory 202
Fernández Marrero, Juan Jorge 51, 69, 77, 193
Ferreira, Roberto 96
Feyerabend, Paul 146, 151
Fill, Alwin 25, 39

Fischer, Michael 59
Five Graces Group 15, 19, 77, 84, 110, 113
Fletcher, Janet 109
focalizers of otherness 181, 183, 186
focalizers of understanding 181, 183, 186
Ford, Marilyn 25, 117
Foreign Language Learners Cluster (FLLC) 201, *201*
formalism 85, 111
forms of address 21, 26, 53, 68
Fought, Carmen 5
Frattini, Eric 159
free scale networks 47
French language 211
frequency 18, 25, 26, 27, 30, 79, 80, 81, 82, 83, 84, 85, 91, 95, 96, 98, 113, 114, 115, 117–118, 124, 132, 134, 135, 141, 142, 188
Frith, Uta 2
functional zone 133, 134–135, 138
functionalism 4, 34, 41, 54

Gallistel, Randolph 2
García, Ofelia 220, 221
Garfinkel, Harold 28
Geeraerts, Dirk 10, 12, 23, 25, 27, 31, 94, 100, 101, 107, 109, 125, 126, 144, 146, 148, 157
Geertz, Clifford 61
generality 91, 151, 152, 156, 202
generalization 79, 80, 82, 110, 112–113, 115, 202
generative grammar 109, 111, 120, 123
generativism 5, 18
genetics 84, 85
geographical regions 19, 141, 196, 198–200, 210, 217
geography 104, 133, 206
geolects 27, 76, 120, 127, 141, 198, 202, 215, 216
geolinguistic variation 77, 203
German language 212, **212**
Ghana 49, *49*, 200
Ghomeshi, Jila 123, 194
Giddens, Anthony 8
Giglioli, Pier Paulo 206
Giles, Howard 24
Givón, Talmy 115
Glasgow, UK 174
Gleason, Henry A. 61
Gleitman, Henry 94
Gleitman, Lila R. 94

Goldberg, Adele 111
Goldstein, Louis M. 131
Goodenough, Ward H. 61
Gordon, Mathew 162, 163, *164*, 206
Görlach, Manfred 200
gradience 122
gradualist model 85
grafos 96
grammar 5, 54, 78, 91, 96, 194, 211, 215, 217; configuration of 111–113; of constructions 109–110; *core* 112; descriptive 123; emergent grammar hypothesis 115; generative 109, 111, 120, 123; linguistic or sociolinguistic? 122–124; prescriptive 123; social dimension of 118–124; sociogrammar and cognition 109–124; usage-based 110, 117, 123
grammatical dynamics 113–118
Granda, Germán de 54
Gras Manzano, Pedro 110
Greenberg, Stephen 15
Greimas, Algirdas Julien 101
Grice, H. Paul 166–167, 168, 177
Grimshaw, Allen D. 43
Guaraní 212
Guibernau, Monserrat 7
Gumperz, John 5, 220
Gutiérrez Ordóñez, Salvador 81
Gutiérrez Rexach, Javier 120

habitat 28
habits 61, 69, 79, 80, 82, 84, 113, 121, 141, 203, 208, 210, 211, 213
habitus 18, 52
Hagège, Claude 122–123
Harris, Roy 24
Haugen, Einar 25, 39
Havana, Cuba 198
Haverkate, Henk 184
Hawley, Amos H. 28, 149, 211–212
hearer 53, 94
Hegel, Georg W. F. 70
Heisenberg, Werner 150
Henry, Alison 117, 120, 123
Herder, Johan G. 70
Hernández Muñoz, Natividad 95
hetero-regulators 181, 183, 186
heterosemic variation 75
Hidalgo, Antonio 175
hierarchy of modality 63
Hilferty, Joseph 2, 8, 115, 198
Hill, Stephen 42

Hindi 211
Hiskens, Frans 215
historicity 211, **212**, 213
history 17, 34, 51, 194; of the language 3, 22, 116, 194, 208
Holm, Kurt 154
homo loquens 8
Homo sapiens 195
homogeneous community 140
homonymy 85, 91, 95
homosemic variation 75, 96, 99, 120, 130, 135
homosemy 75, 90, 121, 138
Hopi 210
Hopper, Paul 110, 113, 115
Horvath, Barbara 5
Hruschka, Daniel 85
Hübner, Peter 154
Hudson, Richard A. 71, 206
Huici, Carmen 202
humanities 1
Humboldt, Wilhelm von 28, 70, 71
Hungarian 212
Hymes, David 22, 165–166, 210, 220
hypercorrection 51
hypothesis of imposed norm 192
hypothesis of inherent value 192

I-language 15
Ibáñez, Jesús 181
Iberian Peninsula 181
ideal speaker 102, 140, 148
idealism 9
identity 5, 35, 36, 37, 45, 49, 50, 52, 67, 69, 82, 132, 142, 156, 193, 209, 210, 211, 220
ideolect 53, 66, 139, *196*
ideologues dialogue 66
ideology 59, 67, 68, 69, 70, 123, 208
illocutionary force 170, 184
immanentism 8
immigrants 49, *49*, 215–216, 217–218, 220
immigration 26, *215*
imposed norm, hypothesis of 192
income level 42
indexicality 28, 94
India 5, 42, 200, 211
indicators 42, 54, 181, 182, 184, 185–186, 187–188
indigenous languages 211
individual behavior 15
individuals, position in society 67–71

Indonesia 200
induction 4
informants 4, 92–93, 139, 155, 171, 174, 175, 176, **176**, 180
inherent value, hypothesis of 192
insider form of language 70
insiders 103, 174, 176
institutions 35, 40, 41, 45, 52, 192
instructions 60, 62, 63–64
integral linguistics 24
interaction 15, 17–18, 27
interactive sociolinguistics 26
interlocutor 8, 17, 24, 25, 53, 62, 63, 64, 66, 69, 71, 72, 99, 115, 122, 123, 153, 155, 159, 161, 163, 165, 166, 167, 168, 169, 170, 171, 179–180, 181, 182, 183, 185, 186, 187, 188, 192, 209, 219
international English 200
international languages 197–203, *201*
Internet 3
interview *see* sociolinguistic interview
Irish English 200
Israel 200
Itkonen, Esa 148

Jackendoff, Ray 86, 109
Janicki, Karol 23–24, 90
jargon 26
Johnstone, Barbara 149
judges 21, 51, 55

Kabatek, Johannes 218
Kachru, Braj 200
Kant, Immanuel 70
Kenya 200, **212**
kinship 45, 70
Kleiber, Georges 94
Kloss, Heinz 212, 213
knowledge 1, 2, 3, 4, 6, 7, 16, 17, 21, 37, 48, 60, 61, 65, 70, 71, 74, 82, 94, 96, 100, 101, 102, 105, 106, 112, 142, 148, 154, 155, 166, 168, 177, 193, 194, 195, 214, 216
koine 45
König, Ekkehard 116
Korea 200
Krashen, Stephen D. 21
Kremmer, Suzanne 25
Kristiansen, Gitte 10, 12, 25, 31, 53, 56, 100, 101, 107, 109, 126, 130, 143, 146, 157, 193, 204
Kuhn, Thomas 151

Laberge, Suzanne 11, 51
Labov, William 1, 3–4, 5, 21, 25, 36, 42–43, 51, 54, 67, 83, 84, 85, 92, *93*, 133, 139, 140, 145, 159, 160–162, *163*, 163–164, 174
labovianism 29, 34, 54, 89, 92, 103, 104, 127
Laclau, Ernesto 69
Lakoff, George 62, 110, 112, 124, 131
Landauer, Thomas K. 95
Landi, Paulo 149
Langacker, Ronald W. 2, 8, 23, 53, 69, 80, 96, 106, 109, 111, 112, 113, 124, 130, 141, 142, 151, 156, 169, 170
language: as a complex adaptive system 11, 18–19, 30; dynamic nature of 15–19; and reality 69–71
language alternation 206, 214
language attrition 26, 218
language choice 9, 26, 72
language contact: cognitive perspective on 207–213, **212**; consequences of 213–216, *215*; languages in contact 10, 206–207, 208, 217
language death 26
language substitution 26
language teaching 119, 138, 210
language usage 15; and social relationships 39–50, **44**, *48*, *49*
language varieties: linguistic attitudes toward 192–194; perceptions toward 194–197, *196 see also* variation
languages in contact 10, 206–207, 208, 217
langue 23, 28
langue légitime 52, 208
langue/parole dichotomy 17
Larsen-Freeman, Diane 15, 84
Latin 43, 211
Latour, Bruno 63, **63**
Lavandera, Beatriz 11, 92, 100, 124
Le Page, Robert 5, 219
Le Poire, Beth 24
leaders 46, 85
learnability 120
learning 2, 15, 25, 48, 61, 76, 77, 209, 213; discriminatory 194, 202
lects 28, 81
legitimacy 213, 216, 220
legitimized language 52
Leko **212**
Levinson, Stephen 2, 63
Lewis, John 174

lexical availability 95
lexical capacity 101, 102
lexical strength 117–118
lexicon 23, 49–50, 54, 69, 70, 91, 95–96, 99, 101, 102–103, 104, 105–106, 109, 111, 112, 117, 194, 214, *215*, 217; relationship with reality 96, *97*, 98, 100; virtual 100, 102, 105
Liberia 61
Lieb, Hans-Heinrich 3
Lieberson, Samuel 206
life-modes 46
life-threatening situations 163
Limited Skills Cluster (LSC) 201, *201*
linguistic attitude 6
linguistic behavior 8, 9, 20, 29, 34, 37, 39, 41, 46, 48, 51, 77, 156, 192, 219
linguistic capital 52
linguistic change 16, 49, 54, 74, 82–86, 131, 156, 193
linguistic competence 5, 37, 52, 86, 133, 140
linguistic contact 206–220
linguistic corpora 148, 153
linguistic correctness 69, 162, 197
linguistic judges 21, 51, 55
linguistic leaders 46, 85
linguistic legitimacy 213, 216, 220
linguistic loyalty 210, 213
linguistic market 6, 46, 51, 53, 218
linguistic meaning 90–92, *93*, 94–96
linguistic relativity 60–61, 70, 210
linguistic selection 8, 62
linguistic usage 16, 18, 24, 25, 26, 42, 43, 44, 50, 52, 53, 54, 55, 75, 77, 86, 115, 123, 135, 194, 214, 219; environments of 35–39, *38*, *39*
linguistic varieties 10, 15, 19, 28, 79, 207, 209, *212*, 212–213, 214, 215, 219; perception of 191–203 *see also* variation
linguistics, definition of 7
Lloyd, Barbara 2
logic 105, 123
Longa, Victor 8
Lope Blanch, Juan M. 139
López García, Ángel 6, 77, 85, 198
López Morales, Humberto 21, 140, 206
Lorenzo, Guillermo 8
Low German **212**
lower class 42
loyalty 210, 213
Lozano, Jorge 62
Luckmann, Thomas 62

McArthur, Tom 200
Macauley, Ronald 5
Madrid, Spain 4, 181, 198, 214
Málaga, Spain 46, 225
Malaysia 200
Malinowski, Bronislaw 62
manipulation 35, 62, 224
Maori 61
maps, cognitive 26
Marcus, George 59
Marina, José Antonio 47
marked interrogations 182, 184
markers of doubt 181
Marouzaeau, Jules 45
Martín Alcoff, Linda 7
Martín Butragueño, Pedro 18, 19, 46, 121, 154
Martín Zorraquino, María Antonia 185
Martinet, Jean 119
Marx, Karl 35
Marxism 4, 5, 34, 51
mass media 50, 192
matched-guise technique 155
mathematics 2
Maurer, Bruno 174
Maxim of Manner 167
Maxim of Quality 166–167
Maxim of Quantity 166
Maxim of Relation 167
Maynts, Renate 154
Mead, George Herbert 8
meaning 10, 17, 23, 26, 28, 29, 39, 60, 61, 67, 71, 82–83, 89–90, 98–100, 105–106, 109, 110, 112–113, 114, 116, 117, 118, 119, 120, 121, 122–123, 133–134, 138–139, 186, 214; communicative 90, 100, 101; contextualized 90, 95, 109; emergent 92, 105, 106; linguistic 90–92, *93*, 94–96; nature of 90–96; social nature of 100–105; stylistic 98, 100
measurement by approximation 150
Meillet, André 115
memory 2, 25, 48, 67, 114, 117, 149, 202
men 44, 188
Mendieta, Eduardo 7
Merriam-Webster Dictionary 98
Merton, Robert 34
Mesthrie, Rajend 3
meta-perception 218
metaphor 34, 62
metatheory 9, 11, 22, 23, 24

methodology 29, 120, 145–157, 159, 162, 189
Meunier, André 151
Mexico 104, 199, 211
Meyerhoff, Miriam 206
Michael, John W. 42
middle class 42, 43, 122
migration contexts 216
migrations 52, 217, 218
migratory environments: perceptions of languages in 216–220, **217** *see also* immigrants; immigration
Milroy, James 46, 57, 77, 88, 193, 196, 204
Milroy, Lesley 4, 45, 46, 54, 162, 163, *164*, 196
mind 17, 70, 80, 95, 119, 120, 135
minimalist syntax 120
mirror, metaphor of the 62
misunderstandings 17, 19, 28, 67, 214
Mitwelt 36
mixed varieties 45, 218–220
mnemonic data 147, 149
modality, hierarchy of 63
modules, thematic 163, *164*, 166, 167
Molina, José Luis 49, *49*
monitor 6, 19, 20–21, 78, 167, 168, 174, 175
monitor theory 20–21, 159, 170, 171
monolingual **217**
Montes Giraldo, José Joaquín 198
Moore, Wilbert 34
Morales Domínguez, José F. 21, 202
Morán, Emilio 195
Moreno Martín de Nicolás, Irene 181
morpheme 20, 96, 110, 115, 117
morphology 1, 11, 91, 117, 121
morphosyntactic level 75, 113, 122, 123
Morris, Pam 9, 90
motivation 22, 44, 84, 115, 219
Mühlhäusler, Peter 25, 39
multilectal competence 29
multilingual communities 208, 212, 219
multiple grammars 6
multiple observer *173*, 176
multiple regression analysis 4
multiple subject interview *173*
Murcia, Spain 199

narratives 60, 63, 65, 66, 180, 199
Nathan, Geoff 129
Native Skills Cluster (NSC) 201, *201*
Navajo 210

network sociolinguistics 47–50, *48*, *49* *see also* social networks
networks 27, 40, 41, 51, 55, 85, 91, 95–96, 97, 100, 102–103, 105, 111, 112, 113, 131, 134, 156, 173, 218; "free scale" 47; brain and computer science 1–3; complex networks 2–3, 30, 85; of modules 163, *164*, 166, 167; social 3, 4, 37, 40, 43–45, **44**, 46, 47, 49, *49*, 55, 83, 84, 85, 103, 163
neuroscience 1–2
New Hampshire, USA 21
New York, USA 216
New Zealand 61, 104; New Zealand English 200
Newman, Isadore 154
Niedzielski, Nancy 163, 171
Nishida, Hiroko 25, 208
nomenclatures 96, 99
Nordberg, Bengt 173
Norman **212**
Norwich, UK 42

O'Keefe, Georgia 146
objective conceptualization 175
objective environment 37, *38*
objectivism 9
observation 66, 147, 148, 149–150, 154, 155, 156, 161, 162, 169, 174, 187; participant 160, 162–163
observer's paradox 149–150, 160, 162, 172
Occam's razor 151
Optimality Theory 78
Ortega y Gasset, José 2, 17
Otero, Jaime 201
otherness, focalizers of 181, 183, 186

palatals 191
Palmer, Gary 34, 71, 95, 166, 169, 177
Panama 4–5
paradox: of contextual meaning 90; observer's paradox 149–150, 160, 162, 172
Paris, France 139
Parodi, Claudia 98
parole 23, 28
parosemy 101
Parsons, Talcott 23, 34, 41
participant observation 160, 162–163
particles 96
passives 61
Pavlini?, Andrina M. 218

Pearce, John M. 202
Peirsman, Yves 10, 12, 100
perceived environments 37, *38*
perception 8, 9, 17, 20, 26, 66, 69, 82, 109, 121, 153, 154, 155, 156, 179, 180, 181, 182, 186, 189, 191–192, 200, 203, 208, 218, 220; of languages in migratory environments 216–220, **217**; of linguistic contact 206–220; of linguistic varieties 191–203; of prototypes in international languages 197–203, *201*; of referential realm 182; of *self* 181, 182; of sociolinguistic interview 168–176, *170*, *171*, *172*, *173*, *175*, **176**; toward language varieties 194–197, *196*; of *you* 182
perception indicators 184–185, 186, 187–188
perceptual dialectology 195, 203
perceptual dynamics of the sociolinguistic interview 179, 185–189, *187*; basics of 179–181; indicators of perception 181–185
performance 28
peripheral meaning 101
periphery 27, 210, 211, 213, 219–220
periphrases 116
perlocutionary force 184
perspective schema 168, 169, 170, 175, *175*, 177, 179, 182
phenomenological sociology 35, 99
phenotypical sociolinguistics 26
Philadelphia, USA 21
Philippines 200, 211
phonemes 29, 46, 128–131, *131*, 132, 133–135, 138, 139, 141, 142
phonetics 54, 127, 135, *215*, 217
phonology 42, 82, 91, 109, 120, 127, 139, 141; configuration of 128–131, *131*; sociocognitive dynamics of 131–138, *136*, *137 see also* sociophonology
phraseology 202
phylogenetic sociolinguistics 26
physics 2, 150
pidgin 45, 200, 206, **212**, 219
Pierrehumbert, Janet 25, 81, 130–131
Pike, Kenneth 149
polilectal grammar 5
politeness 68, 69, 184, 214–215, *215*, 217; politeness signals 181, 183, 186
Pollner, Melvin 180
polymorphism 139, 142
polysemy 85, 90, 103–104, 106

Ponsoda, Juan Villena 225
Popper, Karl 80, 94, 151
popular theory 195
population 28, 42, 46, 207, 209, 220
Portolés, José 185
Portuguese 212
post-colonial English 200
potency 28
Potter, Jonathan 62, *63*
pragmatics 8, 24, 59, 62, 85, 105, 106, 181
predicate 115, 122
predictivity 151, 152, 156
preeminence 70–71, 105, 113
prejudices 191, 192
prepositional phrases 116
prescriptive grammar 123
PRESEEA 181
prestige, covert 51, 52, 84, 119, 162, 193–194, 198, 199, 203, 208, 210, 212, 213, 216
Preston, Dennis 6, 171, 195, *196*, 197
priming 117
principal component analysis 185
principle of accountability 154, 157
principle of communicative efficiency 104
principle of economy 151–152, 156
principle of explicitness 151, 152, 156
principle of factuality 151, 156
principle of generality 151, 152, 156
principle of generalization 202
principle of predictivity 151, 152, 156
principle of preeminence 113
principle of representativeness 154, 157
principle of semantic anteriority 104
principle of semantic posteriority 105
principle of the interview 160–161
principles and parameters 8
principles of semantic identicality 104
probabilistic variation grammar 25
probabilities 4, 114, 117, 133
professionals 42, 44
professions 51, 181
prosody 115, 130
prototype theory 71, 77, 198, 202, 220
prototypes 8, 26, 27; in international languages 197–203, *201*
psycholinguistic processing 15
psycholinguistics 71
psychology 2, 11, 41, 148
Puerto Rico 4, 104
punctuated equilibrium 85
Putnam, Hilary 102, **102**

Putonghua 52
Pütz, Martin 2, 13, 178

qualitative research 148, 150, 154–155, 156, 176
quantification 6, 27, 134, 154, 155, 157, 189
quantum physics 2
Quesada, Montse 159
questionnaires 95, 96, 154, 155, 157, 170
Quine, Willard van Orman 94, 117, 131

Ramón y Cajal, Santiago 145
rational choice model 9
rationalism 2
realist linguistics 18, 154
reality: and language 69–71; lexicon's relationship with 96, *97*, 98, 100
recorders 162, 167, 168, 169, 170, 171, 172, 174
recording 120, 155, 160, 162, 175, 176
referential appeal 182, 183
referential distance markers 181, 183
reflex theory 71
reflexivity 28
regulatory component 38–39, *39*
Reif, Monika 2, 13
religion *164*, 211
repetition 82, 116, 182
replication 67, 75, 76, 79, 82, 83, 84
representation 6, 8, 25, 65, 71–72, 80, 81, 82, 87, 96, 99, 111, 112, 113, 118, 119, 123, 141, 155, 156, 166; speakers' representation of the world 59–64, **63**
representativeness 154, 157, 159
research techniques 154, 155–156, 157 *see also* methodology
restricted code 42, 106, 122
Rex, John 7
Reyes, Graciela 8
rhetoric 63, 183, 184
Rickford, John R. 43
Riley, William 42
ritualization 83, 209
Ritzer, George 35
Roberson, Debi 61
Robins, Clarence 174
Robinson, Justyna A. 2, 13
Rock, Paul Elliot 94
Romaine, Suzanne 6, 11, 92
Rosch, Eleanor 2, 82, 94
Rossi Landi, Ferrucio 51, 70

routines 209
rules 4, 6, 23, 37, 45, 52, 66, 69, 91, 112, 113, 116, 140, 149, 151, 152, 167, 197, 211

Sacks, Harvey 62, 181
samples 15, 79, 81, 95, 110, 113, 120, 145, 160, 162, 163, 176
San Juan de Puerto Rico 4
Sancho Pascual, María 214, *215*
Sankoff, David 11, 51, 86, 92, 119, 121, 140
Sanskrit **212**
Sanz, Gema 193
Sapir, Edward 70
Sapir-Whorf hypothesis 70–71
Saussure, Ferdinand de 9, 28
Saville-Troike, Muriel 120
scenarios 16, 28, 61, 166, 169, 174, 177, 179, 188
Schaff, Adam 71
Schegloff, Emanuel 181
schema 26, 27, 53, 74, 113, 114, 115, 118, 128, 129, 130, 131, 132, 134–137, *136*, *137*, 138, 142, 153; perspective 168, 169, 170, 175, *175*, 177, 179, 182; and the sociolinguistic interview 166, 168, 169, 170, 174, 175, *175*, 176, 177; and variation 79–81, *81*, 85, 86
schematicity 80
Schiffrin, Deborah 62, 165, 166
Schlieben Lange, Brigitte 6, 30, 80
Schmid, Hans-Jörg 23, 113
Schneider, Edgar 200
Scholfield, Phil 155
school 42, *49*, 76, 77, *164*, 192, 194, 195, 209
Schuchardt, Hugo 206
Schütz, Alfred 8, 21, 36
scientific lexicon 96, 99
Searle, John 38, 66
secret recording 162, 176
secular linguistics 18
self 8, 180, 181, 184, 186, 187, 188–189
self-regulators 181, 183
semantic anteriority 104
semantic change 90, 103, 124
semantic equivalence 89, 90, 91, 95, 103, 104–105, 124
semantic externalism 102, **102**
semantic identicality 90, 91, 95, 104
semantic posteriority 105

semantic referential level 75, 122
semantics 28, 90, 94, 101, 102–103, 104, 106, 115; cognitive 90, 94
semi-guided interviews 160, 161, 162–163, 165, 175–176, 186, 188, 189
Senegal 211
sensory data 148, 149
sentences 115, 117
Serrano, María José 100, 108, 206, 222
sex 20, 21, 49, 101, 102, 188
sexism 194
Shaw, Marvin 44
Shepard, Carolyn A, 24
Shuy, Roger 42
sibilants 135, 136, 137, 139
silences 105
Silva-Corvalán, Carmen 206
Silverstein, Michael 28
Simmel, Georg 23, 41
simplification 19, 21, 84, 202
Singapore 200
Singh, Rajendra 5
situation 27, 29, 34, 35, 36, 38, *38*, 43, 55, 59, 61, 64, 65, 66, 67, 76–77, 78, 79, 96, 98, 99, 100, 133, 134, 138, 153, 155; language contact situation 206, 207–210, 213–214, *215*, 216, 219, 220; and the sociolinguistic interview 161, **161**, 162, 163, 165, 166, *170*, 172, 175, 179, 180, 188
situational descriptors 182, 184
Small, Steven 94
Smith, Eric 140
Sobrero, Alberto 43
social brain 2
social change 34–35, 60
social class 6, 9, 20, 21, 29, 36, 37, 41–43, 45, 46, 55, 120, 122; old 41–43
social communication, speakers as agents of 50–55
social environment 1, 8, 25, 27, 36, 37, 47, 49, 68, 69, 94, 123 *see also* environment
social factors 21
social groupings 41, 43–47, **44**, 53, 102, 142
social groups 9, 24, 34, 35, 36, 37, 38, 39, 40, 41, 43, 44, **44**, 45–46, 52, 54, 55, 68, 71, 78, 83, 85, 100, 101, 102, 106, 127, 168, 173, 174, 193, 203, 210–211, 218, 219
social integration 26, 67, 68, 217, 220

social interaction 2, 8, 10, 15, 17, 18, 113, 124, 193
social organization 15
social reality 3, 5, 7, 16, 29, 69, 71; and perception 34–55
social relationships, and language use 39–50, **44**, *48*, *49*
social sciences 1, 149
social status 42, 212 *see also* social class
social strata 30, 41, 43, 103 *see also* social class
social stratification 42, 103 *see also* social class
social systems 23, 40, 41, 44, 45
socialization 15, 61, 76, 122
society 10; individuals' position in 67–71
sociocognitive linguistics 9, 20, 224
sociogrammar, and cognition 109–124
sociolects 43, 55, 193, 197, 211
sociolinguistic competence 6, 86, 133, 141, 156
sociolinguistic interview 159, 177; cognitivist interpretation of 165–168; foundations of 160–165, **161**, *164*; interview dynamics 166, 181, 187–188; interview organizers 181–182; interviewees 159, 160, 163, 165, 166–167, 168, 169, 170, 171–172, 173, *173*, 174, 176, 180, 185, 186–187, *187*, 189; interviewers 160, 163, 165, 166, 167, 168, 169, 170, *171*, 171–172, 173–175, 176, 185, 186, 187, *187*, 188, 189; perception of 168–176, *170*, *171*, *172*, *173*, *175*, **176**; perceptual dynamics of 179–189; principle of the interview 160–161
sociolinguistic monitor 19
sociolinguistic perception 19–21
sociolinguistic reality: four levels of 22; perception of 19–21
sociolinguistic variation 4, 5, 7, 9, 74, 75, 76, 77, 78, 104, 123, 140
sociolinguistics: of complexity 25; future of 3–4
sociology 2, 11, 23, 27, 35, 41, 77, 99, 156; of context 65; of knowledge 148; of language 138
sociophonetic variation 138–142
sociophonology, and cognition 127–143
sociosemantic differences **102**
sociosemantics, and cognition 89–106
Solé, Ricard 3, 47, *48*, 96, 103, 149
solidarity 53, 68, 69, 78, 171, 194

sound 17, 21, 29, 67, 76, 84, 104, 120, 128, 129–130, 131, 132, 134, 135–136, 137, 139, 142, 194, 199
South African English 200
South Carolina, USA 21
Southern American English 198
Southern Hiberno-English 200
space of variability 134, 143n1
Spain 4, 46, 78, 104, 141, 174, 197, 198–199, 210, 214, 216, 219
Spanish 3–4, 46, 77, 78, 84, *97*, 98, 99, 103, 104, 116, 121, 134, 135, *136*, 137, *137*, 139, 141, 181, 197, 198–199, 200, 201, 203, 206, 210, 211, 212, **212**, 218, 219,
speakers: as agents of social communication 50–55; representations of the world 59–64, **63**; role in sociolinguistic methodology 155–156
speech, and social dimension 64–67
speech acts 16, 59, 64, 65, 66, 71, 72, 166, 169, 219
speech community 6, 9, 36, 37, 47, 49, 51, 60, 70, 75, 78, 83, 84, 96, 99, 101, 102, 105, 119, 120, 123, 139, 140, 141, 151, 154, 162, 207, 209, 211
spoken language 19, 21, 29, 64, 66, 145, 153, 154, 160, 163, 165, 176, 189, 225
spontaneity 163, 176, **176**
Stalnaker, Robert C. 99
standard language 52, 138, **212**
standardization 200, 203, 208, 211, 212, **212**, 213
statement 15
statistics 4, 5, 20, 48, 81, 86, 95, 123, 131, 133, 134, 140, 156, 185, 186, 189; of inference 4
Stehl, Thomas 80
stereotypes 61
Stewart, William 211–212, **212**
stimulation model 94
stimulus recording 155
storage 80, 82, 86, 87, 91, 95, 135
strategists dialogue 66
structural functionalism 34, 41
structuralism 9, 18, 127, 130, 133, 139, 140, 141, 142
structure, of sociolinguistic reality 22
Stuart-Smith, Jane 174
Stubbs, Michael 181, 184
style 21, 24, 43, 46, 52, 53, 62, 65, 66, 71, 78, 80, 120, 122, 162, 163–165, 171, 193, 211

stylistic meaning 98, 100
stylistic variation 26, 76, 78, 90
subject 68, 115, 121, 122, 149, 155, 161
subjectivation hypothesis 115
subjective conceptualization 175
subjectivism 9
subjectivity 2, 8, 9
suprasystem 140, 141
surveys 145, 155
syllables 84, 134, 135, 139, 199
symbolic interactionism 35, 41, 94
synonymy 89, 90, 91, 95, 101, 104
syntax 109, 111, 116, 117, 118, 120, 121, 129

Tabouret-Keller, Andreé 5, 219
Tagliamonte, Sali 110, 126, 140, 144
Tajfel, Henri 45
Tannen, Deborah 166
taxonomies 24, 184
Taylor, John R. 94, 130
teaching 119, 138, 210
television 50
Texan English 198
thematic modules 163, *164*, 166, 167
theories of complex system 82
theories of natural categorization 2
thought 2, 16, 70–71, 99–100, 186
Three waves of variation study 3, 25
Tomasello, Michael 25, 32, 34, 58
tourism 209
transcriber 169, 175, *175*
translanguaging 220
translation 94, *97*, 210
Traugott, Elizabeth 115, 116
Trudgill Peter 18, 41, 42, 46, 84, 162, 194, 206
Trujillo, Ramón 104, 105
Tusón Valls, Amparo 66
Tylor, Edward 61

Umwelt 36
uncertainty principle 2, 147, 150, 156
understanding, focalizers of 2, 25, 77, 80, 90, 150, 181, 183, 186, 214
Ungerer, Friedrich 23, 113
ungrammaticality 117
United Kingdom (UK) 45, 103, 104, 174, 200
United States of America (USA) 42, 200; American English 21, 103–104, 121, 141, 198, 200, 210
upper class 42, 78

urban sociolinguistics 4, 145, 211
urbanization 43
Urzúa, Paula 96
usage 27
usage-based grammar 110, 123
usage-based linguistics 11, 23, 24, 25, 81, 87, 141, 146, 155
use 9, 18, 26, 27
usted 218

Valéry, Paul 20, 92
Van Dijk, Tuen 62, 65, 66, 67, 193
Vargas, Roberto 96
variable competence 29
variable rule 4, 6, 29, 133, 140
variation 27, 87; concept of 74–78; origin and place of 86; properties of 78–82, 81 *see also* language varieties; linguistic varieties
variationism 11, 24, 25; weaknesses of 4–6
variationist sociolinguistics 3–4, 6, 8, 25, 55, 101, 104, 124, 140, 160, 195
Vendryès, Joseph 99
verbs 116, 117, 121
vernacular speech 46, 52, 77, 159, 160, 161, 162, **212**
Vic, Spain 49, *49*
Viladot i Presas, Maria Àngel 45
Villena Ponsoda, Juan 5, 6, 30, 37, 45–46, 55, 225
virtual lexicon 100, 102, 105
vitality 208, 211, **212**, 213
voice recorders 162, 167, 168, 169, 170, 171, 172, 174
volapük **212**
Voloshinov, Valentin N. 9, 17 *see also* Bakhtin, Mikhail
voseo 199
Vossler, Karl 9
vowel formants 20

vulgar language 196
Vygotsky, Lev 2, 34

Wallat, Cynthia 166
Walter, Henriette 139
Wardhaugh, Ronald 206
Weber, Max 37
Wei, Li 220, 221
Weinreich, Uriel 140, 207
Wellman, Barry 47
Werlan, Iwar 37
Weydt, Harald 6, 30, 80
Whorf, Benjamin Lee 60–61, 62, 70–71, 210
Wierzbicka, Anna 70, 167, 177
Williams, Glyn 5
Willis, Gordon B. 181
Wittgenstein, Ludwig 27, 34, 70
Wolf, Mauro 28
Wolfram, Walter A. 42
women 20, 44, 104, 188, 193
Woolard, Kathryn 52
Woolgar, Steve 63, **63**
words 17, 23, 24, 29, 51, 70, 71, 76, 82, 84, 85, 91, 92, 94–96, 98–100, 101, 102, 103–104, 110, 111, 115, 116, 117, 121, 135, 141, 214
world representation 59–64
worldview 9, 10, 59–62, 59–64, **63**, 65, 70–71, 154, 155, 166, 207, 208, 210, 214–215, 220
writing 17, 89, 98, 136
written language 25, 148, 153

Yallop, Colin 109
youth 44

Zimmerman, Klaus 211
Zimmerman, Tanja 218

Taylor & Francis eBooks

Helping you to choose the right eBooks for your Library

Add Routledge titles to your library's digital collection today. Taylor and Francis ebooks contains over 50,000 titles in the Humanities, Social Sciences, Behavioural Sciences, Built Environment and Law.

Choose from a range of subject packages or create your own!

Benefits for you
- Free MARC records
- COUNTER-compliant usage statistics
- Flexible purchase and pricing options
- All titles DRM-free.

Benefits for your user
- Off-site, anytime access via Athens or referring URL
- Print or copy pages or chapters
- Full content search
- Bookmark, highlight and annotate text
- Access to thousands of pages of quality research at the click of a button.

REQUEST YOUR FREE INSTITUTIONAL TRIAL TODAY

Free Trials Available
We offer free trials to qualifying academic, corporate and government customers.

eCollections – Choose from over 30 subject eCollections, including:

Archaeology	Language Learning
Architecture	Law
Asian Studies	Literature
Business & Management	Media & Communication
Classical Studies	Middle East Studies
Construction	Music
Creative & Media Arts	Philosophy
Criminology & Criminal Justice	Planning
Economics	Politics
Education	Psychology & Mental Health
Energy	Religion
Engineering	Security
English Language & Linguistics	Social Work
Environment & Sustainability	Sociology
Geography	Sport
Health Studies	Theatre & Performance
History	Tourism, Hospitality & Events

For more information, pricing enquiries or to order a free trial, please contact your local sales team:
www.tandfebooks.com/page/sales

The home of Routledge books

www.tandfebooks.com